The Vision of Christian Unity

The Vision of Christian Unity

A Life Given to the Ecumenical Quest

Essays in Honor of
Paul A. Crow, Jr.

Edited by
Thomas F. Best and Theodore J. Nottingham

Oikoumene Publications
Indianapolis

THE VISION OF CHRISTIAN UNITY;
A LIFE GIVEN TO THE ECUMENICAL QUEST:
ESSAYS IN HONOR OF PAUL A. CROW, JR.

Interior design: Robert Coalson / Broad Ripple Laser
Cover photo: Larry Casey-Allen / International Candle Communication

ISBN 0-9658850-0-3

Published by Oikoumene Publications
130 E. Washington Street
Indianapolis, Indiana 46204

Library of Congress card catalog number 97-68365

Printed in the United States of America

PREFACE

Through this book—a labor of love realized most directly by some thirty persons but with many, many more helping in one or another way—we honor the life and witness of Rev. Dr. Paul A. Crow, Jr.

Dr. Crow's commitments and career have engaged him in every aspect of the faith and life of the churches, taken him to every part of the globe, and brought him into contact with humanity in all its diversity. Paul Crow's life has been one of:

- *leitourgia* (commitment to worship and spritual discipline as its foundation),
- *koinonia* (spiritual bonds and friendship with countless persons around the world),
- *martyria* (witness to God's reconciling will for the churches, the whole human community and all of creation), and
- *diakoinia* (service to the church and its unity, and to the churches' service to all those in need and to the whole of creation).

How best to honor such a life? In this volume we honor Paul Crow in several ways. The first is through furthering ecumenical discussion of issues which have concerned him passionately throughout his ministry. Thus the earlier part of the volume is crafted from a series of incisive essays by a wide range of academic, church and ecumenical leaders, treating many of today's focal ecumenical concerns. A second way is, of course, through direct expressions of gratitude and appreciation from some who have known Paul and prayed, reflected, drafted, and occasionally even disagreed with Paul. Thus the later part of this volume gathers a truly impressive array of warm personal tributes to Paul Crow from Christian leaders the world over.

A third way of honoring Paul Crow is by making manifest his own contributions to ecumenical reflection—and action—throughout his career. Thus the volume concludes with a comprehensive bibliography of Paul Crow's writings. The remarkable scope and richness of this bibliography speaks for itself! The volume includes also a generous selection of photographs illustrating many aspects and stages of Paul Crow's career.

Readers will appreciate the particular challenges involved in gathering together, and producing, a volume including so many distinctive voices speaking from such diverse contexts. In several areas we have not imposed a uniformity of style, so long as the original is clear; for example we have, in most cases, left citations as supplied by the respective authors.

Before concluding, the editors would like to express, each in his own voice and in a more personal and direct way, his gratitude to Paul Crow.

Tom Best writes:

I first met Paul Crow during the mid-1970s when I was a youngish teacher in the Religion Department at Butler University in Indianapolis, with an occasional foray to help out at nearby Christian Theological Seminary. I said at both institutions that the ecumenical movement was a Good Thing. I did not know about it in any detail, but clearly it responded to a command of the Lord (John 17:20-21), and the basic ecumenical "story" I had learned in seminary and graduate school was full of interesting characters, not all men either, who believed passionately that the church should be one, that unity should incorporate a rich diversity, and that unity was not for its own sake, but so that the church could better praise and witness to the triune God, and serve humanity and all creation.

As I taught, I learned more and more about the Scriptures and about the church. And the more I learned, the clearer it became to me that the ecumenical movement had to be brought to the center of the church's worship and life, and acknowledged as God's special calling for the churches today.

Along the way I formed my idea of the qualities which ecumenical leaders would need to survive. These were diverse, demanding, and sometimes mutually contradictory, qualities such as tact, forthrightness, sensitivity, passionate conviction, keen intelligence, simplicity and directness of bearing and expression, spiritual depth, humility, the patience of Job, the impatience of Amos, a comprehensive grasp not only of the Bible, but of how the various churches read and (sometimes literally!) "use" it, a knowledge not only of theology but of the theolog*ies* of countless churches, as well as a mastery of church history, Christian ethics and so on. Imagine my surprise upon finding all these qualities in a single person—for that was, more or less, my first impression on meeting Paul Crow.

There are also other aspects to the ecumenical journey, and Paul knows about these as well. He may have withstood more jet lag than anyone else on the planet. He probably has made more speeches, on less notice, than any five of his friends put together. And there are those famous *postcards* which reflect, I suspect, Paul's longing to keep in touch with family, friends and colleagues, and to keep *them* in touch with the latest developments in the ecumenical world.

Through twenty years of friendship and close collaboration I have been priviledged to see many more of the qualities which make this complex man the gift he has been to his family and his friends, to the churches and to the ecumenical movement. I look forward to the next twenty years!

Ted Nottingham writes:

My first encounter with the work of Dr. Crow was through his book *Christian Unity: Matrix for Mission.* I had entered seminary after a long spiritual search, only to find myself confronted with the dry bones of academia. Upon discovering the writings of a Disciples theologian who quoted the likes of Thomas Merton and spoke of the critical importance of the contemplative spiritual teachings from different traditions within Christianity, I was inspired with new hope for the relevance and future of our denomination.

Dr. Crow's voice was a cry in the wilderness of reductionist rationalism and secular social activism masquerading as Christian wisdom and charity. He was one of the very few who called for a rooting and grounding in the deeper teachings of the Faith, those that carry in their wake transcendent and transforming power for individual lives.

As I later came to know Dr. Crow through my work at the General Offices of the Christian Church (Disciples of Christ), I discovered another prophetic element in his leadership—his relentless insistence that the Disciples recognize at the core of their identity an indissoluble link with the Church Universal. Indeed, Dr. Crow has gone out on the far edge of that proverbial limb and courageously stated that if we do not access the grand panorama of Christian wisdom in all its varied manifestations—Orthodox, Catholic, and so on—our denomination would suffer the tragic fate of becoming a narrow provincial expression of the Body of Christ, little more than an intriguing historical anecdote of questionable value for the future.

Dr. Crow's deep appreciation of the great men and women who lived only a few generations removed from the appearance of the Anointed One, when His teachings were not yet entirely diluted and fragmented, has led him to the radical conclusion that the heart and soul of ecumenism, and of the very future of religious institutions, is to be found in the integration of the vision of Christian wisdom that has been handed down by the saints, martyrs, and lovers of God who have come before us.

Dr. Crow's own legacy is found not only in his long devotion to the development of ecumenism, but in his personal experience and commitment to the teachings of the Faith that belong not to this or that group and culture, but to all followers of the Holy One of God.

And now in conclusion, we offer together heartfelt thanks to all the contributors of essays, tributes, the bibliography and photographs; and to all who have helped with the myriad steps and tasks involved in producing this book. We commend it to its readers, in the hope that this celebration of the life and achievements of Paul Crow may further the cause of Christ's church—its unity, its witness, and its service to all creation.

Thomas F. Best
Theodore J. Nottingham

CONTRIBUTORS

I. *Articles/Editors*

Dr. Charles B. Ashanin is Professor of Early Church History Emeritus, Christian Theological Seminary, Indianapolis, Indiana, and a member of the Orthodox Church, American Jurisdiction Antiochian Patriarchate.

Rev. Dr. Thomas F. Best, a Pastor of the Christian Church (Disciples of Christ), is Executive Secretary for Faith and Order, Unit I, World Council of Churches, Geneva, Switzerland.

Rev. Dr. Emilio Castro, a Methodist Pastor from Uruguay, is a former General Secretary of the WCC and a former head of its Commission on World Mission and Evangelism.

Rev. Dr. Daniell C. Hamby, a Priest in the Episcopal Diocese of Pennsylvania, is General Secretary of the Consultation on Church Union.

Rev. Diane C. Kessler, a Pastor in the United Church of Christ, is Executive Director of the Massachusetts Council of Churches, Boston, Massachusetts

Rev. Dr. Michael Kinnamon, a Pastor of the Christian Church (Disciples of Christ), is Dean of Lexington Theological Seminary, Lexington, Kentucky.

Dr. William C. Nichols has held Professorships in the fields of marriage and the family, and psychology, at Florida State University, the Merrill-Palmer Institute (Detroit), and the University of Alabama in Birmingham. He has been a close friend of Dr. Crow for over 40 years. Athens, Georgia.

Rev. Theodore J. Nottingham, a Pastor of the Christian Church (Disciples of Christ), is Director of Production and Consultation Services in the Office of Communication, Christian Church (Disciples of Christ), Indianapolis, Indiana, and Managing Editor of *Mid-Stream*.

Rev. Dr. William J. Nottingham served with the Division of Overseas Ministries, Christian Church (Disciples of Christ) in the U.S. and Canada, for twenty-five years and was its president from 1984-1994; he is Affiliate Professor of Mission at Christian Theological Seminary, Indianapolis.

Dr. Mary Tanner is General Secretary of the Council for Christian Unity, General Synod of the Church of England, London, and Moderator of the Commission on Faith and Order, World Council of Churches.

Rev. Fr. Jean M. R. Tillard, O. P., is Professor of Dogmatic Theology at the College Dominicain, Ottawa, Canada, and at the University of Fribourg, Switzerland. He is a Vice-Moderator of the Commission on Faith and Order, World Council of Churches.

Dr. David M. Thompson, past-Moderator of the United Reformed Church in the United Kingdom, is Lecturer in Modern Church History at Cambridge University, Cambridge, England.

Rev. Dr. William D. Watley is Senior Minister of the St. James African Methodist Episcopal Church, Newark, New Jersey, U.S.A.

Rev. Dr. Peggy Way is Professor of Pastoral Theology at Eden Theological Seminary, St. Louis, Missouri, U.S.A.

Rev. Dr. Hans-Ruedi Weber, a Pastor of the Swiss Protestant Church Federation, was Director of Biblical Studies for the World Council of Churches from 1971-1988.

II. *Tributes*

His All Holiness Bartholomew of Constantinople is the Ecumenical Patriarch of the worldwide Orthodox Church, Turkey. He has served on the Executive Committee and Central Committee of the World Council of Churches, and has been an officer of the Faith and Order Commission, World Council of Churches.

His Holiness Alexy II is Patriarch of Moscow and All Russia. He has served as chairman of the Presidium and Advisory Council of the Conference of European Churches, and on the Central Committee of the World Council of Churches.

His Eminence Edward Idris Cardinal Cassidy is President of the Pontifical Council for Promoting Christian Unity of the Catholic Church, Rome.

Rev. Dr. Richard Hamm is General Minister and President of the Christian Church (Disciples of Christ) in the United States and Canada, Indianapolis, Indiana.

Rev. Dr. Konrad Raiser, a Pastor of the Evangelical Church in Germany, is General Secretary of the World Council of Churches, Geneva, Switzerland.

Rev. Dr. Vinton R. Anderson is Presiding Bishop of the 2nd Episcopal District of the African Methodist Episcopal Church. He is a President of the World Council of Churches, and a Vice-President of the Consultation on Church Union.

Rev. Dr. Joan Brown Campbell, a Pastor of the Christian Church (Disciples of Christ), is General Secretary of the National Council of Churches of Christ in the USA.

Rev. Dr. Fred B. Craddock, a Pastor of the Christian Church (Disciples of Christ), is Bandy Distinguished Professor of Preaching and New Testament, Emeritus, in the Candler School of Theology of Emory University.

Dr. Vivian U. Robinson is President of the Consultation on Church Union, having taught in colleges of the Christian Methodist Episcopal Church in Georgia.

Dr. Howard E. Short is Professor of Church History Emeritus at Lexington Theological Seminary, Lexington, Kentucky, and Vice President Emeritus of the Christian Board of Publication, St. Louis, Missouri.

The Most Reverend Desmond M. Tutu, Anglican Archbishop Emeritus of Cape Town, South Africa, is Chairperson of the Truth and Reconciliation Commission, South Africa.

Archbishop John Vikström, of the Evangelical Lutheran Church of Finland, is Archbishop of Turku and Finland.

Rev. Dr. G. Hugh Wilson, Senior Minister of the First Christian Church, Norman, Oklahoma, is Chairperson of the Board of the Council on Christian Unity of the Christian Church (Disciples of Christ).

III. *Bibliography*

Dr. Peter M. Morgan is President of the Disciples of Christ Historical Society, Nashville, Tennessee.

The Rev. David I. McWhirter is Director of Library and Archives of the Disciples of Christ Historical Society, Nashville, Tennessee.

Dr. Phil Dare is Librarian of Lexington Theological Seminary, Lexington, Kentucky.

CONTENTS

Howard E. Short   271
Professor of Church History Emeritus, Lexington
Theological Seminary

Desmond Tutu   275
Archbishop Emeritus, Anglican Church of South Africa

John Vikström   278
Archbishop of Turku and Finland, Evangelical Lutheran Church
in Finland

G. Hugh Wilson   280
Senior Minister, First Christian Church (Disciples of Christ),
Norman, Oklahoma, and Chairperson of the Council on
Christian Unity, 1994-1997

Peter Morgan, David I. McWhirter, and Phillip Dare

Ecumenical Issues and Impulses

ESSAYS IN HONOR OF PAUL A. CROW, JR.

CHAPTER ONE

PAUL ABERNATHY CROW, JR. – THE SHAPING OF AN ECUMENIST

William C. Nichols

1931:
- Life and society: The Great Depression was worldwide.
- Baseball: Babe Ruth and Lou Gehrig combined to hit 92 home runs for the New York Yankees.
- Ecumenism: The Anglicans and the Old Catholics entered into full communion.

Who is Paul Crow? "As much as anyone you'll ever meet, Paul Crow is a product of where he came from," says Mary Matthews Crow, his wife of forty-two years. A Disciples pastor, professor, ecumenist, and historian, he entered the world in the midst of the Great Depression (1929-1936). Athletics—especially baseball, "the national pastime"—was a significant part of his developing years in a small milltown in East Alabama, and the South and religion were an early and enduring part of his being.

A longtime member of the board of directors of the Disciples' Council on Christian Unity describes him flatly as "simply the best" in working with diverse and powerful, influential religious leaders and taking a leadership role in the ecumenical movement. Under this leadership the Disciples of Christ have been unusually visible and have exercised influence in the world ecumenical movement and international church affairs far beyond their comparatively small numbers. How did someone who grew up in a small Alabama milltown acquire the ability to move comfortably among the heads and representatives of great world religious bodies, while also thriving on relationships with ordinary people and local congregations in many countries and cultures?

"He hasn't planned out his life as some people do, but has been influenced strongly by a stream of influential people, starting with his parents, and by the contexts in which he has lived" says Mary Crow. Among the earliest and most basic were his family, life in the Chattahooche Valley, and the University of Alabama.

The Basic shapers: the Parkers and the Crows

Both of Paul's parents, Beulah Parker Crow (1910-1980) and Paul Abernathy Crow (1906-1985), came from rural, small town settings. Beulah's hometown, the village of Parker, just outside of Panama City in the Florida Panhandle, was founded by her ancestor, Captain Peter Ferdinand Parker. Her maternal grandfather, Frank W. Hoskins, was an Englishman who arrived in the United States as a young man and as a teacher, postmaster, merchant, civic leader, church organist, and writer-historian played a key role in the development of Bay County, Florida. Included among his writings was *The History of Methodism in West and East Florida* and numerous articles in *The Florida Historical Quarterly.* The third of four children, Beulah moved to Birmingham, Alabama with her parents following high school graduation. A beautiful young woman, she met Paul A. Crow at dances in Birmingham. They formed a skillful, graceful couple who won prizes for their ballroom dancing.

Paul A. Crow, Sr., one of five children—he had two brothers and two sisters—grew up in Hollins, near Sylacauga, Alabama, and graduated from Sylacauga High school, where he played baseball. Moving to Birmingham, he worked for the Israel Decorating Company and played semi-pro baseball. Known as "Daddy Paul" by his grandchildren and probably the greatest single influence in his son's life, he was a mild-mannered, well-liked, and influential presence. The equanimity with which Paul Jr. typically views the world was a readily apparent quality in his father. Mr. Crow deeply loved the southern region of the United States ("the South"), and its traditions and values were always visible in his life. Being Southern gave him a sense of identity and nurtured him, but did not blind him to its racial inequities. As an adult he spoke out for Black people and as a result once was labeled at work with one of the South's most negative epitaphs of the times. This example and influence could be seen decades later when his son emphasized racial inequity as a major issue facing Christianity.

Paul Jr. was born November 17, 1931, in Birmingham, but lived in Lanett, Alabama, from two years of age onward. Beulah suffered from poor health. She had a difficult time with childbirth and almost died from internal bleeding. Paul had to be an only child because of the complications attendant to his birth. His mother was a compassionate woman. Many stories are told by Lanett people about how she brought food and cheer to those who were ill and in needy times, and was kind and helpful to all she knew. In later years, "Momma B," as the grandchildren called Beulah, was "always sick and fearing illness."

Like many others, the Crows suffered greatly during the Great Depression (1929-1936). Although he never mentioned it to his son, "Daddy Paul" later told his grandchildren about the pain and desperation of being out of work for a year. Unemployed in the spring of 1933 and visiting a sister in Lanett, Jude Hammock (Paul Jr.'s "Auntie"), Mr. Crow learned that there might be a possibility of employment at the local textile mill. As the family story goes, it was his baseball skill that tipped the balance for a job, and thus set the Crows' future. At the end of an interview, the mill's general manager asked:

> "What did you say your batting average was?"
> ".355 last season," was the reply.
> "Mr. Crow, I think there is a place for you in the machine shop."

Mr. Crow stayed with the mill for the next thirty-eight years and retired as head of the air conditioning department, spending the final twelve years in management. Largely self-taught beyond the high school level, he took courses on air conditioning and management and read widely on subjects relating to human behavior.

During the summers, Mr. Crow starred in a semi-pro baseball league among area towns. Some professionals such as Hall of Famer Dizzy Dean played in Lanett occasionally on weekends for extra money. Before World War II the towns formed one professional team that played as the "Valley Rebels" in the Georgia-Alabama League. Mr. Crow played right field and Paul learned the skills of baseball as the bat boy.

The Valley and life in Lanett

It is called the "Greater Valley Area" according to the chamber of commerce, but to the 40,000 people who live and work in LaFayette, Lanett, and Valley in Alabama and West Point in Georgia near the Chattahooche River on the border of the two states, it is simply "The Valley." The textile manufacturing heritage, a magnificent climate, and a panoramic countryside of rivers, lakes, and woods give the 600 square mile Valley a strong sense of unity, identity, and powerful appeal for most of its residents. Traditional Southern values of work, family, worship, and play have characterized life in The Valley.

"Lanett meant a lot to me. People appreciated my family and encouraged me. Young people in Lanett knew they were valued and important," says Paul Crow. As an only child, he was, according to his own admission, "pampered." His father once told a colleague that he only disciplined his son once when he was quite young. After that, he said, he never felt that he had to do more than to tell Paul what was expected; even as a child he was very serious and responsible. This demeanor and the open and easy social acceptance insured that the younger Crow would grow up with everybody liking him. Very early, his peers began to seek him out as a leader, establishing a pattern that has continued and make him one of those rare persons who has been "president of practically everything" in which he has been a member. In high school he was popular and was elected president of the senior class.

Mr. Crow later told his son, "We knew you had a destiny when you were in junior high school." Paul recognizes that he fulfilled some of his father's ambitions but never felt a pressure to do so. Both parents celebrated who their son was and what he was doing. He says, "My mother's love was very genuine but became possessive as her illness and psychological needs grew. When I was in college, I had to tell her that I had to be permitted to make my own decisions. She did."

Work was a part of his everyday life. Young Paul had a paper route delivering the celebrated *Atlanta Constitution*. Revealing management skills, he divided his route so he could eat a Southern breakfast at his Aunt Jude's house in the middle of his delivery schedule. Even the newspaper he delivered exerted an influence on his development. When told that Ralph McGill, of the *Atlanta Constitution*, was a great man, he began to read McGill's writings, launching a lifelong pattern of reading the work of important authors. Paul later worked during summers in the mill's weave room and in the dye works. Eventually he gave up his early ambitions to play professional baseball (although offered a contract by the New York Yankees) and decided to enter university to become a chemist.

The Crow network was composed of their friends, relatives and the ministers of the First Christian Church (Disciples of Christ). The Crows lived simply in apartments until Paul was in high school. Then they bought a frame mill house and, in his senior year, an automobile. As long as his father lived, Paul in his adult years spent a week or so of summer vacation painting the house. Although not "upper-class" in terms of income, practically speaking the Crows were upper-class in their social contacts in Lanett. Bankers, physicians, teachers, and others who were prominent in the community were close friends. Paul learned to be comfortable in the presence of eminent and influential people as well as with the more ordinary people of the community.

The Church was the center of the Crows' life. The family attended twice on Sunday for church school and worship, and on Wednesday nights for prayer meetings. Both parents were active lay leaders in the First Christian Church. Mr. Crow sang in the choir and directed it for the last twenty years of his life. Not surprisingly, the ministers always influenced Paul and encouraged his leadership. He remembers Osceola (Jake) Highsmith in particular as "a man of faith who taught the Gospel simply and in ways so that people could relate to the Christian life." Baptized at age 10, Paul became active in the Christian Youth Fellowship and in high school began to attend Christian Youth Fellowship (CYF) conferences and to see the outside world. In the 10th grade he was elected president of the Alabama CYF. When a university sophomore, he served as President of the International CYF and spent four months going across the United States on speaking tours.

A high school English teacher, Charles Martin, also shaped Paul, especially by instilling a love for literature, art, and writing. Also the choir director for the First Christian Church and a frequent dinner guest at the Crows' table, "Mr. Martin touched our lives with creativity," recalls Paul. Martin introduced his students to poetry and Shakespeare, taking the class to Atlanta to see plays by Shakespeare, and played classical music in the classroom. "He gave a sense of integrity to life," Paul says.

Lanett was typical of Southern towns in that athletics played a major role in life. Paul was a starter on the high school baseball and basketball teams. During the summers he played American Legion baseball, twice playing on teams that went to state tournaments. He believed he had to play football in order to get the coach's favor to play on the Lanett basketball team, and was a reserve quarterback. The coach for all sports was Mal Morgan, a former all-star college athlete and World War II Army captain. A great motivator who could develop young people, Morgan reached out to his young player and provided some needed "tough love," emphasizing that "nobody is going to hand anything to you—you have to work for it." The Lannett basketball team played its way into the state high school tournament at the University of Alabama during Paul's senior year. A sports writer at the tournament later said, "Two players stood out on that Lanett team. One was a tall, slender sophomore whose athleticism later carried him to a career in professional football. The other was a chunky, serious senior guard who ran the team on the floor. He was, of course, Paul Crow."

Membership in the Boy Scouts also gave Paul "tough love." His scouting experiences led to one of the pivotal events in his personal and religious life. When he was to be recognized as an Eagle Scout in a service at his church, he eagerly invited his friend Leon ("Mug") to the service. A lasting impression was made when "Mug," a Roman Catholic, had to withdraw because his priest told him that it would be a mortal sin for him to enter the First Christian Church. Would there have been a Disciples of Christ-Roman Catholic Dialogue without this experience?

Mary Crow's assessment of who Paul is as a person is succinct and perceptive: "Being an only child and the center of his parents' life, parents who instilled in him that he was someone special, gave him the drive to leave The Valley. This sense of specialness and drive has caused him to keep growing and developing."

Providence and the University of Alabama

The University of Alabama in Tuscaloosa gave Paul a entirely new and broader outlook. Paul says that "pure providence took me there." He flourished in the new atmosphere, reaching new levels of achievement. Pledging a social fraternity, which gave him a sense of community on a large state university campus, he eventually served as fraternity president and found his leadership development moving to another level. Active in campus intramural sports and religious life, he also became president of the Disciples Student Fellowship at Tuscaloosa's First Christian Church and later served as vice-president of the International CYF and, in 1952-1953, as president.

So also was his personal world expanding. Mary Evelyn Matthews, a member of the Tuscaloosa church, and Paul had met at a state Disciples youth meeting when she was a 14-year-old high school freshman and Paul a year older. They came to know each other gradually through youth meetings and conferences and in the church. Their first date occurred in Mary's senior year in high school when she accepted an invitation from Paul to the spring formal dance of his fraternity. They dated for all four years of Mary's undergraduate career at the University of Alabama, where she was a member of a sorority and a campus beauty, and married on September 11, 1955, after her graduation and Paul's first year of seminary.

Paul's honors list at Alabama was impressive. President of the student body of the School of Chemistry, he went though the stages of the university's honorary societies, progressing from the freshman honorary to Omicron Delta Kappa, the highest honorary, as a senior. Enrolled in the Reserve Officers Training Corps and a member of its highly regarded drill team, he was on the way to becoming a distinguished military graduate and receiving an officer's commission in the Signal Corps when he resigned from ROTC because of his career change toward the Christian ministry.

His parents and members of the Lanett church knew that Paul had been unconsciously struggling with the challenge of ministry for several years. Although Paul was not aware of where he was headed, he did know that he had been greatly influenced during his college days by several campus ministers, including the Baptist campus minister from whom he took New Testament courses, the Roman Catholic campus minister with whom he had a "faith and reason" course, and the Methodist and Episcopal campus ministers. During the summers, in ecumenical United Christian Youth Movement meetings, he was greatly impressed by Vanderbilt University theological professor Nels F. S. Ferré and Hanns Lilje, a German Lutheran Bishop who had been imprisoned by the Nazis. In the summer between his junior and senior years during a communion service at an international youth conference at Champaign-Urbana, Illinois, he felt a call to the ministry.

The new vocation was undertaken immediately. At the University of Alabama Paul was asked to fill the Disciples' vacant campus minister position for 1953-54. He also started preaching on Sundays at the small Cottondale Christian Church, a few miles from the campus. This service as a minister of local congregations lasted from 1953 until 1961, a period in which he served Disciples churches in Alabama and Kentucky, and an historic United Church of Christ congregation in Hadley, Massachusetts.

Ecumenism and concern with the unity of the Church began to grow into a burning desire to unite all believers around the earth in Christ. Paul's ecumenical fellowship began in the United Christian Youth Movement (UCYM), which was part of the National Council of Churches. There he began to meet and to develop friendships with youth leaders of other churches, including Andrew Young and Donald Shriver, who were working for the UCYM and who later became distinguished leaders in the American church and society. While attending a 1954 UCYM meeting, Paul saw John R. Mott and met Toyohiko Kagawa, a Japanese Christian known as "the Albert Schweitzer of Asia," Philip Potter, director of the youth department of the World Council of Churches, D. T. Niles, missionary statesman from Ceylon, A. Dale Fiers, beloved leader of the Disciples, and other major religious figures who had gathered at Evanston, Illinois, for the second assembly of the World Council of Churches.

The flames of unity were focused and fanned during Paul's senior university year by an encounter with Charles Clayton Morrison, editor of *The Christian Century* and world ecumenist, who was the speaker for the University of Alabama's Religious Emphasis Week. As student chairperson of the event, Paul had the responsibility of hosting the famous Disciples lecturer. Mary was involved because her father gave them the use of an old Cadillac automobile for the week. In addition to formal contacts when Morrison lectured on the contents of his forthcoming book, *The Unfinished Reformation,* the young couple engaged in a series of informal conversations with him, starting a friendship that was maintained in subsequent years. Before the week was ended, Morrison had charged Paul to work for the unity of the Church in whatever form his ministry might take. Although the youthful zeal for unity never flagged, it was a few years before Paul Crow's career was focused entirely on ecumenism.

Again in the right place: Lexington and Hartford

For his seminary education, Paul chose The College of the Bible (now Lexington Theological Seminary) in Kentucky because of ministers he had known and because of its emphasis on preaching. Concerned because he was entering the seminary as a chemistry major and without a strong liberal arts background like most other students, he was determined to work hard to overcome his educational deficiencies. He graduated with honors.

With an undergraduate minor in history, it is not surprising that in studying with Professor Howard E. Short, Paul discovered a love for church history and thus set the course for a major theme in his career. He would become a church historian—focussing on patristics and modern church history—and be concerned with teaching the development of the ecumenical movement. Dr. Short, who had been on the faculty of the first graduate school at the Ecumenical Institute Bossey (Switzerland), gave his students a vision of Christian unity. The ecumenical vision also was greatly enhanced during Paul's senior year in seminary when he was part of a youth delegation of the National Council of Churches sent to visit the church in thirteen Latin American countries while en route to the Latin American Ecumenical Youth Assembly in Colombia. While at the conference, he and a female delegate prepared and delivered a paper on racism and the world church.

Regarding his theological experience at Lexington, "I was in the right place again, as I had been at the University of Alabama," recalls Paul. Theological and biblical study aided in his development of a deep pastoral interest. During his first year in Kentucky, he served as student minister of two rural congregations—Moorefield Christian Church and the Botland Christian Church outside Bardstown. The second year in Kentucky (1955) was momentous: Paul and Mary married and the Botland church became a full-time charge, meaning that the young couple would spend their weekends at Botland for the next two years. The Crows formed strong personal relationships with persons in the congregation and still maintain friendships with people from all the churches where Paul was the minister.

Paul had decided to become the pastor of a local congregation when he completed his seminary studies. Other forces were at work, however. He wrote his bachelor of divinity thesis on "The Nature of the Unity We Seek," the theme of the 1957 North American Conference on Faith and Order, held at Oberlin, Ohio. Professor Short and seminary president Riley B. Montgomery urged Paul to secure a Ph.D. degree. Admitted both by the Yale University Divinity School and Hartford Seminary Foundation in Connecticut, Paul accepted a Jaccobus Fellowship at Hartford to study for a master's degree.

Things were beginning to come together. Hartford had a strong emphasis on mission and, with Dr. Matthew Spinka on the faculty, had "the best program in modern church history." Hartford powerfully connected theology, church history, ecumenism, and mission. Paul wrote a master's thesis on the Church of South India, the first united church to reconcile episcopal and non-episcopal ministries. Urged by his Lexington mentors and a retiring Professor Spinka to complete a doctorate degree, Paul stayed, and earned a Ph.D. degree with honors under church historian Robert S. Paul. A leading scholar on Puritanism and ecumenical theology, Dr. Paul came to Hartford from Oxford, England, and from serving on the faculty of the Ecumenical Institute Bossey. With Dr. Paul another close and lasting collegial relationship developed.

During the last days at Hartford, another struggle emerged. During his doctoral studies, Paul had served as minister of the First Congregational Church, in Hadley, Massachusetts, a 300-year-old church and the eleventh oldest in the New England state. A painting of the Hadley church hangs in the Crow living room today, a reminder of the ministry and of the personal relationships formed during the four years of Hadley experience. As the end neared at Hartford, Paul was invited to serve the historic Jonathan Edwards Congregational Church in Northampton, Massachusetts, but he felt that he "had to come back to the Disciples," and this he did—although, as destiny decreed, not to a pastoral ministry.

Back to the Disciples: six years as a seminary professor

The return to the Disciples of Christ was to a teaching position, back in Kentucky's Blue Grass country. Even before he had completed his dissertation at Hartford, Lexington Theological Seminary called him as a professor of church history. He taught early and modern church history and, as the youngest faculty member, also served as registrar for the first two years and supervised bachelor of divinity theses. The first year was probably the hardest; he recalls working nightly from 10 PM to 2 AM to get his dissertation completed. By that time, Mary and Paul had two children, Carol born November 14, 1958 during the Hartford days, and Stephen Paul, born August 16, 1961, just as they returned to Lexington.

During those years in Lexington, Paul came to know Thomas Merton, the Trappist monk and poet, spending retreat days at Gethsemane from time to time. Beginning to see the essential role of prayer and contemplation in the life of the church, he acquired a lasting emphasis on spirituality. His regular discipline is to arise early in the morning and end the night by spiritual reading, contemplating, and praying.

As the Crow family was returning to Lexington, events in American ecumenism were occurring that would shape Paul's life and career for more than the next three decades. In 1960 Eugene Carson Blake's electrifying sermon at San Francisco on church unity launched the Consultation on Church Union (COCU). George L. Hunt, a New Jersey Presbyterian minister, served as a part-time executive for the new church union organization. While on the seminary faculty, Paul was named associate executive secretary and set about staffing COCU's theological commissions, a task that he undertook in addition to his seminary responsibilities. As a young professor he became a friend and colleague with many American church leaders.

Following six years in Lexington, the Crows, now numbering five (with the addition of Susan on January 15, 1965) packed up and went to England, where Paul had scheduled a sabbatical year at Oxford University. That experience, in which he served as a Visiting Fellow at Mansfield College, offered the occasion to interact with many scholars from various backgrounds, and to do important research. This year was one of the highlights of his life: "I reached a level of scholarship—

focussed but relaxed scholarship—I had never before been able to achieve." Paul developed friendships with Anglicans and Congregationalists, such as Michael Ramsay, the Archbishop of Canterbury; Donald Coggan, Archbishop of York; Oxford scholars such as Henry Chadwick, George Caird, John Marsh, David Jenkins (later Bishop of Durham); and visiting American professors such as Gabriel Fackre and Carl Braaten. At several Oxford colleges he engaged in dialogues with colleagues and enjoyed the high table tradition. In that year of immersion in scholarship he learned the contribution that critical thinking can make to one's experience and sharing of the Christian faith.

The Crow family also enjoyed the year immensely, from living in ancient Oxford to playing at the mysterious Stonehenge ruins to taking a cruise to the biblical sites in Greece and Asia Minor. Mary spent countless hours on her knees in churches, making brass rubbings of art, some of which adorn the Crow dining room today. During the sabbatical the family expected to return to Kentucky. Paul says, "When I went to the faculty of Lexington Theological Seminary, I thought I had reached the pinnacle of my career. I thought I would retire as a professor there."

A career in ecumenism: the COCU years

Due to the efforts of George G. Beazley, Jr., president of the Disciples' Council on Christian Unity, and James I. McCord, president of Princeton Theological Seminary, Paul was in effect drafted as the first general secretary when the Consultation on Church Union established a full-time staff. After turning down their invitation three times because he wished to remain at Lexington, he acquiesced. In one of his first acts, Paul chose Princeton, New Jersey, as the site for COCU's offices, primarily because of the foremost theological community found there, with its great resources and its proximity to New York's airports and other transportation hubs. Because of his study of the Church of South India, which had faced all the theological issues that lay before COCU, Paul knew what was ahead. As a nationally visible leader he developed his own leadership style, giving COCU a strong theological component and a strong diplomatic component.

Major international travel began, and Paul Crow became a world presence in the Christian unity movement over the years 1968 to 1974. (By 1997 he had traveled to more than 90 countries in his work, and had delivered more than 25 major lectureships in universities and theological seminaries throughout the United States and around the world.) These "COCU days" were a time of heavy involvement in the task of interpretation, including a great deal of speaking and lecturing on unity. "My task was to nurture the churches toward a church truly catholic, truly evangelical, and truly reformed while working with theologians and church leaders to discover the model of church unity God wants and the churches would affirm," he reflects. And Paul's service for COCU has continued throughout his career; later on he chaired the Church Order Commission which redefined the goal of the Consultation on Church Union as "covenant communion," focusing the COCU vision on a new and creative understanding of "Koinonia ecclesiology."

A career in ecumenism: rooted in Disciples, linked with the whole Church

Following the death of his close friend George Beazley in Moscow while on a visit to the Russian Orthodox Church, Paul was persuaded, largely by two of his mentors, Paul Stauffer and Harold Johnson, to accept the role of president of the Disciples' Council on Christian Unity—a position he has filled from 1974 to the present. He left Princeton and COCU for Indianapolis reluctantly, yet with a feeling of satisfaction, calling his work with COCU "a career gift I could not have anticipated. I was privileged to participate in the most dramatic process toward Christian unity in American history."

Paul's service as president of the Council on Christian Unity has been marked by two themes: first, his determination to make the ecumenical vision a reality for Disciples at national, regional and local levels. He has fought tirelessly within the Disciples to ensure that we are true to our heritage by truly claiming the unity of church, as he said in a notable essay, as our "polar star." He has exercised this leadership at the national level of the church, but equally at the local level. Those who think of Paul as a world Christian leader are often surprised to learn that, in fact, he has often spent twenty or more weekends a year with local congregations—preaching, teaching and interpreting the biblical vision of Christian unity to Disciples and within other denominations.

The second theme marking Paul's tenure at the Council on Christian Unity was his determination to set Disciples at the heart of the modern ecumenical movement. Here he sought both to represent the distinctive gifts and talents of the Disciples vision in the ecumenical arena, and to bring to Disciples a sense of the whole church in the whole world. This has meant service on behalf of Disciples in several "ecumenical spaces." One of these has been the National Council of Churches of Christ in the USA. Paul has been a member of the Executive Committee and National Board of the National Council from 1974, and will continue to serve until in that capacity until 1998, and he was the Moderator of the Presidential Panel which redesigned the National Council as a "community of communions."

Another area of passion for Paul has been his leadership in the World Council of Churches (WCC), its Faith and Order Commission and its Ecumenical Institute at Bossey, Switzerland. Remarkably Paul's first Faith and Order Commission meeting was already in 1960 in St. Andrews, Scotland, where he drafted and presented the report from the Youth Delegation. He was well prepared for involvement in the Faith and Order movement: as noted above his B.D. thesis had been on a Faith and Order theme, and his Ph.D. dissertation at Hartford (1962) was on "The Concept of Unity in Diversity in the History of the Faith and Order Movement 1927-1957." He has served on the Commission on Faith and Order since his appointment in 1968, and will continue as one of its Vice-Moderators through the WCC assembly in 1998. With the exception of Aarhus in 1964, he has attended every one of the Commission meetings since St. Andrews in 1960, as well as attending (and often moderating, or helping to plan) countless Faith and Order consultations. Two programs have been especially close to Paul's heart. One is the path-breaking study programme on "The Unity of the Church and the Renewal of Human Community," which Paul moderated over the decade beginning in 1984. His staff colleague in this study was another key Disciples ecumenist, Thomas F. Best. The other is the work with united and uniting churches; here Paul attended five of their six international consultations from 1967 on, chairing the one in Sri Lanka in 1981 and reading major papers at several, including the most recent, in Jamaica in 1995. In addition he has attended several of Faith and Order's "Bilateral Forums" focusing on high-level international discussions between churches.

Beyond all this Paul has fought over the years to maintain a Disciples presence in the Faith and Order context, through a staff secondment to the commission. Long funded through the Week of Compassion, and in recent years directly through the Council on Christian Unity, this position—held since the 1970s by a succession of able Disciples ecumenists—has been a major witness to the Disciples' commitment to ecumenism on the international scene. All this adds up to an unparalleled record of service in the Faith and Order Commission, that "most representative theological forum in the world."

Paul has also given decisive leadership on the broader World Council of Churches scene. A member of its Central Committee from 1975-1998, and of its Unit I Commission from 1991-1998, he has been the major voice for Disciples within the WCC. He has served as Bible study lecturer for at least one Central Committee meeting. It is typical of the man that during his years of service with the WCC he has become friends with all five of its general secretaries: W. A. Visser 't Hooft, Eugene Carson Blake, Philip Potter, Emilio Castro, and Konrad Raiser.

Of all his WCC commitments, Paul guards a special affection for his service as Moderator and member of the Board of the Ecumenical Institute, Bossey from 1975 to 1983. Paul lead Bossey through its most severe crisis, raising together with his friend Luis Carols Weil (then the WCC finance officer) the Bossey Endowment Fund. It is not for nothing that Paul Crow is remembered by Bossey staff as "the Saviour of Bossey," and a tireless champion of its unique role as a laboratory of ecumenical learning.

But Paul was also active during these years in other areas, making contacts between the Disciples and the great "confessional families" which preserve important aspects of the Christian tradition. He was convinced that it was essential to establish strong relations between Disciples and the Roman Catholic Church, and thus spent eighteen months and five trips to Rome to establish the Disciples of Christ-Roman Catholic International Dialogue in 1977. In those months he became a friend of Cardinal Johannes Willebrands, president of the Secretariat (now Pontifical Council) for Promoting Christian Unity. This dialogue was Paul's special dream. He has been its Co-Moderator on behalf of the Disciples from 1977 on, and will continue in this role in his retirement. He recalls with special affection two reports from this international bilateral dialogue: that on "Apostolicity and Catholicity" (1982), and "The Church as Communion" (1992). All in all, Paul has been well placed to represent Disciples to the Roman Catholic Church—he has had one audience with Pope Paul VI and, if I count correctly, no fewer than 12 with Pope John Paul II!

Paul has also been keenly concerned with the distinctive identity and witness of the Orthodox Church. Enjoying a friendship with virtually all the Orthodox Patriarchs (of Constantinople, Moscow, Alexandria and so on), he has sought to create links between Disciples and their special tradition and understanding of the gospel message, and the wider ecumenical movement. He remembers in particular the official visit of Disciples to the Russian Orthodox Church, which he arranged in 1988. It is typical of Paul's gift for building bridges that he linked the major event then being celebrated by his hosts—the thousand-year anniversary of the Baptism of Rus in 988 A.D—with the 200th Birthday of Alexander Campbell, born in 1788!

During these years Paul's travels and worldwide ecumenical leadership reached extraordinary proportions. And in the midst of all this international involvement and witness, Paul comes back again and again to his home in the Christian Church (Disciples of Christ). He says he has struggled harder as president of the Council on Christian Unity than in any other position because "The issues are more complex, the ecumenical movement more diverse, and church diplomacy more demanding." He describes his vocation and role in terms of the larger Christian world picture in these terms: "Ironically, I have been friends with two popes, most orthodox patriarchs, and major Protestant leaders, yet I have maintained ties with local congregations because I need the contacts with local Christians."

How does Paul Crow relate effectively both with world religious leaders and local congregations? The answer can be stated simply: he maintains a genuine respect for all people; he treats the highly visible and the humble alike with respect and warmth, whether they are a shy couple invited over to share Christmas at their home in Hartford or Bishops at the 1988 Lambeth Conference. He thrives on the contacts with people, saying, "It is enriching, energizing to have an international circle of friends."

Reflections

Some of the major moments in Paul's life have occurred in large meetings. One was in 1986 at Assisi with Pope John Paul II, who had invited a hundred global leaders of all faiths to gather and pray together for peace. Another was a meeting of 3,000 people at the sixth assembly of the World Council of Churches at Vancouver, British Columbia, in 1983 when the Lima Liturgy was celebrated. "Even though some did not partake of communion," Paul says, "I knew for that one moment that the church was the way it ought to be—one in all things."

Paul expresses surprise that he has achieved the level of academic and theological status that he has gained. "I'm the first Crow in our immediate family to graduate from college." He adds, "My self-image would never have pushed me in the direction of a Ph.D." Some friends remember how difficult it was for him to conceive of the possibility of going beyond a master's degree. He asks, "What is the role of scholarship and how did I happen to go into that?" and adds, "I never had an ambition to be a scholar, but others pressed me in that direction." In reflecting on his years with the Council on Christian Unity, he provides another part of the answer. "The years here have been fulfilling; the role of the president of the council and chief ecumenical officer has a theological/academic component. It could never have been simply an administrative role. The ecumenical movement requires critical thinking."

Those who spent time with the Crows over the years quickly learned to appreciate the openness and nurturing qualities of Mary Crow. Open to an extent that can make Paul uncomfortable, she mixes humor and teasing with explicit expressions of caring and loving that are models for some of their more "constricted" friends. It is impossible to avoid feeling welcomed in their home. Mary has enjoyed experiences they have had because of Paul's work, including some of the traveling she has shared as well as some of the people they have met and the relationships they have maintained through the years with former parishioners. Basically steering clear of Paul's work, she has carved out appropriate roles for herself in church endeavors. Her nurturing qualities have found expression in a role as the first laywoman to chair a Disciples' regional Commission on Ministry and, twice, as director of overseas guests for the Christian Women's Fellowship (CWF) Quadrennial. She also has been local president of the CWF.

Many of Paul's characteristics come from his Southern heritage and experiences. These include his interest in developing people, young theologians, and involving them in ecumenism; his commitment to the Disciples; an abhorrence of racism, which is a deeper issue to him because of being Southern; and qualities of caring and hospitality. It has not been accidental that Paul has included mention of Lanett and the American South in lectures and sermons around the world. Nor has it been accidental that his courtesy, caring, and loyalty have been manifest in many friendships and collegial relationships lasting for decades. He believes his Southern heritage equipped him for living in the Church Universal.

Both Paul and Mary have found it hard to accept the jealousy of colleagues, political fights, and infighting in the church—things which have marred the life of all churches in recent decades. Paul has said, "The hardest times are when anybody calls into question my integrity," but he quickly adds, "I don't have many memories of really tough times. By and large I have experienced many more good times than bad times." Reflecting on the jealousies and political game-playing by some colleagues (whatever the reasons might have been) he says, "Perhaps I expect too much of other people." His claim about all sorts of difficulties—that he "felt I could handle them, this-will-pass kind of thing"—has a ring of authenticity for those who know him. Like his father, Paul demonstrates no tendency to engage in continuing bitterness, and moves on with life instead of dwelling on the past.

What is Paul Crow like as a person? Reflective, caring, at times secretive. And social, for he enjoys people. He always works with a sense of history, tradition, and destiny. While he has a serious side, he also enjoys and practices humor. Once, for example, he arrived home for Thanksgiving after an extended overseas trip and burst through the door with an exuberant and characteristic cry: "Break out the clam chowder!" Two close friends then struggled into the room with a sagging fishnet containing 50 cans of clam chowder in honor of his 50th birthday, leaving the honoree momentarily speechless.

The creativity that was nurtured in his youth is visible today in Paul's concern with art, music and literature. He has studied the major French impressionists for the past twenty-five years and continually delves into Southern literature from William Faulkner to Reynolds Price.

Retirement: another phase in the journey

The public announcement of Paul Crow's forthcoming retirement in December, 1998 as the Disciples chief ecumenical officer said, in part, that his retirement:

> will bring to a close a career that has included extraordinary service as a pastor and seminary professor, in key posts with the World and National Council of Churches, and as general secretary of the Consultation on Church Union. The Disciples General Assembly 1995 ratification of the COCU covenanting plan advanced Crow's signature personal and professional passion— the unity of the Church. The plan seeks to reconcile the mission and ministries of nine US denominations including the Disciples of Christ ecumenical partner, the United Church of Christ.

Paul Crow's unique legacy will include unparalleled perspectives. His personal notes and records contain sufficient material to keep him occupied in a second career: writing and interpreting much of the history of the Ecumenical Movement from the perspective of his personal participation in, and contributions to, the search for church unity over the past half-century.

When Paul Crow "passes the torch" to his successor in 1998—to begin another phase of his service to the Church and humanity—he will undoubtedly focus his vocation on a predictable mixture of reading, writing, teaching, contemplation, travelling to Cape Cod (a place where the Crows vacationed for twenty years and which has mystic qualities for Paul), visiting with friends, and sharing in the lives of children and grandchildren. To this point his life and ministry have been an incredible journey. Surely the God who gave him breath will lead him to other years and marks of faithfulness within the *oikoumene*, the whole inhabited world.

CHAPTER TWO

ECUMENICAL CHRISTIANITY AND THE ROLE OF A CHURCH HISTORIAN

PERSONAL REFLECTIONS AND REMINISCENCES

Charles B. Ashanin

I

One significant characteristic of Christianity is that from its very beginning it has understood itself as being universally relevant and therefore called to a universal mission. This is all the more striking when one considers its numerically small membership and its origin in a remote province of the Roman Empire, surrounded by far greater provinces and ancient civilizations.

But the Christian dream of its universal application was not just an idle dream. We know that in one generation following the crucifixion of its founder by the Roman authorities and the Jewish religious establishment, Christianity had become strong enough for the Roman Emperor Nero to issue, in 64 AD, a decree aimed at destroying its adherents in the city of Rome. And from that time forward, for the next two hundred and forty-nine years, the Roman Empire, one of the mightiest powers of the time, continued to persecute Christianity in an attempt to stamp it out.

And yet, with even greater persistence, by the early fourth century Christianity had compelled the Roman Empire to grant it the status of a tolerated religion through the famous Edict of Milan, issued by the Emperor Constantine and his colleague, Licinius. Not only was the spread of Christianity, in spite of adverse circumstances, phenomenal, but it achieved internal unity, in spite of its being scattered widely throughout the Empire and beyond it into the neighboring Persian Empire. This is not to say that, in the eclectic and philosophically pluralistic intellectual atmosphere of the Graeco-Roman world, Christianity did not suffer fragmentation by dissident groups, but these were not able to shatter its catholic ecumenical unity and oneness for a long time. It took a millenium and more before, under the pressure of political ideas copied by the Church from the Roman imperial theorists, there was a major split within the Christian commonwealth. This occurred in 1054 AD when the Greek-speaking Eastern part and the Latin Western part separated.

Since that time there have occurred, in the fifth and sixth centuries, considerable divisions within the Church, such as the formation of the Nestorian and Monophysite churches of the Middle East. These separations were aggravated by the rise of Islam in the seventh century. But the most shattering event in this decline of Christian unity occurred at the time of the Reformation in the sixteenth century, and the process has continued up to our own time as the American church historian, Martin E. Marty, has described in the second edition of his book, *A Short History of Christianity* (p. 307).

But in spite of all this unwelcome fragmentation Christianity never lost its original sense of being one faith delivered to the saints. History testifies that numerous efforts were made to heal the schism within Christendom, even among the most ardent antagonists among the Orthodox and the Roman Catholic Latins. Evidence of this are their attempts at reunion at the Councils of Lyon in 1274 AD and Florence in 1439 AD. In our own time, in the relationship between the Orthodox and the Roman Catholic Church there continue to be several "gestures," I would call them—rather than real efforts—to bring these two branches of Christianity together. The most important of these occurred in the 1964 when the Greek Ecumenical Patriarch Athenagoras and Pope Paul VI met in the Holy Land and declared that the mutual excommunications of 1054 AD were lifted. And in Roman Catholic Christianity there has been a significant lowering of barriers in regard to both the Protestant and Orthodox worlds following the Second Vatican Council in the 1960's.

But the most significant event in dramatizing the ecumenical character of Christianity came in 1948 when the first World Assembly of

Churches was founded in Amsterdam. Its aim was to cement the sympathies Christians had developed during the Second World War due to their own and the world's impotence to prevent the suffering and crimes which were caused by that war. The most tragic example of these occurred in my own native country of Yugoslavia where the Croatian Roman Catholic clerical party, in collaboration with Nazi Germany, authorized the formation of the so-called "Independent State of Croatia" under the Croatian Nazi leader Ante Pavelich. Pavelich and his S.S. band of Ustashi murderers destroyed over 700,000 Orthodox and 70,000 Jews in the territory of Croatia. This crime did not receive much attention in the West, such being at that time the Christian indifference toward groups other than their own. To my own agony, I was a witness to these events in which I lost many friends of my own age. After the war, when I left Yugoslavia for the West, I found only one article, published in *The Christian Century*, about the genocide that was carried out by the Croats against the Serbs with the full support of officials of the Roman Catholic Church.

I mention the above because it had a profound impact on my own future, for it led me to consider how I could contribute toward Christian solidarity so that Christians, at least, would not be guilty of destroying one another. I decided to become a church historian. It is in the service of this cause that the rest of my life, since 1945, has been spent, first as a student until 1955 and then as a University and Seminary professor until my retirement in 1990.

I am happy that now, in my retirement, I have the opportunity to write these words in the cause of ecumenical Christian solidarity in honor of a remarkable colleague and personal friend, Dr. Paul A. Crow, Jr. He was an invaluable supporter in my teaching ministry when I came to teach Early Church History at Christian Theological Seminary, a school of his own denomination, then under the leadership of an elite group of ecumenical Disciples who had decided to open it up to a wider ecumenical embrace and service.

Coming, as I do, from the Orthodox Christian tradition, this was a big challenge for me, for I soon realized that historically, the 19th century religious movement known as the Restoration, led by Thomas and Alexander Campbell and their collaborators and now known as the Disciples of Christ, was still deeply embedded in the ideology of their original leaders. According to them, essential Christianity was New Testament Christianity, and the subsequent Christianity of the next 15 centuries was an historical subversion and distortion.

So there I was, thrown into this situation to impart the historical memory of the church history of those very centuries which were considered to be a falsification of Christianity. Truly it might be said of me in this situation that "fools rush in where angels fear to tread."

But while the religious ethos was steeped in the tradition I have described, the picture was much brighter for me thanks to two remarkable men who were my colleagues. One of these was the president of the Seminary, Dr. Beauford A. Norris, Ph.D. of Edinburgh University in Scotland, who knew and valued the scholarly tradition of Scottish universities and appreciated the fact that I held Ed.D. and Ph.D. degrees from the University of Glasgow, Scotland.

For the next six years, while Dr. Norris was the president of the Seminary, I could not have had a more gracious and supportive leader. Dr. Norris passed away several years ago. May his memory be blessed. The other colleague, who at the time of my appointment was the Dean, was Professor Ronald E. Osborn, Ph.D., a historian by training and a recognized intellectual and denominational leader among the Disciples. He extended to me his broad personal and academic sympathies, by which I was encouraged to lay before my Protestant students the riches of the lost 15 centuries of pre-reformation church history. Osborn was a medievalist by training, and while absolutely devoted to the Disciples tradition, he did not hesitate to criticize its historical perspective. He felt that the Disciples were too wrapped up in the ethos of the Enlightenment and the rationalism of Thomas Jefferson and the "Manifest Destiny" of America to realize that church history, from its beginning until today, is not an irrelevant appendix to Christianity—and still less a subversion or distortion of it—but rather what I call "The third Testament."

Osborn was determined that under his leadership the school should include the chair of Early Church History, and after a long search I was appointed on the recommendation of Harvard Divinity School colleagues who knew me from my sojourn there in the 1960's on a post-doctoral program. But the best commendation in my favor among CTS Disciples was the fact that in the late 1940's I was the student of a remarkable English Disciples theologian, William Robinson, who was my first mentor in the Western tradition of Christianity. In 1951 Robinson came to America to teach in the same school where, 16 years later, I came to teach, and this connection reassured my Protestant colleagues that a student of William Robinson's, though an Orthodox Christian, would not subvert their traditions and mores.

I apologize for this biographical intrusion, but in no other way could I have explained my theme of the role of a church historian in the history of the Christianity of our time. For me as a Christian believer, church history is not just a record of the Christian past: it is a laboratory which uses the lessons of the past to enable each Christian to make his or her own contribution to the world of their own time in the spirit of its own genius.

II

Although Christianity is intrinsically ecumenical in its character, it has not escaped, because of the peculiar circumstances under which Christianity had to live in history, the fragmenting forces which are ever present among human groups. British Disciples theologian William Robinson (d. 1956) described it in terms of a *Shattered Cross*, the title of his book describing the divisions within the Christian commonwealth, a legacy of the turmoil and conflict of cultures in societies which have tried, and often succeeded, to exploit Christianity for their own self-serving purposes. Nicholas Berdyaev was a Russian philosopher with a lifelong obsession with the spirit of Christianity as the most humanizing promise in history. He saw the pathological aspects of Christian history as due to the fact that, in spite of the advent of the New Testament two thousand years ago, humanity, spiritually, psychologically, and ethically, is far behind in its ability to implement its spirit in the life of the societies in which it has been preached for so many hundreds of years. Berdyaev says that human beings still live essentially in the Old Testament and are more attuned to its ethos.

This does not mean that Christianity has failed, but it challenges humanity in its hope for moral and spiritual evolution. This also does not mean that the New Testament has not found a realization of its ideal among human beings. On the contrary, from the very beginning of Christian history a great many devotees of Christ—as the icon of what human beings should aspire to be—have been the *leaven* which has kept the Church recognizably adhering to God's covenant with humanity through Jesus of Nazareth, whom it proclaims to be the Christ. However, the Christian core referred to earlier as the "leaven" is in fact the *remnant*—the saints, whom St. Augustine considers to be the spiritual elite who "rule the world on behalf of Christ until the consummation of the world." This is not the Kingdom of God but only its foreshadowing: a leaven working through the lump of humanity, permeating it with the power of the Holy Spirit. The saints are not necessarily a clerical order, although there may be saints among the ecclesiastical functionaries who guide the political, social, and liturgical structures of the church as the school of Christian discipline and education. The saints of the church are more perceived than seen. Their gifts to the church are charismatic, diffused as an influence rather than embodied visibly in institutionalized structures.

Although this is not consciously promoted in the present state of Christianity, the spiritual destiny of Christianity depends chiefly on whether Christendom will be able to beget, from its genius, the saints it needs to give it inspiration and the hope that the Kingdom of God is on the horizon of its vision. Here is where the church historian's role is essential—not that church historians are to be preachers as such, although some have been, nor are church historians mere chroniclers, although as someone has said, there is no history without chronology. Church historians who deserve this highly-prized title are the guardians of Christian historical memory in its *catholic* sense. Even when the historian deals with a particular period of history or a particular movement or group within it, for example the rise of the medieval monastic orders, he or she must always see this in the context of previous history. For history, religious or secular, abhors disconnection and discontinuity.

Those church historians who do not adhere to and respect this proviso are in danger of inventing a new religion, even when they appear to give it fully Christian credentials such as "Biblical authority." Those who do this appeal to the Bible to buttress their argument. They forget that the Bible, especially the New Testament, arose from the life of the Church and was written for the life of the Church, to give it a Messianic calling as a missionary movement. This includes implicitly the consequent history of the Church, which must be neither ignored nor arbitrarily dismissed as a falsification of the earliest revelatory event which had set the history of the Church in motion.

On this issue the catholic and sectarian views of history differ and are no longer partners in the guardianship of the historical memory of the Church. Wherever the sectarian principle has cut its moorings to the history of the Church and has declared it "fallen" (and therefore no longer valid), a new religion, albeit *called* Christian, has been established. This is not to say that the history of the Church could not be *hijacked* by certain groups and coteries in the Church who proclaim themselves to be the legitimate guardians of its apostolic deposit, so to speak. Or to put it another way, "guardians" of its apostolic tradition—that which must always be regarded as the very core of Christian history and Christian corporate memory. When this usurpation occurs it is the duty of church historians, above all others, to help the Church recapture its *original* historic past, removing those arbitrary blockages to the earlier flow, so that the artesian wells, the living waters, of Christian history may continue to refresh new generations and help them benefit from the full treasury of the Christian past that is their birthright. Should church historians fail in this task by giving up the quest and surrendering to the usurpers, they lose and betray their commission as trustees of the catholic integrity of the Christian revelation which, while once delivered to the saints in the person of Jesus Christ, is dispensed continually to the saints of all ages of the Church as the never-diminishing fullness of God's truth, grace, and love. One reminder of this is the continuous celebration of the Holy Eucharist as the continuation of the last supper before the Lord's crucifixion and resurrection.

In this regard the task of the church historian is more important than that of the theologian, for all good Christian theology must be informed by the history of the Church. If it is not, it is an exercise in a vacuum and not the guardianship of the intellectual truth which the Church must possess. It must possess this truth in order to help the human mind comprehend the revelatory outreach of the Divine mind, that is, the Divine *Logos*—and through it to find the source of its life, its destiny, and its meaning. This implies that a good church historian must also be a theologian.

III

Having described the role and responsibilities of the church historian to the catholic, that is to say, ecumenical, vocation of the church, it is now my duty to respond to the request of those who have entrusted me with the present task. Now I must say something about my contribution to the study of the early church by my ecumenical hosts, among whom I exercised, from 1967 through 1990, the teaching ministry as a Professor of Early Church History. I refer, of course, to the Disciples of Christ.

I approach this task with fear and trembling because, while I did work with my colleagues who, in large majority, were and are Disciples, I am not a student of their tradition. Here I can offer only the observations of a scholar who is deeply given to Christian ecumenical concerns. I feel grateful to God that during my life I have been privileged to exercise my Christian teaching vocation on three continents—Europe, Africa, and America—in institutions of churches other than my own Orthodox Christianity. The chief of these was Christian Theological Seminary, a Disciples of Christ institution in Indiana.

For material for this report I am indebted to my distinguished former colleague and special friend, Professor Ronald E. Osborn, a distinguished American church historian and a bridge over which I have walked into the Disciples' world in order to serve as a teacher of Early Church History to a body of ecumenical American students. The majority of the students were Disciples, but they were matched in number by a godly company of the spiritual and religious descendants of John Wesley. However, I will confine my remarks to the Disciples because the honoree of this *Festschrift* is a distinguished Disciples church historian by profession, as well as a foremost ecumenist by calling and orientation: Dr. Paul A. Crow, Jr., whom I have for many years called *Brother* Paul since he came to Indianapolis to occupy the position of President of the Council on Christian Unity of the Christian Church (Disciples of Christ).

IV

When I left my native country of Yugoslavia in 1945 at the age of 24 due to the Communist conquest of the country, the hardest thing to bear was the fear that I would not be able to continue advanced work in the history of Christianity, which I saw as the only antidote to the godless spirit of atheism, the religion of triumphant communism. By the providence of God my exile brought me to Great Britain. There I was introduced to a remarkable Englishman, Charles Raven, Professor of Divinity at Cambridge. He was a naturalist and philosopher of science who took me under his wing and suggested that I go to Birmingham, to an ecumenical center where the various British Christians had entered into an alliance to educate persons for missionary service under a unified faculty. My first contact in Birmingham was with Professor Arthur H. Curtis, who taught New Testament. He insisted that I should study with Professor William Robinson, whose field was Christian doctrine. So I did. That was the fall term of 1948-49. Robinson was an elderly man and a very witty eccentric who wore a tattered academic gown which his women students spent hours mending, much to the amusement and annoyance of Robinson, whose view of Christianity demanded identification with the poor of the world.

Robinson received me graciously as an Orthodox Christian. He knew a great deal about the Orthodox tradition, for British and Russian Orthodox Christians had already established an ecumenical forum called the Fellowship of St. Alban and Saint Sergius. St. Alban was a fourth century British martyr and Saint Sergius was the fourteenth century creator of a remarkable monastic community in Russia which, even today, is a spiritual center of Russian Christianity. Robinson was theologically versatile and intellectually stimulating. His earliest academic training was in science. Although he studied theology in Oxford as a resident of a Unitarian college, his teaching was catholic of the patristic period, especially regarding Augustine. He would mention how, as a young man, he would seek privacy to read the "Letters of Saint Ignatius" by the first century Bishop of Antioch and martyr (d. 115). Robinson was a former Anglican who had joined an American-based movement headed by Thomas Campbell and his better-known son, Alexander.

After a year of study with Robinson I thought well of the church to which he belonged, although I did not study it in depth. I moved from England to the University of Glasgow and in 1955 , after receiving my Ph.D., I went to Ghana, in West Africa, where I taught at the newly-founded University College of Ghana. During all this time I kept in touch with Robinson, who would send me offprints of his publications. In 1960 I emigrated to the United States and spent seven years teaching in South

Carolina in Allen and Claflin Universities, both black schools to which I was drawn by sympathy for the tremendous suffering of black people, uprooted as they were from their native soil. So was I, which made my empathy with African-Americans deep and abiding. The racial troubles of that period saddened me but did not discourage me.

In the meantime Robinson had moved from Britain to the United States following his retirement in 1951, and had begun teaching at Butler University's School of Religion, a school which had been founded by the Disciples of Christ. After seven years in South Carolina I felt that I had done all I could do there and sought a graduate school of theology where I could give myself to my first love, academically speaking. Thus I made inquires at the very school where Robinson had taught earlier. It so happened that the school was looking for a Professor of Early Church History. Eventually I was appointed and my twenty-three-and-a-half year career at Christian Theological Seminary began. I did not initiate the program in Early Church History, for when I arrived the curriculum for Pre-Reformation Church History was already on the agenda (despite the fact that most followers of the Campbells considered this period a wasteland from which distortions had crept in and corrupted Christianity). I learned that this discipline had been introduced by Professor Frank Albert, a former Orthodox Christian who had become a Disciples but who, as quoted by Professor Ronald Osborn, maintained that in becoming a disciple he (Albert) did not cease to be Orthodox.

Be that as it may I was grateful to Albert, who had died a few years earlier, for legitimizing the study of Early Church History by Disciples instead of leaving it to me, a non-Disciple, to introduce a program of study of a period that had such negative connotations in the minds not only of my students, but of many Disciples colleagues as well. Fortunately for me, I was shielded by the two remarkable men whom I have previously mentioned, President Beauford Norris and Dean and Professor Ronald E. Osborn. They gave me tremendous moral support both as a scholar and a member of the Orthodox Christian communion. Osborn was a trained historian and showed me every support which colleagues working in the same field should show to one another. The six years that I worked with these two men were exciting ones. In 1973 both Norris and Osborn left Christian Theological Seminary—Norris to retire, and Osborn to move to the School of Theology in Claremont, California. At that time I was on sabbatical in England, where I researched the Constantinian period of Christianity.

On my return I found, to my disappointment, that the new administration was hospitable neither to me nor to my subject. Personally, I was not considered to be a "liberal," whatever that meant, and in addition I was a member of the Eastern Orthodox Church, which in the opinion of most of my colleagues is a most reactionary form of Christianity. The climate was one of returning to the "dogma" ascribed *to patriarch* Alexander Campbell: that the study of pre-Reformation Church History was a waste of time. With the departure of Norris and Osborn, some felt, came the chance to repair the damage and restore the traditional Campbellite ignorance of the fifteen centuries prior to the Reformation.

Fortunately for me, I had tenure and the support of two remarkable men, both of whom held the office of President of the Council on Christian Unity. The first was Dr. George G. Beazley, Jr. (d. 1973). George was intrigued by the ancient and Semitic character of Orthodox Christianity and was conversant with the Coptic Churches in Egypt and Ethiopia. Dr. Beazley's last earthly journey was to visit the Orthodox Church of Russia in order to lend moral support to the hierarchy and people during the difficult period of persecution of the Church by the Communists. He died in Moscow during that visit and his wife, Charlotte, told me that the Russian Orthodox Church did everything they could to help her cope with such a sad event and gave to George a memorial service as if he were one of their clergy—a rare event in the protocol of the Orthodox Church. Dr. Beazley was succeeded by Dr. Paul A. Crow, Jr., a well-known ecumenist who has contributed so much to COCU—the fellowship of Protestant churches pledged to promote Christian Unity, including serving as its general secretary. But as far as I was concerned, he was a trained church historian and had taught church history at Lexington Theological Seminary. One of his assignments there had been to develop a course on Patristic Christianity. He was well informed about the Orthodox world, and we developed both a personal and a professional relationship which has sustained me greatly as the environment in which I worked became more ambiguous. I firmly believed that the forces which desired to eliminate the study of early church history were held at bay for a while by Paul's support for my work at the Seminary.

I have already mentioned the negative attitude of the earliest Disciples toward pre-Reformation Church history. However, according to a survey of Disciples Theology by Professor Ronald Osborn, published in Dr. Beazley's *The Christian Church (Disciples of Christ)* (Bethany Press, 1972 pp. 81-116), it was obvious that as Disciples availed themselves of greater theological education they produced leaders who matched their brethren in other Protestant churches intellectually, and consequently changed their views on pre-Reformation Church History. Ronald specialized in Medieval history under Professor Quirnius Breen at the University of Oregon, and his thesis was on the great medieval preacher, Peter Damiani (d. 1072). In later years Ronald wrote on such patristic themes as "The Influence of Classical Tradition on Patristic Christianity." In 1981 he lectured at a convocation in Claremont on St. Macrina, the famous sister of Basil the Great and Gregory of Nyssa. His forthcoming four volumes on the *History of Preaching* include a treatment of the earliest preachers of the second and third centuries: Ignatius, Polycarp, Perpetua, Eulalia, Quadratus, Aristides of Athen, Justin, Athenagoras of Athens, Tertullian, Minucius Felix, Arnobius, Lactantius, Marcion, Maximilla, Priscilla, Melito of Sardis, Cyprian, Clement of Alexandria, Origen, and Anthony. Mention should also be made of Dr. Richard White of Lexington Theological Seminary and his publication *Melito of Sardis— Sermon on the Pascha.*

This does not mean that the traditional, negative view of Church History does not prevail, nor is this lost on American church historians. One of these, Professor Horton Davis of Princeton University, once asked me how I managed to function among the (as he called them) "non-historical Disciples." I told him, "by the grace of God and some historically better-informed Disciples." I will not say more on this subject except that in my case the problem was exacerbated by the presence in the seminary's administration of individuals who abominate the Orthodox Church as a bastion of obscurantism. In addition to this the South American adherents of Liberation theology, who were favored as visiting professors, often taunted me as a reactionary for my anti-Communist views.

Looking back upon my teaching career at Christian Theological Seminary, I can say that I do exemplify how difficult it is to be an ecumenically-oriented Church historian in a Christendom which speaks of ecumenism on one hand, and dismisses it on the other. I write this in order to warn other would-be church historians of the challenges they will face if they are concerned about Christianity as an ecumenical commitment.

As someone who has experienced the Christian ecumenical spirit, and through it was able to make some contribution to the study of church history, not the least through an ecumenical student constituency, I am convinced that where early church history is not studied or respected ecumenism loses its Christian evangelical perspective and becomes a chess game seeking a "Union of Churches" on a secular pattern. The study of early church history reveals how painful the path of Christian history has been in every age and how brave and faithful people have fought to preserve its savor by reminding the world of "One Lord, One Faith and One Baptism"—as the Protestant hymn says. Such testimony in the fragmented state of present day Christendom is costly, but it is the only worthy enterprise for the church historian.

V

At this stage of my discourse on the Disciples contributions to the study of early church history, mention should be made of the contributions of scholars of the Independent Christian Churches which traces its descent, as do the Disciples, from Alexander Campbell. We can only acknowledge them and some of their publications. Among these scholars stand the names of Dean Walker, Everett Furguson, Frederick Norris and others. The significance of this group lies in the fact that, for the purpose of studying Christian origins, they have established an Institute in Tubingen (Germany) where Christian origins are given a wider context than just the New Testament text. Of their publications let me mention only three: *The Second Century*, 1981 to 1992; *The Journal of Early Christian Studies*, 1993; and the *Encyclopedia of Early Christianity* of which the second volume, edited by Everett Furguson, has come out in 1997. This is of interest not only in terms of the contents of these publications but of the promise it offers that this group, which like others who called themselves a "Restoration movement" were locked into the period of the New Testament, are now attempting to reclaim the vistas of church history beyond the first century. It took Alexander Campbell's followers to realize that church history did not stop developing after the last New Testament book was written.[1]

The Disciples branch of "Restoration Christianity," with the exception of its historically-trained scholars, are resolving their quarrel with church history by seeking an alliance with the sixteenth-century Protestant bodies in the United States. This alliance is being made with the United Church of Christ and the New England Calvinists who consider themselves the originators of American Christianity. In this regard, it is the opinion of this writer that the Independent branch of the Restoration movement is on sounder ground.

Conclusion

Since I became an exile in 1945, most of my life has been lived under the aegis of ecumenical Christianity. It was this spirit which helped me become a church historian in the catholic sense. I have personally experienced its vision as well as the power of its detractors, and I am happy to say that the ecumenical world of Dr. Paul A. Crow, Jr. is richer for his presence in it. In spite of Orthodox Christians' suspicion of Protestant deviation from the catholic historical tradition, many Orthodox leaders and scholars from various ethnic backgrounds have welcomed Dr. Crow as a personal friend and Christian brother, this writer included. It is my hope that Dr. Crow's and my own contributions to the life of each other's communities will be taken up by younger generations and that there will arise among them scholars of church history who will not use church history polemically, but comprehensively, in the spirit of the Anglican Archbishop William Temple, whose motto was: "I consider nothing Christian alien to me."

In my lifetime I have especially admired the ecumenical spirit and contribution of three church historians: the Russian Orthodox Dr. Nicholas Zernov, (1898-1980), the Lutheran Professor Martin E. Marty (1928-) and the Disciples Dr. Paul A. Crow, Jr. It is their example, as church historians of the ecumenical nature of Christianity, which convinces me that a church historian has no greater privilege than to seek to serve its cause.

In the case of Dr. Paul A. Crow, Jr. this is especially remarkable, coming as he does from the tradition of the Restoration movement which had written off the older traditions of Christianity, such as the Orthodox Church. But Paul Crow transcended this historical prejudice. Within these rejected, older traditions he discovered spiritual forces which make the search for ecumenical Christianity a never-ending task. My own contribution as a church historian in one of Dr. Crow's Disciples institutions has been made possible only by ecumenically-minded Disciples like him.

In this tribute to Dr. Crow I would like to also acknowledge all those Disciples who have embraced the history of universal Christianity through the centuries as being the best gift which their tradition could give to itself. For that task its church historians must be trained with the ecumenical vision of Dr. Paul A. Crow, Jr. Well done, *Brother* Paul!

Notes

[1] I am indebted to Professor David Bundy, Librarian of Christian Theological Seminary for information on the non-Disciples Restoration movement scholars.

CHAPTER THREE

FROM SEOUL TO SANTIAGO—AND BEYOND

THE UNITY OF THE CHURCH AND JUSTICE, PEACE AND THE INTEGRITY OF CREATION

Thomas F. Best

Paul Crow's leadership has come at a time of unprecedented challenge to Faith and Order's self-understanding and role within the ecumenical movement. Faith and Order works for the unity of Christ's church. But what, in the modern and post-modern eras, is "unity"? How does Faith and Order relate to—no, *serve*—the ecumenical movement as a whole? And recently with special sharpness: how does the search for Christian unity relate to the mission and service of the church today, to its prophetic witness and engagement in the struggles of our time?

No one has done more than Paul Crow to ensure that Faith and Order face these questions squarely.[1] He has insisted, not seldom at personal cost, that action and reflection belong together, that unity is intrinsically linked to prophetic witness and service, and that the two founding "wings" of the ecumenical movement—Faith and Order, Life and Work—share a common calling and destiny.

This essay honors Paul Crow by exploring an area in which he has given major leadership over the past quarter century: the relation between the search for Christian unity and the Church's ethical reflection and action.[2] Focusing on the interaction between Faith and Order and the WCC program on "Justice, Peace and the Integrity of Creation," or JPIC, it is in part an exercise in the recovery of ecumenical memory. But it is not innocent: for my aim is first to *disturb* the conventional memory of these years by "reading" Faith and Order not from its own perspective, but in light of the challenge put to it by the program on

JPIC; and second, on this basis, to *identify* issues crucial for the future of Faith and Order and, I believe, for the ecumenical movement as a whole.

But let us begin with a story.

An African bishop's tale

Faith and Order Commissioner Bishop T. S. A. Annobil of Ghana was once asked why *Baptism, Eucharist and Ministry*[3]—with its focus on church doctrine and practise—was important for "everyday Christians" in his country. In reply he told the following story:

> An illiterate old woman reflecting on the Eucharist confronted me with a serious theological argument and asked some serious questions. She told me that since the priest of her own denomination could visit their congregation only once a month, she sometimes went to the service at another church since their priest (who had a car) was able to visit there more often.
>
> She said: "On one such occasion Father X visited and that morning I felt spiritually hungry so I went to the other service. When it was time for hold communion I felt I should partake, so I got up to go to the altar. The priest, who knew me personally and also knew that I am from another church, sent one of the servers to tell me not to go for communion.
>
> I was not only embarrassed but I felt spiritually rejected and let down. What worries me is that when there was a shortage of food in 1984, Father X brought rice and beans to this village and when I went to the mission house, he gave me enough rice and beans to last me and my family for about two weeks. And yet when I got up to go for communion he refused me.
>
> "Bishop, I do not believe that you bishops, priests and ministers make the things of the altar holy, they are made holy by God. Is the Jesus you clergymen preach the same Jesus who went about doing good, the Jesus who received the Samaritan woman, Mary Magdalene, the publican Zacchaeus, the Jesus who was a friend of publicans and sinners? I do not believe that the Lord himself would have refused me."

The old lady concluded by saying, "May God's kingdom come quickly and then we will know who is right."[4]

More vividly than tomes of theology, this extraordinary account links koinonia with diakonia, the churches' search for visible unity with their common calling to prophetic witness and service. It shows that unity is the basis for common Christian witness and service, that work towards unity is incomplete unless it issues in such witness and service, and that such witness and service must be complemented by the search for visible unity. How striking that this testimony comes not from a professor of ecclesiology, but from the instinctive Christian wisdom of an "illiterate" church member! *The "grassroots" have spoken: and they want unity.*

The imperative to unity, witness and service

This woman challenges us to explore the relationship between unity and witness and service. I begin by noting that while the form of Christian unity is intensely debated today,[5] *the imperative for Christian unity* is no longer in question. It is necessary on at least six grounds: (1) *doxologically*, in obedience to God and to the praise and glory of God, who wills that God's people be one; (2) *Biblically*, in obedience to Christ's command that his disciples might "be one . . . in order that the world may believe" (John 17:20-24), and the New Testament picture of the church struggling to "be of one heart and mind . . . " (Acts 4:32), and truly the body of Christ; (3) *theologically*, recognizing that the life of the church is grounded in the vision of the life of the Trinity, a life of unity-in-diversity and sharing, a vision belied by the divisions among Christians; (4) *ecclesiologically*, recognizing that the harmful divisions between churches are wounds in the body of Christ, crying out for healing, a healing which involves just behaviour and right relationships between the different members of Christ's body;(5) *missiologically*, because disunity contradicts the Christian proclamation of wholeness and healing based on the restoration of right relationships among human beings and between humanity and the whole created order, and may degenerate into competition among rival Christian groups;[6] and (6) to enable a *more effective witness*, because disunity leads to duplication of effort, if not unseemly competition, while co-operation and united effort enable Christians to speak as one, both to persons earnestly seeking the meaning of life or to the "principalities and powers" governing a society indifferent—or hostile—to the gospel and its values. Thus the search for Christian unity is not an "addition" to the Christian faith, but an essential part of it, an integral element of the churches' life.

Strikingly, institutional or bureaucratic "needs" do not appear on the above list; indeed, church union efforts based primarily on grounds of efficiency or the "imperative for downsizing" are unlikely to succeed. Church unions are sometimes promoted as a way to save on costs of administration and facilities. They are not.

The fundamental motivation for Christian unity is the conviction that our institutional divisions are a contradiction of the very message we proclaim, a scandal (*skandalon*) or "stumbling block" for both the churches and the world. We are rejecting not the necessary variety which enriches the one body of Christ, but the harmful divisions which are wounds in and of that body. We are rejecting the fact that so many Christians in the world today are unable to share the Eucharist—the supper of their common Lord—together. The theological claim of the Vancouver (1983) WCC assembly that "Christ—the life of the world—unites heaven and earth, God and world, spiritual and secular"[7] "renders even more scandalous the fact that Christians are not able to come together at the Lord's table."[8] We are rejecting the fact that, even today, membership and ministry are not mutually recognized between many churches. We are rejecting a too-narrow self-understanding of the churches which tempts them to identify Christian truth with a particular theological, confessional, cultural, national or ethnic identity, making them prey to being used by one side or another in political, social and economic conflicts.[9]

Often those most deeply committed to the unity are driven by a personal experience of belonging to the one body of Christ in spite of, and beyond, the divisions of the churches. They have had a foretaste of Christian communion, and can no longer accept the comfortable accommodations we make to our divisions. Consider this testimony:

> Ecumenism [in Malaysia] was born in the common experience of Christian leaders interned in Changi prison during the second world war. [Up to then] their denominational differences had centred on varying interpretations of baptism, communion, etc. When there was no bread, no cup, no wine to be had,

when the only water for baptism was that from the toilet in their cell, they experienced their primal unity as Christians rather than their separate identities as Anglicans or Methodists.[10]

Those who share this "divine discontent with disunity" experience our continuing separation as painful and wrong; they hunger for unity, and will not grow weary in working for it.

But *the Christian imperative to witness and service* is equally fundamental to the identity and life of the churches today. Although convictions may differ as to goals and methods, no church within the ecumenical family would now deny that it is called to witness and struggle for justice between individuals and groups, for a true peace (a *shalom* rooted in justice), and for the nurturing of creation. Because God wills that God's creatures live in harmony and right relationships with one another, and that Gold's creation should flourish and prosper, Christians are called to translate these convictions into practical results in specific situations here and now. Thus the call to witness and service is not something "extra" to the Christian faith, but an essential expression of that faith and integral to the life of the church.

And there is more. Since its beginnings the ecumenical movement has insisted that *the call to unity* and *the call to witness and service* are inseparable. This was affirmed already at the first world conference on Faith and Order in Lausanne in 1927, which saw the early stages of a discussion leading, in 1948, to the formation of the World Council of Churches. Some at Lausanne felt that a council of churches incorporating these two dimensions of the ecumenical movement should be formed quickly while, as the report noted,

> others believe that, for the present, it would be wiser for the movements represented by Stockholm [Life and Work, e.g. common witness and service] and Lausanne [Faith and Order, e.g. the search for visible unity] to develop in independence, each following its own way; *but there is general agreement that ultimately life, work, faith and order are expressions of an existing spiritual unity, and that each requires the other for its complete fruition.*"[11]

The "unity" of unity, witness and service remains a fundamental ecumenical principle, reasserting itself when necessary for the health of the ecumenical movement. It reappears, for example, with special force in *Church and World*, the culminating text from the Faith and Order study program on "The Unity of the Church and the Renewal of Human Community":

> These two issues—the search for unity and the search for renewal—are often seen as being separate and distinct, and with this goes the tendency to consider either one *or* the other as the most important or urgent ecumenical task. This contradicts, however, the long-held ecumenical conviction that God's will, revealed in Jesus Christ, calls the churches both to visible unity among themselves and to common witness and service for the renewal of human community.[12]

But the very strength of the appeal betrays the presence of a problem: despite the conviction that these two "wings" of the ecumenical movement belong together there has, in fact, been a persistent tendency to see them as separate. Worse yet, they have become institutionalised in the lives of the churches and ecumenical organizations; indeed, they often co-exist as different "divisions" within the same church or council of churches, carried by separate and distinct structures, each feeling a sense of rivalry—if not outright competition—with those carrying the other "part" of the ecumenical agenda. One cause of the "ecumenical malaise" of the 1980s and early 1990s was surely the continuing division between these forces.[13]

Up to now I have insisted upon, and I hope demonstrated, the coherence of the ecumenical efforts towards unity with those focussed upon witness and service. And I have warned that this coherence, while required by our faith, is often not realized within the life of ecumenical movement. To probe this dynamic more fully, let us take a closer look at two central "carriers" of the concerns for witness and service and for unity respectively. We may begin with JPIC and move then to Faith and Order.

Seoul and the JPIC process: its ecumenical significance

The WCC program on "Justice, Peace and the Integrity of Creation" (JPIC), developed after the Vancouver assembly in 1983 and culminating in a global consultation in Seoul in 1990, linked churches with Christian movements and action groups to address issues such as racism, violence, and the destruction of the earth's ecosystem. Despite some practical and conceptual difficulties, the process was of immense significance to the churches and the ecumenical movement. It generated creative theological and ethical reflection, not to mention networks of common concern, through the preparatory gatherings in Latin America, the Pacific, and particularly Europe; from Reformed, Orthodox and Roman Catholic confessional perspectives; and from women's regional meetings.[14] The commitments made at the Seoul world convocation on JPIC[15] have great symbolic power, as well as considerable tactical and political potential for bringing Christian pressure to bear on crucial ethical issues today. But even more instructive, I believe, than these "results" are three ways in which the JPIC process brought fresh life and energy to the ecumenical scene.

First, it restored a sense of the ecumenical endeavour as a *movement* rather than a bureaucratic system "belonging" to the institutional churches and their professional staffs. Consider this stirring call from the world convocation on JPIC in Seoul:

> Now is the time to recognize that there is a long process still before us. We will take to our churches and our movements the affirmations and commitments we have made in Seoul, inviting others to join us. Together with them we struggle for the realization of our vision. We are accountable to one another and to God. We pray that we do not miss the *kairos* to which we have been led by God.[16]

These are "marching orders." They criticize the institutionalization of ecumenical work, call for the deeper involvement of the whole church in the process, and plead for a renewed sense of excitement and commitment. Notably this reaction was aimed not only against the classic "unity movement," but also against the ecumenical aid and development structures—recognizing that their programs can be every bit as bureaucratized as those of "the theologians" who seem, to some, mainly interested in the number of doctrines which can fit on the head of a pin.

Second, Seoul expressed a powerful longing for renewed connections with others working for the same cause. It noted that "not every church or group can be engaged at all points of the struggle for JPIC at the same time. Each engages at some one point knowing that by so doing it belongs to a covenant solidarity that is worldwide."[17] Thus against the sense of apathy and despair, the fear that the problems faced by the world and the churches are simply too big for anyone to tackle, Seoul insisted that Christians and others of good will could make a difference. In "covenant solidarity" lies hope and new energy for the struggle.

Third, the JPIC process offered those working on various "fronts" in the struggle against injustice a sense of wholeness and integration. Indeed, it broke down barriers *within* this "wing" of the ecumenical movement, easing tensions between those struggling with issues of justice and those working for peace. In the context of the Cold War, the Northern hemisphere's concern for "peace" seemed to some a diversion from the struggle against the injustice wreaked upon the South—by *both* of the North's political systems! Here the Seoul message sought a breakthrough, saying that "there are no competitive efforts for justice, peace and the integrity of creation. There is one single global struggle."[18] Much of the power of the JPIC vision came from its uniting of related but differently organized, and sometimes frankly competing, agendas of ethical engagement.

JPIC: the limits of a common vision

Thus the JPIC process has important lessons to teach the whole ecumenical movement. And yet it also revealed some limits to common ecumenical witness and service, as was apparent with the two theological concepts which should have provided the foundation of the entire JPIC process: the ideas of covenant and of JPIC as a "conciliar process."

The Seoul gathering had to admit that "in spite of all the attempts made, there were still some unresolved differences in the understanding of 'covenant'."[19] The use of this term was grounded in the experience of delegates to the WCC sixth assembly in Vancouver in 1983, where Christians from various regions of the world made solemn commitments to one another ("covenanted" together) to work for specific religious/ethical and political goals. The term reflects the creative focus of Reformed theology on the biblical theme of God's covenant with God's people. But as the JPIC process developed the term proved difficult: for several confessional families it was not familiar theological coinage; and some of those comfortable with the image of God's covenant with Israel—a covenant between a superior and a dependent party—found it dangerous when applied to covenants made between human beings or between churches. Did it not inevitably imply that one party was "superior" and the other "inferior?" And was this not exactly what those those covenanting between North and South, developed and developing countries, "rich" and "poor" were trying to avoid?

Another problem came from the Vancouver model of covenanting, which was based upon personal commitments between individuals to achieve specific goals on which they basically agreed. It proved difficult to translate this personal dynamic into the lives of churches or Christian organizations, large and complex institutions encompassing a variety of views and encumbered with maddeningly slow decision-making processes. The JPIC process simply did not have enough time to deal with these realities of institutional life. True, "it was indeed remarkable that this diverse group [at the Seoul convocation] was able to enter into and set in motion a global process of covenanting as an expression of their mutual commitment . . . ";[20] and that is to be celebrated. But the process fell seriously short of the level of engagement of the churches *as churches* which was hoped for.

Perhaps even more serious was the fact that, as the Seoul final document put it, "the term 'conciliar process' . . . had to be abandoned for theological reasons."[21] The term reflected JPIC's desire to be not only a personal but also an official process, a vehicle through which the churches could grow together, formally and officially, in their common commitment to the struggle against injustice, violence and the manifold threats to life. Some saw a parallel to the Faith and Order study process on "Baptism, Eucharist and Ministry," thorough which many WCC member churches explored the degree of ecumenical convergence in areas of church doctrine and practise:[22] could not the churches grow together also in the field of social witness? There was, after all, a consensus in some areas—that theological support for apartheid was, in quite a precise sense, heretical, and that there is a Christian responsibility to respect and protect creation. Could not the agreement among the churches in such areas be deepened through a process of ecumenical discussion? Could not the process lead beyond discussion to common commitment, and even action?

Again the time factor was a significant problem; there was insufficient time to consolidate, and broaden, the consensus emerging in some specific areas amongst the churches.[23] But more serious were the difficulties inherent in the term "conciliar" itself. The term is sensitive, it has many meanings and it is very dear to the theological hearts of the churches. WCC central committee moderator Archbishop Aram Keshishian discerns no fewer than five meanings in current ecumenical usage.[24] The two fundamental senses of the term were already well expressed by the Faith and Order Commission meeting at Bristol in 1967:

> The conciliar process in the ancient church took place in a still unbroken fellowship, generally speaking . . . [there were differences, but] the conciliar process . . . took place, nevertheless, on the basis of the existing fellowship. Today, however, the point of departure is one of plural ecclesiastical communities in confrontation with one another. They differ in their confession of the truth . . . The restoration of fellowship is the task with which they see themselves faced in the ecumenical movement.[25]

Thus for some the term "council" refers to the "fellowship of divided churches," gathered in modern-day "councils of churches" for common reflection, witness and service. These bodies, at the local, national regional and world level, provide an essential forum for churches to cooperate in witness and service, and to discuss the theological issues which still divide them. But for others the meaning of the word "council" is deterermined by the councils of the ancient, undivided church: a council is a "representative gathering of the one church," come together to state its common mind on specific issues of faith and life.[26] The term "conciliar," then, could refer either to a process by which the churches worked towards unity, or to an event which expressed a unity already achieved. The result was that some churches never accepted that the word "conciliar" could be used in the present ecumenical situation at all, while others never quite saw what all the fuss was about.

The institutional fate of the JPIC program after Seoul is also instructive. At the heart of Vancouver's call for a JPIC process, and still hoped for at Seoul, was the vision of JPIC as an "umbrella" program capable of focusing and unifying the ecumenical social agenda.[27] But it did not achieve this, not even within the WCC, where (through the 1991 WCC reorganization) JPIC became one among seven programs within a large administrative unit, the other six continuing previous work in the traditional areas of development, ecumenical opposition to racism, and so on. Certainly JPIC "lives on" among Christian movements and action groups around the world. There it continues to offer an inspiration and unifying vision for Christian social engagement, *and that is probably the most important thing.* But it is striking that JPIC, for all its vision, did not really succeed in institutionalizing itself within the "official" ecumenical movement. Or is that precisely *why* it has endured so well at the local level? And if so, what does that tell us?

After this review of the importance and complex results of the JPIC process let us look at that other classic ecumenical agenda, the search for visible unity, as reflected in the Faith and Order movement. This is particularly appropriate because, being also lodged within the WCC, Faith and Order was that part of the unity movement most directly related to JPIC.

Faith and Order:
the search for unity as a call to witness and service

The above critical appreciation of the JPIC movement has prepared us, I believe, to look at Faith and Order's story in a fresh way. The "voice" of JPIC helps Faith and Order recover aspects of its own history which it has tended to forget—perhaps not always unintentionally. Read from this perspective, the history of Faith and Order is a struggle to bring the search for unity into dialogue with the challenges posed by the world for Christian faith and for the churches. Above all, it is a struggle to take seriously the deep divisions within the human community, and their impact upon the life of the church and upon the churches' work towards visible unity.

It is well to begin with a consideration of the third world conference on Faith and Order (Lund, 1952). The discussion of the "function" of Faith and Order first focused on the "essential oneness of the church of Christ," on questions of doctrine and worship, on difficulties and possible steps towards union.[28] But to this agenda a certain Disciples of Christ theologian, Dean S. J. England, added a crucial element:

> To study the social, cultural, political and other apparently non-theological factors which affect the actual relationship of the churches to one another . . . and to consider the theological implications of these factors for their bearing on the movement towards the unity of the church.[29]

Today this theme, in even stronger language, occupies a key place in Faith and Order's by-laws.[30]

In response to this imperative, a long series of studies from the late 1960s wrestled with the realities of human brokenness and division in relation to the search for unity, including the work on the community of women and men in the church (in collaboration with the WCC sub-unit on women in Church and Society), on issues of racism (in collaboration with the WCC's Programme to Combat Racism), the inclusion of the differently-abled in the life of the church, the intrusion of ethnic and caste divisions into the life of the local church, and many others.[31] Questions of method were central to these studies; all of them, but especially the "Unity and Renewal" study, grappled with the challenge of integrating the so-called "contextual" and "classical" theological approaches.

For some within Faith and Order the attention paid to these issues and to diverse theological methods has been controversial, a "diversion" from its traditional, proper agenda. But the Faith and Order movement as a whole has affirmed this broader approach to the search for unity, agreeing that:

> . . . churches today are divided not only over the traditional theological issues of transubstantiation or the proper age and forms for baptism but also, and often with more tragic results, by the alienation between ethnic groups, social and economic

classes, and the sexes: the divisions of the world are, insofar as the church is a human institution, church-divisive realities. This did not mean that Faith and Order was shifting its attention to "non-theological" factors, but a new awareness that sexism and racism raises precisely theological and ecclesiological issues, and that work towards greater visible unity of the churches must also take account of these realities.

The point is that the search for Christian unity, and the struggle to overcome the brokenness of the human community (a brokenness which leads to divisions within the church as human institution) are part of one and the same response to the gospel of Jesus Christ. The two must not be left to different "wings" of the ecumenical movement, thus reinforcing the old, destructive, tragic and false division between "theologians" and "activists." Nor is this a new theme for Faith and Order, but the direct response to a challenge already sounded in its by-laws . . .[32]

Thus Faith and Order insists that the concern for human renewal is not a "sidelight" for the unity movement, but is an integral part of its theological and ecclesiological reflection, standing at the heart of its own life and work. From this perspective it has *necessarily* addressed many of the concerns identified with JPIC for they belong, equally, on Faith and Order's own agenda.

Let us look briefly at several of these, taking first the question of justice. Referring to the technical discussion of models of unity (organic unity, reconciled diversity, communion of communions), *Church and World* insists that:

> . . . the criterion by which the vision of the unity which Christians seek will be judged is nothing less than the radical renewal and fulfilment of the human community. The connection between unity and justice makes it necessary to ask of every expression of visible unity: *"Does it promote justice* in the light of the gospel of Jesus Christ, both within the church and the world?" And secondly: *"Does it foster the engagement of the church* in God's work for justice?"[33]

Thus the promotion of justice has become one criterion by which the search for visible unity must be judged. That is, a true unity must provide for justice within the life of the church; churches may have come close to each other in traditional matters of faith and order, but if they remain divided, "in their living out of the faith and their ordering of church life," by racism "or other forms of human brokenness," then "such 'unity' is not yet the visible unity to which Christians are called by their being one in Christ."[34]

The link between unity and justice is so central to the future of the ecumenical movement that it is worth examining one more affirmation of their relationship. This comes from the united churches who, having moved from denominational separation, through the sacrifice of their former identities, to a new identity, are perhaps uniquely qualified to testify to the *cost* of unity. In their fifth world consultation (Potsdam, 1987), they addressed courageously the continuing doubts about the "relevance" of the search for unity today:

> Many Christians today, engaged in their mission and service with the major problems of human individuals and groups, are unable to perceive any urgency in the quest for visible unity. Prolonged reflection on the theology of church, ministry and sacraments, so prominent in union negotiations, seems to them a distraction from pressing Christian duties. Members of the consultation declared their conviction that the quest for visible unity is related, and must be seen to be related, to the overcoming of human divisions and the meeting of human needs. This does not mean that the unity of the church is only functional: it is also a direct reflection of God's own unity and unitive love. Relating unity to mission, service and sharing the sufferings of humankind is precisely an expression of the love of God which calls the church into being, as the sign, foretaste and instrument of a new humanity in the kingdom of God.[35]

Significantly, this perspective has also informed a critique of the churches' "cultural captivity" to forms of injustice and oppression, forces which threaten to impose themselves within the churches' *own* life as human institution. Thus the fourth Faith and Order world conference (Montreal, 1963) addressed the issue of racism in its working section on "All in Each Place: the Process of Growing Together," asking pointedly:

> But does the life of the church in each place assert the dignity of the human person as God's gift? . . . We are shamefully divided by racial prejudice and discrimination . . . In Christ there is no defence or excuse for the wilful continuation of groups, church meetings or fellowships which are racially exclusive. We therefore call upon Christian in their local churches to show the marks of Christian discipleship whatever the cost.[36]

From this has come a vision of the local congregation as the place where one's doctrine of the church is incarnated in tangible, experiential form:

> For it is here that the love, justice, reconciliation and "new being" offered by the gospel should be available; it is here that ecclesiology ceases to be an abstract system, and takes on a "human face," that its theological categories and truths become embodied in Christian sisters and brothers who incarnate God's challenging, enabling love and redeeming grace. It is not too much to say that the "quality of Christian life" within a Christian community is the primary test of its faithfulness, more important than tests of doctrinal "correctness" (cf. Matt. 25:31-46, 7:21-23, cf. Luke 6:46-49!).[37]

And in a nutshell: "If the church is to be faithful to its calling it will need, as a community of shared faith, to exhibit God's justice in its own corporate life."[38]

As a second example of Faith and Order's broader concern, we note that its vision of unity and wholeness has not been confined to the church, but has sought to encompass the whole created order. Already 30 years ago the Bristol Faith and Order Commission meeting, developing its programme on "God in Nature and History," affirmed:

> Christians should support all those responsible for nature conservation in various countries in their long-standing struggle

against the pollution of air and water, in their demand for an afforestation which counteracts the denudation and erosion of vast regions, and in their plea for a policy of habitation which takes into consideration the much endangered biological balance of many areas. What these groups claim for biological reasons, the church has to support for basic theological reasons.[39]

Later vocabulary and issues may differ, but Bristol's intent is clear and just as relevant today: to call the churches to an ecological responsibility, and to do so within the context of their continuing search for visible unity. This call was continued, and anchored firmly within the context of the search for justice, in *Church and World*:

> This new life in Christ and his justice should also be manifested in a new life-style of Christians and their communities. Such a life-style will express today an awareness of the injustice done to creation by unlimited exploitation, and will seek to support all efforts towards a responsible stewardship of creation. Such a life-style will be a contribution to a more just sharing of the resources of this earth between rich and poor, within the framework of a new world economic order. Such a life-style will in itself become a credible witness to the readiness of the church to be used by God as an instrument of the renewal of the human community.[40]

In a third area of broader concern, Faith and Order moved beyond the conventional ecclesial landscape in touching on one of the most sensitive issues raised in the JPIC process, namely the role of Christian movements and action groups working, in large part, outside the official structures of the churches. Already at its Louvain plenary meeting (1971) the Commission suggested "that the World Council of Churches explore still further the ways in which it can provide fellowship, support and guidance for those individuals and groups which are seeking new forms of Christian obedience for which existing ecclesiastical structures provide no opportunity."[41] This basic openness to the witness of Christian movements and action groups, and indeed of persons of other faiths or no faith, continues through to *Church and World*, where we are reminded that:

As Christians in different situations confront their tasks they become aware that they are not alone in their struggle. They are part of human communities in which the search for justice is urgently pursued and where often Christians need to learn from others outside the church what are the issues to be addressed. Indeed, Christians should expect in this co-operation to have their own limited vision of God's justice judged and renewed, and their theological perspectives deepened and enriched.[42]

As a fourth and final example of Faith and Order's wrestling with broader issues, we may consider its attitude to conflict—to tension and sharp disagreement arising within the search for Christian unity. That search *must* prove threatening to those who are comfortable with the present divided state of the churches, who prefer not to face differences openly or who fear the risks involved. This means that a serious struggle towards unity must expect opposition. Faith and Order's 1963 Montreal world conference acknowledged this courageously:

Unity is the fruit of Christian discipleship, and the latter takes various forms. A common protest against unjust laws which create or enforce racial divisions will make clearer the oneness in Christ . . . co-operative activities in ministry and fellowship, when done *even in advance of consensus within a denomination or of the strict interpretation of canon law*, can promote unity.[43]

Faith and Order, to be sure, has not always been able to bear such tension as the cost of pursuing its vocation. At times it has been attracted to (not to say seduced by) a consensus style of work in which conflict is minimized, and sensitive issues avoided. From a later vantage point it is striking how far, in the stormy 1970s, some degree of conflict was understood to be inevitable as we work towards unity. Faith and Order then knew what it has since sometimes tried to forget: how to speak of the search for "unity in tension." It was recognized that Christians might disagree strongly on specific ethical and social issues, and that some might be called to forms of witness which others would find unacceptable. Such witness, said the Accra Faith and Order Commission meeting in 1974, must not be sacrificed to a false understanding of "unity" which sought, above all, to avoid conflict: "An ecclesiastical unity which would stand in the way of struggles for liberation would be a repressive unity, hindering the just interdependence which Christians are called to serve."[44]

This survey has explored how the unity movement has wrestled with some issues of social witness and action. I end with a close look at one more unity document, the text "The Unity of the Church as Koinonia: Gift and Calling" which was drafted by Faith and Order, revised and then adopted by the WCC Canberra assembly in 1991.[45] This is the latest in a series of assembly statements restating afresh, for each ecumenical generation, the imperative and vision for visible unity.[46] It is remarkable how thoroughly this "Canberra unity statement" has integrated imperatives from the JPIC process into its powerful call for Christian unity. Identifying unity as " . . . a koinonia given and expressed in the common confession of the apostolic faith; a common sacramental life . . . and a common mission witnessing to the gospel of God's grace to all people *and serving the whole of creation*," it calls on churches to "take specific steps together . . . as they learn from one another, *work together for justice and peace, and care together for God's creation.*"[47]

Of the classic assembly unity statements, Canberra's is by far the most concrete and specific in its challenges to the churches. Claiming the ecumenical movement "as a reconciling and renewing movement towards full visible unity," it calls the churches to a number of practical steps towards unity. Several deal with the life of the churches, calling for mutual recognition of baptism and the apostolic faith, and urging progress on recognition of ministries and appropriate exploration of Eucharistic hospitality; but these are then related to an urgent call for the churches

> to recommit themselves to work for *justice, peace and the integrity of creation*, linking more closely the search for sacramental communion of the church with the struggles for justice and peace.[48]

This statement was one of the few officially adopted at Canberra by the WCC member churches meeting in assembly—if not yet in council—and it at last claims unity, witness and service in their full integrity and inter-relationship.

Aided by perspectives from the JPIC process, this "reading" of Faith and Order history has confirmed the relation between the search for Christian unity and the churches' engagement in the world. And I trust that our review of JPIC and Faith and Order has shown the value of bringing these prominent "actors" on the ecumenical scene into close conversation. In a final section I want to explore three further topics suggested by these reflections, and of special promise for the next stages of our ecumenical journey.

The ecumenical movement: towards a fresh Christocentric perspective

First, the ecumenical movement needs to move towards a fresh Christocentric perspective. This is suggested by problems in recent ecumenical reflection on creation. JPIC, for example, stood courageously for creation's inherent goodness, emphasizing how creation's "mysterious ways, its life, its dynamism—all reflect the glory of its Creator."[49] It rejected "the abuse of some biblical statements . . . to justify destructive actions towards the created order,"[50] as well as an instrumental view of nature which has encouraged its exploitation by the human species. This was linked with other JPIC commitments, for example to indigenous peoples who live integrally with nature, particularly the land.[51]

But there is another side to nature, and it is here that further reflection is called for. We noted above Faith and Order affirmation at Bristol of Christian responsibility to care for creation in its goodness as a gift from God. But Bristol was also aware of the ambiguity of nature for human life: for nature produces not only beautiful sunsets but "the hurricanes, the floods, the droughts, the earthquakes . . . "[52] The questions come immediately: if God is both good and the creator of all that is, why is there so much destructiveness in the created order? Why so much suffering and pain for God's creatures? While some suffering of human beings may follow from their having free will, what about the suffering caused by an apparently indifferent, or hostile, natural order? And what about the suffering of animals, who live so largely within their programmed patterns of ancestral instinct? And why is the whole natural order threatened incessantly by—and finally, in natural terms, delivered up to—decay and death? Or are these very questions inappropriate, a reflection of our chauvinistic focus upon the importance of the human species?

What, in short, is the nature of *Nature*? Ecumenical reflection must move beyond its present tendency to glorify nature, and take far more seriously nature's "shadow side."[53] And this requires, I suggest, a clear Christocentric perspective, a vision rooted in the biblical picture of the cosmic Christ (John, Colossians, Ephesians) whose death and resurrection is at the heart of the divine plan of redemption for the whole created order, and who lives today in the hearts of his followers. Faith and Order wrote in preparation for its Santiago world conference:

> Because of the redemptive work of Christ, Christians expect the final healing, liberating and restoration of the whole of creation from the destructive powers of darkness and evil and look forward to the day when Christ is to recapitulate and consummate the whole creation in the eternal kingdom of God.[54]

This eschatological perspective enables us to celebrate the goodness of creation, and to face squarely its terrible aspects, by holding both realities within the framework of Christ's Lordship over the cosmos, anchored in God's redemptive plan for creation. *And it relates that plan to the unity of the church,* showing how our continuing divisions are judged also from the perspective of the integrity of creation:

> The division of Christians weakens their effectiveness in caring for creation; it subverts the sign of the unity of creation, and humanity remains without a challenge to its own striving . . . The churches by their divisions obscure the lordship of the Lord of creation. The problem is thus not only one of a divided witness before the world: it is also the problem of being faithful before God to our calling to live as a koinonia of healing and caring in relation to creation.[55]

This shows how a fresh Christological vision would further link the search for visible unity with the imperative for witness and service. Some such Christocentric perspective was at the heart of the original ecumenical vision as we see, strikingly, from the Life and Work conference held at Oxford in 1937. This declared that:

The first duty of the church, and its greatest service to the world, is that it be in very deed the church—confessing the true faith, committed to the fulfilment of the will of Christ, its only Lord, and united in him in a fellowship of love and service.[56]

This was not meant to claim centrality for the church, but to call the churches "to an intensely self-critical procedure" through which they are "summoned, in obedience to their one and only Lord, to become a fellowship of love and service. This fellowship, however, is nothing less than *the practical and ethical reflection of the unity of the church.*"[57] Christ, the body, Lord of the Church and of all creation, calls us to a life of service and witness. This points to the vision by which we search fervently for visible unity, to the glory of God and for the sake of the world which God has made, and by which together we give ourselves in witness and service to others, and to the whole of creation, as a sign and foretaste of our final oneness in Christ, who is all in all.

The search for unity: beyond koinonia to union

Second, the ecumenical movement needs to move beyond koinonia towards a fresh exploration of *organic union* as its goal. This requires a *recovery* of the very term "union." From at least the WCC's Uppsala assembly (1968), ecumenical concepts of unity have developed in dialogue with developments towards unity in the human community. As "one world" has become more and more a surprising reality, the church was challenged to reflect on its own distinctive understanding and experience of unity:

> In a time when human interdependence is so evident, it is the more imperative to make visible the bonds which unite Christians in universal fellowship . . . The ecumenical movement helps to enlarge this experience of universality, and its regional councils and its world council may be regarded as a transitional opportunity for eventually actualizing a truly universal, ecumenical, conciliar form of common life and witness.[58]

Uppsala's view of "the world" was remarkably positive, with its reference to "secular catholicity" and "instruments of conciliation and unification" produced by secular society.[59] This raises a first problem, namely that since Uppsala the notion of unity, in both the secular and Christian arenas, has become problematic: the "oneness" we are being offered looks increasingly questionable, and the methods to attain it increasingly dubious. Already at the first Faith and Order Commission meeting held after Uppsala, at Louvain in 1971, a critical note was sounded about the "unity" being developed within the human community:

> . . . modern technology has forced all mankind into a tight interdependence which constantly threatens freedom and individuality. The church's unity must be of such a kind that there is ample space for diversity and for the open mutual confrontation of different interests and convictions.[60]

Today we could add a long list of unitive impulses (political, economic, social, ethnic, national, ideological, valuational) which "the world" is only too ready to provide, and which are urgently in need of critique from the perspective of the gospel.

There is a second, related problem with the concept of unity: for many it is no longer a positive term, but appears rather as a threat to their identity and growth. Persons and peoples now demand that their unique voice be heard; and for all that is good in this it has also led, as the Santiago working document noted, to the emergence of centrifugal, divisive tendencies among peoples and within nations, to the point where unity and diversity are no longer seen as compatible. This *divisive particularism* now threatens the churches and the ecumenical movement:

> For a number of years there has been a growing proliferation of narrowly particularistic concerns within churches or regions. This is even more serious when it is linked to a resurgence of exclusivistic and militant nationalism or ethnicity as indeed seems to be the case in some parts of the world.[61]

Clearly the ecumenical movement has lost a viable and attractive understanding of unity. Partly in response, the term "koinonia" has recently emerged as the central visioning language for the churches' growing together. Variously—and always partially—translated as "communion," "community," "fellowship," the term "koinonia" has been used since the WCC New Delhi assembly in 1952 to indicate the "dimension of depth" in the relationship among the members of Christ's body, pointing to their common participation in Christ as the church's source and sustaining power. Thus New Delhi:

> The word "fellowship" (koinonia) has been chosen because it describes what the church truly is. "Fellowship" clearly implies that the church is not merely an institution or organization. It is a fellowship of those who are called together by the Holy spirit and in baptism confess Christ as Lord and Saviour.[62]

Yet the language of koinonia has its own problems. Its meanings are many, to the point that the Santiago Faith and Order world conference, whose theme was "koinonia," was in effect an exploration of possible (including some contradictory) meanings of the term. The latest gathering of united and uniting churches surveyed an astonishing variety of approaches to visible unity—all of them understanding themselves as expressions of "koinonia."[63] This diversity of meanings is inevitable since koinonia is, fundamentally, a term about relationships rather than structures; it suggests the *quality of relationship* which should obtain within the "household of faith." But by the same token it lacks the structural component proper to a model of unity, which can clarify and sharpen our reflections on how the churches should order their common life.

It is exactly at this point, touching issues of mutual accountability and structures of decision-making, that we have much to gain from a return to the discussion of "models of unity," and particularly of organic union. The understanding of unity as uniformity has seriously distorted the perception of this model, reading into it a rigid, monolithic quality which was never intended.[64] "On the contrary, what we desire," said the original definition of organic union, "is the unity of a living organism, with the diversity characteristic of the members of a healthy body." That is, the term "organic" is used not to suggest uniformity but to insist precisely upon a *flexible, dynamic diversity* among the churches so "united."[65] Of all the models it is, in my view, the most helpful in combining freedom in the expression of Christian faith and life, with the mutual accountability required of those who truly belong to the *one* body of Christ.[66]

The churches: beyond conversion to kenosis

Third, the churches need to move beyond conversion to kenosis. Spurred by movements such as the *Groupe des Dombes*, churches have recently begun to consider "conversion" as the basis for both their own identity and their growth toward unity.[69] But conversion points beyond itself to kenosis.[70] Because it requires giving up one's claim to be the standard for one's own life, *and to be right* by that standard, it finds its source and completion in the act of kenosis, in that complete self-giving which seeks only the good of the other, asking for and expecting no reward.[71]

I am increasingly convinced that the churches' lives need to be shaped by the notion of kenosis; indeed, that they are called to a *kenotic ecclesiology* which, taking as its starting point Philippians 2:5-11, places at the center of their self-understanding the picture of Jesus as suffering servant.[72] This would require a radical re-evaluation of the idea of "service" in the church, where often "service" means one thing for the "humbler" members of the community and quite a different thing for the "more exalted."[73] It would require a radical re-thinking of attitudes to power, not least as exercised within the church itself, and of attitudes toward property and possessions, including those of the churches. Would it not also require a re-examination of the exclusions—especially the exclusion from the Lord's Table—which the churches practise against one another?

The fifth world conference on Faith and Order just touched upon the theme of koinonia, affirming that:

> the encounter with the other in the search to establish the [*sic*] koinonia, grounded in God's gift, calls for a kenosis—a self-giving and a self-emptying. Such a kenosis arouses fear of loss of identity, and invites us to be vulnerable, yet such is no more than faithfulness to the ministry of vulnerability and death of Jesus . . . As individuals and communities, we are called to establish koinonia through a ministry of kenosis.[74]

This stops well short, however, of calling the *churches* to a fundamental re-examination of their own values, internal patterns of human relations, and structures of power in light of the gospel.

Let us return in conclusion to the story with which we began. The "old woman" knew instinctively that the diakonia practised among Christians is an expression of their koinonia within the one body of Christ. She knew that that koinonia was incomplete—no, *damaged*—for the priest could not match his gift of material food with the gift of spiritual food, the very body and blood of our Lord Jesus Christ. And she did well to reproach Bishop Annobil for the continuing divisions of the church. What would a kenotic ecclesiology demand of the priest in this story? What would it demand of his *church*? "If"—as Paul asks in Philippians 2:1—"there is any koinonia in the Spirit," is it not high time we found out?

Notes

[1] For example as Moderator of the Faith and Order study program "The Unity of the Church and the Renewal of Human Community" (1984-1992) and a principal architect of its culminating text *Church and World: The Unity of the Church and the Renewal of Human Community*, Faith and Order Paper No. 151, 2nd, revised printing, Geneva, WCC 1992; as staunch advocate of the Faith and Order/WCC Unit III study on "Ecclesiology and Ethics" (1992-1996) (on this see note 12), and as Moderator of the upcoming Faith and Order (in collaboration with Unit III) study on "Ethnic Identity, National Identity, and the Unity of the Church."

[2] This essay makes use of material published as: Thomas F. Best, "From Seoul to Santiago: The Unity of the Church and JPIC," in *Between the Flood and the Rainbow: Interpreting the Conciliar Process of Mutual Commitment (Covenant) to Justice, Peace and the Integrity of Creation*, comp. By D. Preman Niles, Geneva, WCC Publications, 1992, pp. 128-152, and on some other material as indicated.

[3] Faith and Order Paper No. 111, Geneva, WCC, 1982. The text, sent to WCC members churches for official response in 1982, has become the most widely-distributed ecumenical text. Some 185 churches have replied officially, and literally thousands of "unofficial" responses have been received. Anglican Bishop T. S. A. Annobil was a Faith and Order commissioner from 1983 to 1991.

[4] T. S. Annobil, "An African Bishop's Story," featured in *Church and World: The Unity of the Church and the Renewal of Human Community, op. Cit.*, p. 11.

[5] See for example Paul A. Crow, Jr., "Reflections on Models of Christian Unity," in *Living Today Towards Christian Unity: The Fifth International Consultation of United and Uniting Churches*, ed. By Thomas F. Best, Faith and Order Paper No. 142, Geneva, WCC Publications, 1988, pp. 21-37.

[6] This point is made with special sharpness in the working document for the fifth world conference on Faith and Order. See "Towards Koinonia in Faith, Life and Witness," draft of a working document (April 1992), in *On the Way to Fuller Koinonia: Official Report of the Fifth World Conference on Faith and Order*, ed. By Thomas F. Best and Günther Gassmann, Faith and Order Paper No. 166. Geneva, WCC Publications, 1994, IV.2, para. 88, p. 289.

[7] David Gill, ed., *Gathered for Life*, Geneva, WCC, 1983, pp. 44. It is this element of contradiction, the way in which our divisions belie the message of justice, reconciliation and wholeness which we proclaim, that justifies *Church and World*'s description of them as "demonic forces that diminish the church's effectiveness as sign and instrument." See *Church and World, op. Cit.*, chapter VII, para. 1, p. 75.

[8] *Ibid.*, chapter IV, para. 31, p. 48.

[9] For an indication of future Faith and Order work in this area see Thomas F. Best and Alan Falconer, "Ethnicity and Nationalism in Relation to Christian Unity," Geneva, Faith and Order, 1996 (forthcoming).

[10] Thomas F. Best and National Correspondents, "Survey of Church Union Negotiations 1983-1985/86," Faith and Order Paper No. 133, Geneva, WCC, Faith and Order Commission, 1986, pp. 1-2; reprinted from *The Ecumenical Review*, pp. 456-479; see pp. 456-457.

[11] See the final version of the text in "Reports of the World Conference on Faith and Order, Lausanne, Switzerland, August 3 to 21, 1927," published by the [Faith and Order] Secretariat, Boston, No. 55, January 1928, pp. 17-24. See also the earlier versions of the report of section VII in H. N. Bate, ed., *Faith and Order: Proceedings of the World Conference, Lausanne, 1927*, London, SCM, 1927, pp. 396-403 and 434-439 (emphasis mine).

[12] *Church and World, op. Cit.*, chapter I, para. 10, p. 4.

[13] The work on "Ecclesiology and Ethics" (see also note 1!), which addressed this issue directly, is an important, but later story. See *Costly Unity: Koinonia and Justice, Peace and Creation*, ed. By Thomas F. Best and Wesley Granberg-Michaelson, Geneva, WCC Unit III and Faith and Order (Unit I), 1993. "Costly Unity," Report of the Consultation, pp. 83-105; *Costly Commitment: Ecclesiology and Ethics*, ed. By Thomas F. Best and Martin Robra, Geneva, Faith and Order/Unit I and Unit III, WCC, 1995. "Costly Commitment: Report of the Consultation," pp. 61-81; and "Costly Obedience," report and papers to be published in 1997 by WCC Publications and in *The Ecumenical Review*, respectively.

[14] "Now is the Time: The Final Document and Other Texts from the World Convocation on Justice, Peace and the Integrity of Creation," Seoul 1990, Geneva, WCC, 1990, p. 3.

[15] See the "Act of Covenanting" and the four specific "concretizations" of that act in "Now is the Time," *Ibid.*, pp. 22-33.

[16] "Message" from the Seoul JPIC convocation, in "Now is the Time," *Ibid.*, para. 7, back cover page.

[17] "Now is the Time," *Ibid.*, p. 5.

[18] "Message," *op. Cit.*, para. 2.

[19] "Now is the Time," *op. Cit.*, p. 4.

[20] "Now is the Time," *op. Cit.*, p. 3.

[21] "Now is the Time," *op. Cit.*, p. 4.

[22] See note 1, and the summary review of the official church responses to date in *Baptism, Eucharist and Ministry 1982-1990: Report on the Process and Responses*, Faith and Order Paper No. 149, Geneval, WCC, 1990.

[23] BEM was almost 15 years old (in fact a first draft had already been through one round of response) when it was sent officially to the churches in 1981. Indeed the process of translating the text into local languages, not to mention receiving responses and evaluating them, has continued into the 1990s.

[24] Aram Keshishian, *Conciliar Fellowship: A Common goal*, Geneva, WCC, 1992, pp. 2-5, esp. P. 4.

[25] *New Directions in Faith and Order: Bristol 1967*, Faith and Order Paper No. 50, Geneva, WCC, 1968, p. 57.

[26] On this see *Conciliar Fellowship, op. Cit.*, p. 4. English has only one term for the two meanings of "council"; French, for example, uses "conseil" for the former meaning and "concile" for the latter.

[27] JPIC was envisaged at Vancouver as a unifying theme which "should be a priority for World Council programmes." A vast range of programmes (most already existing) was suggested for inclusion in its purview, from political ethics to the church and the poor to faith, science and the future, the perspectives of children, young people and women, the Programme to Combat Racism, and others. See *Gathered for Life, op. Cit.*, p. 255.

[28] Oliver S. Tomkins, ed., *The Third World Conference on Faith and Order*, London, SCM, 1953, p. 226.

[29] *Ibid.*, p. 232.

[30] See *On the Way to Fuller Koinonia: Official Report of the Fifth World Conference on Faith and Order, op. Cit.*, pp. 309-313, esp. P. 309.

[31] For a survey, bibliography, and interpretation of these developments within the overall history of Faith and Order see Thomas F. Best, "Beyond

Unity-in-Tension. Prague: The Issues and the Experience in Ecumenical Perspective," in Thomas F. Best, ed., *Beyond Unit-in-Tension: Unity, Renewal and the Community of Women and Men*, Faith and Order Paper No. 138, Geneva, WCC, 1988, pp. 1-33. Of special importance was the "intercontextual" method, through which Faith and Order sought to incorporate reflection on contemporary Christian experience into its work on the unity of the church. See John Deschner, "'The Unity of the Church and the Unity of Mankind': An Appraisal of the Study," in *Uniting in Hope: Commission on Faith and Order, Accra 1974*, Faith and Order Paper No. 72, Geneva, Commission on Faith and Order, WCC, 1975, esp. Pp. 85-86; and Mary Tanner, "The Community Study and the Unity of the Church and Renewal of Human Community," in Michael Kinnamon, ed., *Towards Visible Unity: Commission on Faith and Order, Lima 1982*, vol. 2, Faith and Order Paper No. 113, Geneva, WCC, 1982, p. 154.

[32] Thomas F. Best, "Beyond Unity-in-Tension," *op. Cit.*, p. 13.

[33] *Ibid.*, chapter IV, para. 32, p. 49 (emphasis mine).

[34] *Ibid.*, chapter IV, para. 5, p. 39.

[35] *Living Today Towards Visible Unity: The Fifth International Consultation of United and Uniting Churches, op. Cit.,* "Report of the Fifth International Consultation of United and Uniting Churches," para. 8, p. 6.

[36] P. C. Rodger & L. Vischer, eds., *The Fourth World Conference on Faith and Order: Montreal 1963*, Faith and Order Paper No. 42, London, SCM, 1964, pp. 85-86.

[37] "Beyond Unity-in-Tension," *op. Cit.*, pp. 19-20.

[38] *Church and World, op. Cit.*, chapter IV, para. 12, p. 42.

[39] *New Directions in Faith and Order: Bristol 1967, op. Cit.*, p. 17.

[40] *Church and World, op. Cit.*, chapter IV, para. 27, p. 47; see also chapter II, paras. 29-30, p. 19, and chapter III, para. 22, p. 27.

[41] *Faith and Order: Louvain 1971, Study Reports and Documents*, Faith and Order Paper No. 59, Geneva, World Council of Churches, 1971, p. 229.

[42] *Church and World, op. Cit.*, chapter IV, para. 21, pp. 44-45.

[43] *The Fourth World Conference on Faith and Order, op. Cit.*, p. 87 (emphasis mine).

[44] "Towards Unity in Tension," statement of the conference, *Accra 1974: Uniting in Hope, op. Cit.*, pp. 90-94; the quotation is from para. 10, p. 93. The ecumenical movement, then, is finally "dependent on the Spirit for the

strength to reconcile within the one body of the church all whom the forces of disunity would otherwise continue to drive apart"; see para. 12, p. 94.

[45] See "The Unity of the Church as Koinonia: Gift and Calling (Canberra 1991)," *On the Way to Fuller Koinonia: The Fifth World Conference on Faith and Order, op. Cit.*, pp. 269-270.

[46] The central texts in ecumenical discussion have been those from New Delhi ("all in each place") and Nairobi ("conciliar fellowship"). See W. A. Visser 't Hooft, ed., *The New Delhi Report: The Third Assembly of the World Council of Churches, 1961*, London, SCM, 1962, p. 116; and David M. Paton, ed., *Breaking Barriers: Nairobi 1975*, London and Grand Rapids, SPCK and Wm B. Eerdmans, 1976, pp. 59-61. Also important is the statement on catholicity from Uppsala; see Norman Goodall, ed., *The Uppsala 1968 Report: Official Report of the Fourth Assembly of the WCC, Uppsala, 1968*, Geneva, WCC, 1968, p. 13. The Vancouver assembly referred to a "Eucharistic vision"; cf. *Gathered for Life, op. Cit.*, p. 44.

[47] "The Unity of the Church as Koinonia: Gift and Calling," *op. Cit.* (Emphasis mine).

[48] *Ibid.*

[49] "Now is the Time," *op. Cit.*, affirmation VII, p. 18.

[50] *Ibid.*

[51] *Ibid.*, affirmation VIII, p. 19.

[52] *New Directions for Faith and Order: Bristol 1967, op. Cit.*, pp. 17-18.

[53] This has begun in the recent WCC study on HIV/AIDS, where constant contact with matters of life and death—including the death of a member of the study team—brought an acute awareness of these realities. For example: "The whole creation, for all its beauty and the marvellous order which it reveals, groans in 'labour pains' (Rom. 8:22). Both living beings and non-living material objects are subject to decline and decay. There is disease and illness. Many creatures live—and *can* live—only at the expense of others: indeed, many can live only through the *death* of others." See *Facing AIDS: the Challenge, the Churches' Response*, a WCC Study Document, Geneva, WCC Publications, 1997, p. 34.

[54] "Towards Koinonia in Faith, Life and Witness," *op. Cit.*, chapter IV. 5, para. 106, p. 293, referring to *Confessing the One Faith*, Faith and Order Paper No. 153, new revised version, Geneva, WCC Publications, 1991, para. 82, p. 41.

[55] This formulation is taken from the earlier (April, 1992) version of "Towards Koinonia in Faith, Life and Witness," see chapter IV.2, para. 84, p. 31.

[56] *The Churches Survey Their Task: The Report of the Conference at Oxford, July 1937, on Church, Community and State*, Second Impression, London, George Allen & Unwin Ltd., 1938, p. 57.

[57] Geiko Müller-Fahrenholz, "Retrospect: Motives and Themes Leading to the Emergence of the Theme 'Unity of the Church—Unity of Mankind' 1937-1967," in *Unity in Today's World: The Faith and Order Studies on: "Unity of the Church-Unity of Humankind*," ed. By Geiko Müller-Fahrenholz, Faith and Order Paper No. 88, pp. 15-16 (emphasis mine).

[58] *The Uppsala 1968 Report, op. Cit.*, p. 17.

[59] *Ibid.*

[60] *Faith and Order: Louvain 1971, op. Cit.*, pp. 226-227.

[61] "Towards Koinonia in Faith, Life and Witness," *op. Cit.*, para. 13, p. 268.

[62] *The New Delhi Report, op. Cit.*, p. 119.

[63] See *Built Together: The Present Vocation Of United and Uniting Churches (Ephesians 2:22), The Sixth International Consultation of United and Uniting Churches*, ed. By Thomas F. Best, Faith and Order Paper No. 174, Geneva, Faith and Order Commission, WCC, 1996.

[64] See the statement on "corporate union" or "organic union" from the second world conference on Faith and Order at Edinburgh, 1937: "These terms are forbidding to many, as suggesting the ideal of a compact governmental union involving rigid uniformity. We do not so understand them, and none of us desires such uniformity . . . ," (Leonard Hodgson, ed., *The Second World Conference on Faith and Order*, London, Student Christian Movement Press, 1938, p. 252). Archbishop Aram Keshishian notes the effect of this misunderstanding: "The model of organic unity had started to lose ground . . . mainly because of the fear that organic unity could mean, for some churches at least, the development of structures that might hinder the diversity of Christian life. The model of conciliar fellowship affirms diversity" (see *Conciliar Fellowship, op. Cit.*, p. 21). But in fact conciliar fellowship was proposed an explication and development *of the meaning of organic unity*. As the Nairobi assembly noted: "[Conciliar fellowship] does not look towards a conception of unity different from that full organic

unity sketched in the New Delhi statement, but is rather a further elaboration of it" (*Breaking Barriers, op. Cit.*, p. 60).

⁶⁵ *Ibid.*

⁶⁶ The work on catholicity—diversity within the wholeness of the people of God—begun at the Uppsala 1968 assembly will be crucial in further work in this area.⁶⁷ And it is significant that Faith and Order's reflections on conciliarity developed in close connection with its study on "The Unity of the Church and the Unity of [Hu]mankind," a predecessor of the "Unity and Renewal" study. See *Unity in Today's World, op. Cit.*, sections I (pp. 11-13) and II (pp. 14-27). Further, the experience of JPIC in shaping partnerships for reflection and action needs to be joined with that of the unity movement.

⁶⁷ "Since Christ lived, died and rose again for all mankind, catholicity is the opposite of all kinds of egoism and particularism. It is the quality by which the church expresses the fullness, the integrity and the totality of life in Christ," *The Uppsala 1968 Report, op. Cit.*, p. 13.

⁶⁸ For a careful summary and evaluation of the unity of the church—unity of [hu]mankind studies through the 1970s see Geiko Müller-Fahrenholz, ed., *Unity in Today's World: The Faith and Order Studies on: "Unity of the Church-Unity of Humankind,"* Faith and Order Paper No. 88, Geneva, WCC, 1978, chapters I (pp. 11-13) and II (pp. 14-27).

⁶⁹ See *Groupe des Dombes, For the Conversion of the Churches*, trans. By James Greig, Geneva, WCC Publications, 1993.

⁷⁰ Strikingly, the *Groupe des Dombes* introduces kenosis as an instance of conversion—should it not be the other way around? See *For the Conversion of the Churches, op. Cit.*, paras. 164-168, pp. 69-71.

⁷¹ The language of self-giving is not innocent; it has been abused by some, that they might benefit from the sacrifice of others. But the language must be purified and recovered, I believe, not discarded.

⁷² I have used here material from my article "Koinonia and Diakonia: The Ecumenical Implications of two Biblical Perspectives on the Church," in *Faith in Practice: Studies in the Book of Acts, A Festschrift in Honor of Earl and Ottie Mearl Stuckenbruck*, ed. By David A. Fiensy and William D. Howden, Atlanta, European Evangelistic Society, 1995, pp. 347-375; the text is from p. 365.

[73] See *Church and World: The Unity of the Church and the Renewal of Human Community, op. Cit.*, pp. 69-70.

[74] *On the Way to Fuller Koinonia: Official Report of the Fifth World Conference on Faith and Order, op. Cit.*, p. 233.

CHAPTER FOUR

NEW PERSPECTIVES IN MISSION

Emilio Castro

In 1961 the International Missionary Council (IMC) integrated into the life of the WCC. From that moment on an intense missiological discussion has taken place in ecumenical circles inside and far beyond the WCC. "Mission in six continents" was the slogan of the first conference of the Commission on World Mission and Evangelism (CWMC) as part and parcel of the WCC. It was an attempt to indicate the missionary nature of Christian being, and of the very life of the church, so that everywhere, in the local church or through ministries abroad, we are compelled to be engaged in world mission.

Pretty soon came the discussion about *Missio dei* ("the mission of God"). The real thing was to discover *God's* missionary outreach, embracing the whole creation, and bringing all into the search for Shalom, the all-embracing blessings of God. It was an attempt to enlarge the horizons, to see beyond the upward growth of the church, or the internal concerns of the church, to the reality of the whole world as the arena where Christians and non-Christians were called to walk together toward the horizon of the kingdom of God. The church's ministry was perceived to be at the service of a wider mission.

It is no surprise that at this moment a big debate developed about the relation between evangelism and social action. Was the concern for the total human development one way out of the Christian obligation to "name the name" and call people to faith in Jesus Christ? Could we talk about "priorities" between evangelism and the social manifestation of Christian love? Was the participation in human development the paramount manifestation of our missionary strategy, or should this always be accompanied by the planting of the church? Together with this debate came the big polemic about church growth: could we develop methodologies for such numerical growth? Would such methodologies facilitate the growth of the church at the potential expense of the content, the sacrificial demands, of the Gospel?

In fact the very notion of salvation was explored in the world missionary conference in Bangkok in 1973, because a radical questioning of the whole missionary strategy of the church was at stake. Two other main issues fed this intensely polemic period. One was the concern for dialogue with other religious people and people of other ideological convictions. Fear was expressed that this could lead to a relativizing of the gospel, a diminution of our missionary zeal, finishing eventually in a radical syncretism. Meanwhile a parallel debate was taking place, especially in Africa, about the need for a "moratorium" in international mission.

The desire was expressed that Western, "sending" missionary agencies should stop sending people and material resources, and consider afresh their whole participation in the missionary outreach of the world church. This they should do in full awareness that the situation was radically changing, because the church was *already* planted in most countries on earth.

The whole of this exciting period came to be summarized in concrete ecumenical affirmations in the document *Mission and Evangelism: An Ecumenical Affirmation*,[1] which was approved by the WCC Central Committee in the early 1980s. A knowledge of this document is an essential foundation for my discussion, and in looking to the whole future of the missionary enterprise, so I shall review and discuss some of its central points.

The *Affirmation* begins by recalling the total horizon of God's purpose for creation and humanity, and goes on to discern the particular vocation of the church. Thus the Preface notes:

> The biblical promise of a new earth and a new heaven where love, peace and justice will prevail (Ps. 85:7-13, Is. 32:17-18, 65:17-25, and Rev. 21:1-2) invites our actions as Christians in history. The contrast of that vision with the reality of today reveals the monstrosity of human sin, the evil unleashed by the rejection of God's will for humankind.

The church is sent into the world to call people and nations to repentance, to announce forgiveness of sin and a new beginning in relations with God and with neighbours through Jesus Christ. This evangelistic calling has a new urgency today.[2]

Very clearly, lessons from the mission of God debate are taken—but with a clear concentration on the missionary responsibility of the church, and the centrality of Jesus Christ as the revelation of God in history. And so we read in the section "Call to Mission":

There is a growing awareness among the churches today of the inextricable relationship between Christian unity and missionary calling, between ecumenism and evangelization. "Evangelization is the test of our ecumenical vocation."[3]

The starting point of our proclamation, affirms the document, is Christ and Christ crucified:

The Cross is the place of the decisive battle between the powers of evil and the love of God. It uncovers the lostness of the world, the magnitude of human sinfulness, the tragedy of human alienation. The total self-surrendering of Christ reveals the immeasurable depth of God's love for the world (John 3:16).[4]

From this basic affirmation follow a series of clear convictions about conversion, described in this way: "Jesus' call is an invitation to follow him joyfully, to participate in his servant body, to share with him in the struggle to overcome sin, poverty and death."[5] There is also a clear affirmation of our vocation to announce the gospel in all realms of life, to provide a public witness to Jesus Christ. Thus in Para. 15:

The Evangelistic Witness is directed towards all of the *ktisis* (creation) which groans and travails in search of adoption and redemption . . . The transfiguring power of the Holy Trinity is meant to reach into every nook and cranny of our national life . . . The Evangelistic Witness will also speak to the structures of this world, its economic and societal institutions . . . .
"

The church and its unity in God's mission are part and parcel of the common convictions of the ecumenical family. In Para. 20 the internal life of the church is perceived as a missionary existence:

> **Thus Christian mission is the action of the body of Christ in the history of humankind—a continuation of Pentecost. Those who through conversion and baptism accept the Gospel of Jesus partake in the life of the body of Christ and participate in an historical tradition.**[6]

It is very interesting to see that "tradition" is here perceived in its *missionary* meaning of passing on a message, and a lifestyle, that belongs to the people of God. And at the very centre of the Christian church, of Christian spirituality, the celebration of the eucharist is perceived to be

> bread for a missionary people. We acknowledge with deep sorrow that Christians do not join together at the Lord's Table. This contradicts God's will and impoverishes the body of Christ. The credibility of our Christian witness is at stake.[7]

So naturally the unity of the church is essential for the mission of the Church:

> **. . . common witness should be the natural consequence of a unity with Christ in his mission.** The ecumenical experience has discovered the reality of a deep spiritual unity. The common recognition of the authority of the Bible and of the creeds of the ancient church and a growing convergence in doctrinal affirmations should allow the churches not only to affirm together the fundamentals of the Christian faith, but also to proclaim together the Good News of Jesus Christ to the world. In solidarity, churches are helping each other in their respective witness before the world. In the same solidarity, they should share their spiritual and material resources to announce together and clearly their common hope and common calling.[8]

Because the mission and evangelism to which we are called is the continuation in history of God's invasion of love in Jesus Christ, the style that corresponds to that mission is Christ's own way. So in the chapter called "Mission in Christ's way," the affirmation says:

> "As the Father has sent me, even so I send you" (John 20:21). The self-emptying of the servant who lived among the people, sharing in their hopes and sufferings, giving his life on the cross for all humanity—this was Christ's way of proclaiming the Good News, and as disciples we are summoned to follow the same way . . .
>
> . . . an imperialistic crusader's spirit was foreign to him. **Churches are free to choose the ways they consider best to announce the gospel to different people in different circumstances. But these options are never neutral. Every methodology illustrates or betrays the gospel we announce. In all communication of the Gospel, power must be subordinate to love.**[9]

One of the points of focus in the spiritual and intellectual pilgrimage of the church in the last decades has been the re-encounter with the poor of the earth and the re-discovery, in them, of the face of Jesus Christ. "Good news to the poor" belongs to the very essence of the Gospel and comes as God's priority for the church. Thus Para. 32:

> There is also a tragic coincidence that most of the world's poor have not heard the Good News of the Gospel of Jesus Christ or they could not receive it because it was not recognized as Good News in the way in which it was brought. This is a double injustice: they are victims of the oppression of an unjust economic order or an unjust political distribution of power, and at the same time they are deprived of the knowledge of God's special care for them. To announce the Good News to the poor is to begin to render the justice due to them.

Let me add here a quotation from an essay by Kurt Cadorette in the book *Mission in Bold Humility, David Bosch's Work Considered:*[10]

The preferential option for the poor is often construed as a social-political statement or decision. It is neither. It is really a Christological and soteriological assertion whose foundation lies in the God revealed in both Hebrew and Christian scriptures. What Medellin claimed and Puebla and Santo Domingo reiterated in 1979 and 1992 is that to understand Jesus and the reign of God he proclaimed, Christians must live as he did, among and committed to the poor . . . A disciple does not opt for the poor and oppressed out of a sense of *noblesse oblige* or some romantic assumption about their intrinsic goodness, but because in their midst Christians encounter the God Jesus proclaimed.[11]

We mentioned above that the Mexican conference in 1962 on "Mission in 6 Continents" was the first after the integration of the International Missionary Council with the WCC. The basic affirmations from this gathering remain with us and are taken up by the *Ecumenical Affirmation of Mission and Evangelism*, which indicates that mission is "in and to" six continents.

The Christian affirmations on the world-wide missionary responsibility of the church will be credible if they are authenticated by a serious missionary engagement at home . . .

Every local congregation needs the awareness of its catholicity which comes from its participation in the mission of Jesus Christ in other parts of the world. Through its witnessing stance in its own situation, its prayers of intercession for churches in other parts of the world, and its sharing of persons and resources, it participates fully in the world mission of the Christian church.[12]

It is within this awareness of the reciprocal belonging of home and foreign mission, and of the responsibility of every local congregation to be part of the international mission of the church, that the debate about a "moratorium" on mission arises.

This was not an attempt to stop mission, but to give to the missionary outreach of the church a new moment of reflection, of consideration, to see if a new beginning could free resources to confront new challenges. Thus the text insists that:

> Moratorium does not mean the end of the missionary vocation, nor of the duty to provide resources for missionary work, but it does mean freedom to reconsider present engagement and to see whether a continuation of what we had been doing for so long is the right style of mission in our day.

> Moratorium has to be understood *inside* a concern for world mission. **It is faithfulness of commitment to Christ in each national situation which makes missionary concern in other parts of the world authentic. There can never be a moratorium of mission, but it will be possible, and sometimes necessary, to have a moratorium for the sake of better mission.**[13]

Mission and Evangelism: An Ecumenical Affirmation is a landmark in ecumenical missionary thinking, and I think it is the best possible summary of where our common conviction has led the "ecumenical ship" in the most recent decades. However that document is dated 1982. The world continues to go on; changes are happening, and the pilgrim people of God continues in its missionary journey, facing old and new situations, thinking ever again afresh about its missionary vocation and the way in which it should be performed.

Therefore "new perspectives"—the title of our article—are needed. I offer the following not as a substitute for the common ecumenical wisdom we have already described, but as adaptations of that wisdom, or advances upon it, or as a basis for confronting the new challenges of the day in the same spirit.

First, let us face the reality: we do not have any more the benefit of an historical "inerrancy" in transmitting the Christian tradition or the basic elements of the Christian Gospel. Look at Western Europe: the cathedrals are there. For those who know, or who dare to look carefully, every door, every column speaks in symbols of the Christian tradition. But for most of the inhabitants of Europe, and for most of the tourists passing by, they are only manifestations of a certain craftsmanship and beauty, which do not convey the significance of the Christian symbols.

Allow me to quote from the chapter "The Missionary Challenge to the Church at the End of the 20th Century," which I wrote for the book *Reconciliation: Essays in Honour of Michael Hurley.*[14]

> Let me begin by indicating what to me is the most important challenge with which we are already confronted now, and which will be with us in the years to come. This is well summarized by one of our old Sunday School hymns: "Tell me the old, old story, tell me of Jesus and his love." I do not see any greater urgency than to develop the capacity of transmitting the story of Jesus Christ within and outside the Christian community. While we are well aware of the secularization prevailing in Western Europe, we are also aware of the fact that the majority of the population still likes to be called Christian. In some countries of continental Europe this can be measured even by the payment of Church taxes. Those taxes are these, providing for many services which the churches are able to offer, but the bodies, the minds, the hearts of the people are not there. Make an inquiry about the meaning of some of the official holidays celebrated in some of our countries, like Pentecost or Ascension Day or even Christmas and your will get the most extraordinary responses from the people.
>
> But we are talking only of the region called previously Western Europe. We need to look also to the regions belonging to Central and Eastern Europe. We are obviously excited by the new perspectives which have opened up for the Churches there as a result of the overthrow of the party monopoly, with its ideological system. However, we should not be blind to the fact that for the past 45 or even 75 years the population has been deprived of a living relationship with the Church. Today we are witnesses of a great religious revival; we have a tremendous unity of ethnic groupings and religion. We can watch great feelings, great emotion and the attempt to recover the tradition, but without the actual content, without the actual knowledge. There is curiosity, there is even partisan passion, but there is no knowledge. It is very significant that the Churches in those countries are concentrating their efforts on getting of vast quantities of Bibles

and religious books . . . [through] the Amity Printing Press, a joint effort of the China Christian Council and the United Bible Society . . . millions of Bibles are being printed for the benefit of the Chinese people. The National Council of Churches of (South) Korea is coordinating a big campaign among Churches of that country to raise together the means to provide one million bibles for the Churches in the former Soviet Union.[15]

We could add here the need of fast-developing Pentecostal and African-Instituted churches for substantial basic knowledge of the Christian tradition. I do not need to elaborate the rapid growth in world population, which represents enormous challenges for the formation of Christian communities and the evangelistic task of the Church. Training, Christian education, the spreading of the bible: all these are today a fundamental challenge in our missionary outreach.

We know that there are many dimensions of the mission of the church which have greater glamour, but the sterling work of bible distribution and the Sunday School teacher is fundamental as we go into the new millenium. As a Pentecostal leader from Brazil used to say: "We do not need help for our evangelistic work. We know how to do it. What we need is help in training the converted Christians into Christian citizens, into people who know what the gospel means for private, public and family life." This Christian formation is one of the most exciting missionary challenges for today.

For centuries the missionary expansion of the church from the West was supported and helped by Western colonial and commercial expansion. As is evident from the well-known story of that expansion in the 16th to 18th centuries, that expansion was facilitating the parallel, simultaneous expansion of the Christian church. Today the expansion of the West—and not only its political and commercial influence, but especially in terms of the new communication possibilities and the entertainment industry—is tremendously powerful. But now it proceeds practically without reference to any Christian values. The forces behind the expansion y have developed their own system of values, their own consumerist society, and thus they are in reality competing for the minds, souls, and loyalty of people everywhere. The task of the church, which (with all the ambiguities of the colonial and commercial period, was somehow facilitated by the communication means then available) is made more and more difficult by the values prevailing in the communications systems of today. We read of efforts made to plant the proclamation of the Gospel in the electronic world of the mass media and of the Internet; but we need to realize that, for Christian formation, nothing today can replace the potential—and responsibility—of the Christian family, the Christian local community, and the vocational groups which gather around a particular missionary frontier, or a particular spiritual discipline, to strengthen their knowledge of the Gospel and their attempt to be faithful servants of Jesus Christ.

Second, a series of events or facts have come together to produce a certain "loss of nerve" in the church's missionary consciousness. Perhaps the classical motivation for mission, the conviction of the "lostness" of all humankind and the need to send to all human beings a saving message, has not survived our relatively new proximity to people of other faiths. In today's pluralist society it is much more difficult to speak of the "darkness" of others while their children who play with our children often behave much better than ours. It is also true that a certain "tiredness" prevails as we have so many efforts to develop programs for justice in so many countries of the world, yet see that—despite all our efforts—the present economic model continues to generate marginalized people and to increase poverty.

And also: slogans like "the evangelization of the world in this generation," which was the inspiration and the calling of the generation of Edinburgh in 1910, or the later slogan "Reaching the unreached," that motivated so many Christians in the last decades, have not produced a significant difference in the religious map of the world. The traditional religions of Islam, Hinduism, Buddhism and so on are there to stay, and indeed they are now sending missionaries to do "outreach" in areas traditionally considered "Christian." Again, in the 1960's it was possible to think of the movements of the Spirit of God among the poor of the earth and opening history to create new possibilities; but today, after the fall of the Berlin wall and all of the radical changes experienced in the world, it seems that South Africa formed the last confrontation between the Christian faith and a form of political and cultural life which was clearly evil or heretical. Now we are called to live our Christian life within more ambiguous situations, where of course there are injustices to be denounced, and hopes to be rekindled—but all within a "realistic acceptance" of the ambiguities of history.

We seem to be the first generation which is no longer "naive" in its consideration of the world and the impact of the Christian mission upon that world. Realism is absolutely necessary; but for Christians realism goes not only to the cross, where all evil is unmasked, but also to the resurrection, where the power of God is fully manifested. On this basis our missionary consciousness does not depend on the historical "success" of our efforts, but comes from our belonging to God's movement of love, God's own missionary being, God's own self-disclosure in Jesus Christ. It is this which calls us to be a part of the "missionary" movements within history. The "loss of nerve" will not recovered by arguments about the "darkness" of the world or by all the "success stories" which could be told. Rather the recovery will come through a deeper rooting of our spiritual life in the very life of God in Christ, in the mystery of the Trinity, so that we can be taken by the Holy Spirit and led into new missionary situations. It is, first of all, the recovery of our *Christian missionary identity* that is required in order to cope with the missionary challenges of today.

Perhaps in our situation we could recover something of the psychological and spiritual perspectives which belonged to the early Christians. They were minorities confronting the power of the Roman empire. The could not develop a "master plan" for the whole world. They knew only from whence they were coming: a personal encounter with Jesus Christ, the reception of the Holy spirit, and the internal motivation to share with others what they had received. It is from a sense of sharing blessings received, and a wish to see many others praising God (Phil. 2), that we are involved in our missionary outreach. It is no arrogance or claim of superiority, but only the awareness of God's love, that involves us in same passionate outreach, in the same sharing through the cross in the pains and sufferings and, through the resurrection, in the hopes and dreams of humankind.

Third, as the world becomes a "global village" we are challenged to realize a different type of inculturation, one that means the interaction of the gospel with the themes which now affect the whole of humankind. In an era when the "local" transcends international borders, the credibility of the gospel message depends upon Christians participating actively in the discussion of the values which will shape this world community and the whole of humanity. Specifically we need to engage critically with the prevailing anthropology which reduces human beings to the role of consumers, and proclaims the independence of the market from any voluntaristic control. The mood of society today calls constantly for increasing productivity and competitiveness, treating human beings in terms of an economic variable . At stake is a vision of personal society which is in collision with basic tenets of the gospel.

In today's consumer society the church has new opportunities to speak the name of Jesus Christ, whether in caring for the victims of economic developments, or engaging in the debate to uphold human values. Thus the conciliar process for Justice, Peace and the Integrity of Creation has been, and is, the affirmation of a new relationship between human beings and creation, a new covenant of responsibility between present and future generations. In fact, it is a new way of proclaiming the Gospel message.

Fourth, there is another aspect of this global consideration, one coming from the scientific developments of today. We have to speak the name of Jesus and show the newness of life offered in him in a world where the vision of reality is measured in billions of years, and where genetic manipulation can condition life. Yet it is in the ingenuousness of this story of Jesus that we find the freshness we need to confront contemporary perceptions and to testify to a reality which calls for their creative transformation.

There are two inseparable dimensions to the current debate on biotechnology: bioresearch and its possible consequences, and the economic power which sets the options for such research. Science has the potential for good and for evil; but we are talking here also about the very definition of humanity, about the affirmation—or denial, as in the more extreme expressions of biotechnology—of human freedom and integrity. The advent of biotechnology calls the churches to re-examine the fundamental Christian understanding of creation, and the relationship between God, humanity and the created world. In confronting the challenges of globalization we are called to engage in a theological- philosophical debate but also in the defence of the human spirituality and freedom, and to affirm that justice must be the commanding category in terms of priorities for investigation, research and application.

In the process, the resources of the biblical witness and the declaration of the ancient creeds of the Church must be reaffirmed. Exactly in this context, the affirmation of new life in Christ is an evangelising vocation that challenges us and calls for our cooperative effort.

Fifth, closely related to the inculturation debate is the permanent question, already mentioned in the *Ecumenical Affirmation on Mission and Evangelism*, of the place of other religions in God's plan. In Vancouver, and later on in San Antonio and Canberra, the discussion centred on the recognition of the person of God in other people's religious experience. So Vancouver was able to affirm God's creative hand in the thirst for God, in the acts of searching for God, in the religious aspiration of other people. But the debate today tends to be concentrated on the classical questions: is there revelation in other religions? Is there salvation? Are religions alternative ways toward God? What about the uniqueness of Jesus Christ? If all religions are somehow the "same," what about our missionary vocation?

Part of the difficulty is the Western style of debate, which privileges theological discourse, a discourse that pretends to master reality and does not allow space for the mystical, for the spiritual nature of human relations. When we consider the so-called "exclusivist" texts ("no one comes to the Father except through me," John 14:6; or "There is salvation in no one else, for there is no other name," Acts 4:12) we might be tempted to forget who Jesus was, what was his style, and what is our calling. But let us ask: what could those expressions have meant for the first generation of Christians, who were reading them in the midst of persecution?

If we read those texts confronted with the temptation to worship Caesars in order to survive, the testimony is clear: "only in Jesus there is salvation." Those texts are strength and consolation in persecution, they resound with the awareness of Jesus' death for all, and affirm that in surrendering our own life we are identifying with him. Inside the total life of Jesus, in a loving community, Jesus who cares for others, loving them to the utmost, those texts assume a testimonial value rather than a judgmental one. They are the "open arms," a joyful announcement, an invitation to a life of service. The total life of Jesus is self-surrendering, the style of the servant, and in this style the claims to the final revelation of God in Jesus Christ must be understood not as imperialistic pretensions, but as the joyful confession of faith.

I have found it very important for my own theological reflections, and for my practical relations to people of other religious convictions, to follow Paul in Romans 9-11. Here Paul recognizes that God has been at work from the beginning in the people of Israel, and that God will be at work with them in the eschatological consummation. The Holy spirit has had, and has, a ministry outside the church. Of course I know this because of the revelation of Jesus, which indicates the freedom of the Spirit. Knowing Jesus in the tradition of the Church, I am free to realize the action of the Holy Spirit, the Creator Spirit, in the creation and in the life and cultures of other peoples. Romans 9-11 is a recognition of the past covenant with Israel, an eschatological disclosure of the role that Israel will be playing to the end, and meanwhile both a clear witness and announcement of what God has done in Jesus Christ and an invitation to join the new people of God. This is, for me, a very constructive recognition of God's freedom to operate outside the church, which takes seriously the promise that God's plan will be fulfilled and calls for a new readiness to understand that plan and the role other peoples play within it, But at same time it calls for the joyful acceptance of the mission entrusted to the church, which is to provide a witness to the wonderful disclosure of God's will in Jesus Christ.

As we grow through more existential encounters with people of other religious convictions we gain fresh resources for our theological reflections, and see new, as well as the old, perspectives on both our specific Christian mission and our common human responsibility.

Six: *Mission and Evangelism: An Ecumenical Affirmation* boldly declares that common witness should be the natural consequence of the church's unity with Christ in his mission. Theological reflection concerning common witness, and our common conviction that this is the only way forward in the modern world, has been dramatically tested by the events in Central and Eastern Europe. In Ukraine, Slovakia and many other countries the prevailing theology was not able to bring Christians together in the new situation which followed the fall of the socialist regimes. There is now a different reading of past history, one which brings forward dramatically the events of the 16th century and considers them from a totally different perspective than that of the Orthodox or Catholics.

At the same time there is a clash of ecclesiologies. For the Orthodox churches it is clear that the division of the 11th century gave missionary responsibility and ecclesiastical jurisdiction over the Eastern part of Europe to Constantinople and the national Orthodox churches, while the Western part of Europe, and subsequently the part of the world colonized by Europe, were under the missionary and catechetical responsibility of the Western Church. The classical understanding has been shaken terribly by an invasion of Western mission-based groups which have carried proselytizing and missionary work into the former territories of the Soviet Union and into Eastern Europe. In less than two years, in Romania alone over 400 missionary groups from the West were active and at work. Of course we recognize that the situation between the Roman Catholic and Orthodox churches is a little different because the conflict is not a new one, but is the present manifestation of a centuries-long conflict between churches recognising allegiance to Rome and those belonging to the patriarchates of the East. In any case we are confronted with a serious test of our ecumenical belonging, and after so many years of searching for the unity of the church we run the risk of having to start again from zero.

In this essay our main concern is with the mission of the church and the proclamation of the gospel in today's new situation. Precisely because of this missionary angle we will plead for a historical reading of the situation, and for a missionary response that which corresponds to the situation and conditions today, independent from the more classical debate on ecclesiology which obviously needs to take place. I will insist that in the plural situation of Western Europe the testimony of the Orthodox churches is absolutely essential. Traditionally the Orthodox churches do not want to carry on missionary work in Western territories because they do not want to be objects of proselytism, and do not want to be accused of committing the same things in other territories. But the situation is such that many people have become totally secularized and out of touch with the traditional Christian church. At the same time many young people are searching for mystical experience, looking for oriental cults or esoteric groups. They know nothing of the beauty and the drama of the liturgical life in the Orthodox communities, which could be a real response to the search for mystery and at the same time an excellent mediation of the basic tenets of the Christian gospel.

It is for the sake of mission in pluralist, secularized Western Europe that the Orthodox church needs to revise its position on missionary outreach. But with the same conviction we will call for respect for the Orthodox and classical Christian churches, helping and working in Eastern Europe to allow them to recover the territory taken from them by Socialist regimes, to grow from their own classical roots, to express fully the religious identity of the people, and to strengthen both their internal life and their missionary capacities. Our "missionary service" in Eastern Europe should take the form precisely of restraining our own institutional church life, and our attempts at proselytizing, in order to support fully the work of the classical Churches which have long been established in that area.

The time will come to discuss the relation between geography and ecclesiology. But today—and precisely for the sake of *mission*—total priority should be given to the strengthening of the local churches. Their mission is our mission. Of course we know that there are ecclesiological difficulties in reciprocal recognition. But the ecumenical experience that we have shared so far, the love and solidarity exercised during years of oppression, the commonality of our baptism in Christ, provide sufficient foundation for accepting their mission as our mission, their accepting our support for their mission, and converting that into our common mission. Once again, unity is the test of real mission (John 17:21).

In November 1997 the latest WCC conference on mission and evangelism took place in Salvador, Baihia, Brazil. This time the main topic was "Called to one Hope: the Gospel in Different Cultures." A dominant theme came from the reference to D. T. Niles' famous phrase: "the gospel has reached us in Western pots. We need now to break those pots to enable the gospel to take root in Asian soil." This generation has dramatically "broken all pots," allowing new flowers, new colours, to appear. In fact the question is: how to recognize all these manifestations of the gospel as belonging to the same unbroken tradition of the church. The problem is not new; in fact what we have today in most of the historic churches is a synthesis between various cultures and the gospel—

an interaction with present-day culture. based upon an identity sacralized in a synthesis reached centuries ago. In the ethnic-national expressions of Christianity so dear to many Orthodox churches, we have a cultural amalgamation and adaptation of the gospel, manifesting its power to change and shape culture. The Christian faith has provided the power to preserve national cultures, not only in Eastern Europe but also in the Scandinavian countries. Many of the cultural features of the Mediterranean countries are present in the liturgical drama of the Latin tradition. In Latin America, obviously the popular religion is permeated by Afro, Indian and Latin elements. Many other examples could be given today.

In the missionary history of the church, this process of inculturation has been a normal one. New attention perhaps should be paid to the attempt made by the Jesuits in China in the 15th century. Ricci and his successors spent long years gaining access to the imperial court, and in the study of Chinese classics. While not discouraging Chinese conversion to Christianity, they believed that generations of study by themselves and their successors would be necessary before the "way of Christ could be taught fully in ways appropriate to China." And they embarked on exactly this plan. As noted in *Mission in Bold Humility*:

> In retrospect one sees that Ricci had embarked on a program of reconceptualizing Christianity for the Chinese world in ways as radical as the hellenization that was Christianity's first major hermeneutic and inculturational milestones. It would be anachronistic to say that the Jesuits in China were consciously carrying on what we today call inculturation. But *mutatis mutandis* that was the effect of their entire process, and they were doing it at a depth analogous to that of every Greek and Latin church father.[16]

Today the issue is alive again. Christians of the East are trying to recover their past history—be it personal, family or national history—and to bring it into living dialogue with the Gospel. Attempts are present in Latin America to recover pre-Columbian cultures, both indigenous and African. New syncretism is appearing in Africa, following the model of the African Independent churches. Everywhere in the world women are demanding that their particular perspectives should be taken into consideration, and their interaction with their culture is producing expressions of Christianity which tend to shake our assurances but at the same time opens new ways of communication to the surrounding community. The meeting in Salvador noted that:

> some practises and customs which were once negated and rejected as pagan and superstitious are now recognized as authentic elements of people's spirituality. The use of certain musical instruments and forms of traditional worship are cases in point. The profound need of people to keep the living presence of their ancestors in an organic and holistic vision of reality is not seriously considered in some Christian churches. Other Christian traditions, however, provide for this need through commemorative feasts, family prayers, liturgical celebrations, or visual arts. It is the task of the church to give theological meaning to this profound need through the incarnated Lord who is crucified and risen from the dead and gives promise of eternal life. In rediscovering the catholicity of the church in its cultural contexts, elements such as this play a crucial role. Destructive and death-dealing elements within every culture are critiqued by the gospel. The incarnation, life, death and resurrection of Jesus Christ, all together, constitute the known standard in Christian tradition for such discernment.[17]

In the present debate on mission and inculturation, some are demanding that a limit to diversity be clearly established. Others, like myself, are demanding clarity about the centrality of Christ and then, from this Christological centre, are recognizing joyfully the gift of God in creation and the wonderful creativity of the Spirit through the many cultural manifestations of yesterday and today.

Obviously in this new period in the Christian church we will go through an "organized chaos"—a time of exploration and searching for new approaches and perspectives—within the enduring tradition of the church. Our challenge is to ensure that it will be as fruitful a time for the proclamation of the gospel, and for the application of the gospel to all realms of life, as any period since its original proclamation so many years ago.

Notes

[1]Geneva, Commission on World Mission and Evangelism, 1982; also in *Mission and Evangelism: An Ecumenical Affirmation—A Study Guide*, comp. By Jean Stromberg, WCC Mission Series No. 4, Geneva, WCC, 1983.

[2]P. 1 (emphasis original).

[3]Para. 1. The quotation is from Philip Potter's speech to the Roman Catholic Synod of Bishops, delivered in Rome in 1984 (emphasis original).

[4]Para. 8.

[5] Para. 11.

[6] (Emphasis original).

[7] Para. 21.

[8] Para. 23.

[9] Para. 28 (emphasis original).

[10] Ed. By Willem Saayman and Klippies Kritzinger, Maryknoll, Orbis Books, 1996.

[11] P. 65.

[12] Para. 37 (emphasis original).

[13] Para. 38 (emphasis original).

[14] "The Missionary Challenge to the Church at the End of the 20th Century," in *Reconciliation . . .* , ed. By Oliver Rafferty, SJ, Dublin, The Columba Press, 1993, pp. 130-139.

[15] Pp. 132-133.

[16] *Op. Cit.*, p. 133.

[17] Report of Section IV, para. 20.

CHAPTER FIVE

ECUMENICAL SPIRITUALITY
THE QUEST FOR WHOLENESS OF VISION

Diane C. Kessler

When Paul Crow was asked to talk about life experiences which propelled him into the ecumenical movement, he recalled the occasion of receiving his Eagle Scout award. It was

> to be presented during the Sunday service at my congregation. I invited my best friend Mug, a Roman Catholic of Italian descent, to be present and sit with my family during the presentation. I remember even now the deep pain and hurt when several days before the service Mug sadly told me he could not come into our church because his priest said to do so would be a mortal sin. The Disciples were separated from the true Church. At that moment I learned a divided Church hurts lives and relationships. Experiences of disunity—then and now—have motivated me and countless other Christians to work for the full reconciliation and *koinonia* (communion) of the Body of Christ.[1]

Ecumenism deals with healing relationships—between Christians, among churches, for the sake of the world. Christian spirituality deals with a relationship—to the Triune God we know through Jesus Christ—and through God, to each other. Both ecumenism and spirituality recognize that all too often our relationships with each other, indeed with the whole created order and thus with God, are broken and in need of mending. A loving God beckons us to the Godhead and also to our neighbors.

The Eagle Scout story Dr. Crow tells is a concrete example of the way in which our experiences energize us for the ecumenical task. Christians confess that God works through such encounters. Part of the challenge of Christian spirituality is recognizing and responding to such signs of God's presence, God's activity, and God's will for ourselves, for our churches, and for the world around us. When we do, we find ourselves drawn to a reconciling Spirit which is at the heart of the ecumenical movement.

Definitions

The words "ecumenism" and "spirituality" often are used indiscriminately. A colleague of mine once heard an interracial boxing match referred to as "an ecumenical bout." The word spirituality now suffers from similar carelessness. The term is used to cover anything vaguely "otherworldly." So when one writes about "ecumenical spirituality," the danger of sliding into sloppy definitions increases exponentially!

In an effort to steer through these murky waters, I want to define terms at the outset. Christian spirituality is the personal quest for understanding God, seeking closeness to or communion with God, and following the will of God in one's own life as it is lived in the community of the church and in society. Prayer is a traditional, primary means to engage in this quest. Prayer, however, is not the only means. Christians have relied on a variety of personal and communal ways to seek God and to conform to God's will.[2]

Ecumenism is the healing of the divisions among the Christian churches for the sake of the world. More precisely, it

> is the variety of efforts within and among the Christian churches
> to give visible expression to their unity in Jesus Christ, in response
> to the Holy Spirit, through diverse acts of reconciliation to heal
> all their divisions, and through common witness and service to
> the world.[3]

Thus ecumenical spirituality encompasses all the ways that Christians and Christian churches approach the beckoning, reconciling God we know in Jesus Christ through the Holy Spirit; listen to God's will in the varied ways that it is conveyed to us, with particular attention to what this means for divided Christians and their churches; respond to God's call in our own behavior, and as we live together in Christian community, in this reconciling spirit; and attend to the ways that God beckons us to bring this reconciling spirit into the world around us. Ecumenical spirituality should provide both the grounding and the environment in which we pursue the quest for Christian unity.

This definition is consistent with one we find in the chapter on "Spirituality and Ecumenism" in Dr. Crow's book, *Christian Unity: Matrix for Mission*. He defines spirituality as follows:

> It means a personal and corporate communion with God through Christ, given by the Holy Spirit and leading to a life motivated by God's will. Such a spirituality is marked by prayer, devotional readings, adoration, repentance, forgiveness, sharing the Eucharist or the Lord's Supper, meditation and theological reflection. Out of this seedbed genuine ecumenism flowers and takes shape in the world.[4]

He makes the point that "the power toward unity comes from living in the presence of God."[5] He goes on to say that our communion with God enables us to "transform our relations with others."[6]

Dr. Crow's lifelong grounding in the Disciples tradition has made eucharistic celebration central to his own spirituality. Yet the Lord's Table is one of the most obvious places where Protestant, Roman Catholic, and Orthodox churches are divided. The glaring chasm between what we believe and how we behave at the communion table has been a motivating force for Dr. Crow's commitment to the ecumenical movement, as it has for so many ecumenists.

Ecumenical spirituality is related to a variety of Christian disciplines, yet it is distinct. It involves theology, because the quest for God implies a certain understanding of the nature of God as healing, reconciling, just, and loving. It deals with ethics, because the struggle to know and do the will of God forces us to wrestle with concepts of morality and justice. It goads us to examine the ways in which our behaviors are corrosive to the human spirit, undermine right relationships, and erode human community in both church and world. Ecumenical spirituality draws us into issues of ecclesiology, because assumptions about the church and its ministry affect the forms of spirituality—sometimes exacerbating our divisions, sometimes enriching the whole through our diverse understandings. It prompts us to consider liturgy, because expressions of spirituality are shaped by sacramental assumptions, with the power to divide or unite. Ecumenical spirituality touches the field of history. The memories we hold continue to influence our relationships, and provide keys to unraveling past problems. It entails Biblical studies, because hearing and studying the Word together as it calls us to unity can be a source for spiritual meditation, contemplation, and growth. Ecumenical spirituality touches all these fields. Yet it is distinct, with its own focus.

The forms of ecumenical spirituality are consistent with the means Christians have used to be open to the presence and leadings of God. Some of these include prayer, Scripture reading and study, meditation (the pondering of the texts read), giving and hearing sermons, composition and singing of hymns, and worship. They appropriately are called "ecumenical" when their intention is consistent with the aims of ecumenism—to heal divisions among Christians and their churches for the sake of the world.

Theological assumptions

An ecumenical spirituality makes certain irreducible faith claims. How Christians understand the nature of God as revealed in the life, death, and resurrection of Jesus Christ has everything to do with how Christians understand themselves and the world around them. A beckoning, forgiving, healing, redeeming, righteous, reconciling, compassionate God draws us to Godself and to each other in this same Spirit. Thus, all ways that we foster community, heal brokenness, live with integrity, and redress injustice are consistent with God's nature and intention.

Christian faith is incarnational. We confess that God acts in history. Furthermore, God comes to us in human flesh, through God's Son, in a unique way. God's Holy Spirit continues to work through us, in the life of the Church, and in the world.

These basic assumptions about God and Christ have implications for an authentic ecumenical spirituality. As Philip Sheldrake asserts in his excellent book *Images of Holiness*, "Christian spirituality as such is social as [sic] its very roots—reflecting the society of equal relationships that is God (and which we call 'Trinity') . . . "[7]

We expect to see signs of God's presence in the created order, in the church, and in human beings. We look for such signs. Furthermore, we know from the experience of Christians through the ages that God does not always give us glimpses of Godself in predictable places. Thus, we have been schooled to be attentive to the unfamiliar, the unantici-pated, even to that which is unlovable (from our limited vantage point). Thomas Merton, whom Paul Crow admires and quotes regularly, puts it this way: "I must learn that my fellow man, just as he is, whether he is my friend or my enemy, my brother or a stranger from the other side of the world, whether he be wise or foolish, no matter what may be his limitation, '*is Christ*.'"[8] The doctrine of the incarnation schools us to this perspective, so necessary for the ecumenical vocation.

Christian Tradition is a major means of conveying the story of God's disclosures and their significance through the generations. Through his training as a church historian, Dr. Crow is particularly mindful of this. Tradition codifies and carries the experiences and testimonies of the faithful over the centuries. Tradition teaches us about the Godhead, and about possibilities for our relationship with the Holy One and with each other. Tradition is our touchstone of faith.

Tradition involves not only authoritative teachings, but also dynamic teachers. All Christian churches have been blessed with rich spiritual leaders who have shed light on the journey of faith, much as a flashlight spreads its beams to illumine our steps. The ecumenical movement enables Christians in all times and places to be enriched by the diversity of these spiritual witnesses.

One of the ironies about faithful adherence to Tradition is that it teaches us to be respectful of change as one of the ways in which God works. Christian theology says that God is ever-transforming. God is not finished with us yet. The Holy Spirit is at work in the world. In an essay on ecumenical spirituality, Emmanuel Sullivan, S.A. develops the implications of a doctrine of the Holy Spirit for tradition, change and growth in the ecumenical movement:

> Recognition must be given to the continuing activity of the Holy Spirit over long periods of separation among churches. Such recognition leads to a mutual evaluation and appreciation of particular spiritual gifts and practices found in various churches and Christian communities. Such traditions are acknowledged as gifts preserved or bestowed by the Spirit. As

various Christian churches sought to reform and renew themselves in fidelity to the gospel, the Holy Spirit granted certain valid insights and spiritual gifts proper to authentic Christian life. Subject to spiritual discernment, such gifts and insights may well be intended for the future life of a visibly united church. Spiritual ecumenism respects the work of the Spirit uniting God's people in a diversity of gifts and ministries.[9]

Thus we are called to be modest in our truth claims, aware that new light may be shed on God's word and will, and that some of that light may come through diverse perspectives in the variety of Christian churches.

Ecumenism and holiness

Ecumenists who are attentive to the classic spiritual disciplines, prayer chief among them, often experience over the "long haul" a certain fruitfulness for unity in very concrete ways. When we offer our honest thoughts and feelings about our ecumenical experiences to God in prayer, God takes this raw material and uses it for God's reconciling intentions. We then bring this fruitfulness into the life of our churches.

Philip Sheldrake describes what happens in this process. He says

contemplation is such a vital activity, for it is there where time and eternity, the particular and the universal intersect that we can recognize this God-given oneness as a prelude to recovering visible unity. Contemplation offers the possibility of a wholeness of vision that means we need no longer be cut off from large parts of our collective Christian inheritance but rather have access to all.[10]

For example, in my role as director of a state council of churches, I often find myself invited as a Protestant ecumenical guest at Roman Catholic and Orthodox eucharistic services. I love the liturgies. I am often a friend of the celebrants and of many persons in the congregation. I participate as fully as possible in worship—until the distribution of the elements of communion, which I may not receive according to the rubrics of these churches. At this point in the service, all of us are reminded painfully of the power of our remaining divisions.

My pain has increased over the years. So has my fervent prayer for Christian unity—prayer I silently offer during these services. The effect of these experiences has been to increase my zeal for the ecumenical task. I have discovered that God uses this pain as a witness to the scandal of our divisions, and as a goad to heal them. The channeling of pain into constructive paths is a mark of a fruitful ecumenical spirituality.

On other occasions, usually in intimate gatherings among friends where our behavior is understood and does not scandalize the faithful, the eucharistic rules get bent. This is a foretaste of the time when divisions among our churches will be healed. It is blessed food for the journey.

It happens among friends. Fr. Emmanuel Sullivan has observed that "friendship has proved itself an indispensable element in the process of Christian unity."[11] Dr. Crow is a master of Christian hospitality, and has paid special attention to this ancient and artful tradition—an essential element in the cultivation of Christian friendship—throughout his ministry.

Although ecumenical friendships are a gift of grace on the way, ecumenical encounters plunge us just as often into the unfamiliar, into contact with unfamiliar people, whose styles of worship, cultures, languages, beliefs, and customs are different from our own. This can be disorienting, anxiety-producing, and challenging. I never will forget the first time I, of staid Congregational background, experienced the charismatic fervor of African Methodist Episcopal worship. At first it was intimidating. The Holy Spirit was careening around the sanctuary in rolling waves of unbridled emotion, and I did not quite know what to do with all that passion for God. The second time I experienced this, however, I could anticipate what might be coming. This enabled me to relax into the experience. And I discovered in myself untapped emotional depths of prayer and praise to Jesus which I had not known were there. In this way, ecumenical encounters deepen and broaden our spirituality. They enhance our appreciation for the array of spiritual traditions. If we give these initially unfamiliar experiences a chance, they enrich our capacities for worship and human relationships.

Like latter-day Abrahams and Sarahs, we must be willing to venture into strange lands to encounter afresh the living God, and to jar us out of our fixed ways of being and doing. In this process we become open to new ways of seeing what God wants us to see. We must be willing to endure the uncomfortable if we are going to grow. This, in itself, is a spiritual discipline.

In an oft-quoted sentence from Vatican II's *Decree on Ecumenism,* we read that "There is no ecumenism worthy of the name without a change of heart." This statement provides an intriguing convergence between contemporary Roman Catholic and Protestant thinking about the spiritual concept of conversion and its implications for Christian unity. When we venture into the ecumenical arena, we and our churches must be open to the possibility of conversion—a turning away from sin, a reorientation towards God, and a transformation of our relationships with each other and in society. In this process, we are drawn to conform our hearts more closely to the heart of God we know through Jesus Christ.

Dr. Crow observes that getting down on our knees together in common repentance is not the typical image of what it means to be ecumenical. We would rather assume that the first act is to appoint a high-powered ecumenical committee, to begin some social program, or to be asked to make a jet trip to some far-away place—all, of course, in the interest of Christian unity. But, if we are to say something worth saying when the appointment does come or the right meeting is convened, we must be prepared. Only as Christians purify their hearts can they find the grace to overcome prejudices, hatreds or lethargy.[12]

When we allow our hearts to change, we also may find ourselves evidencing a quality of catholicity, of inclusiveness, of bringing others into the circle, of mentoring new generations of leaders. This inclusive spirit is in imitation of Christ. He gathered disciples from all walks of life, with different personalities and temperaments, strengths and weaknesses, political and economic backgrounds. Their unity was in the God they came to know through Jesus Christ, not necessarily in their natural affinities toward each other. This quality of inclusiveness may stretch us beyond our natural limits. We can get wearied by theological, liturgical, and cultural diversity. It takes more time and energy to understand people who are unfamiliar. And yet by widening our perception of the Christian circle, God brings renewal to Christians and their churches.

One of the qualities which is a precondition for a catholic spirit is humility. It also is a product of a healthy spiritual life. Humility is an active virtue. It suggests that our pilgrimage as individuals and churches is a living, growing thing. It is not a static achievement, once accomplished, never in need of reformation. The life of holiness is one of movement, process, imperfection, failure, longing, searching for God and for each other. Personal and corporate humility are necessary components in a full spiritual life and in responsible ecumenical engagement.

Another dimension of this change of heart to which we are called is in the realm of the material world. Contemporary writing on Christian spirituality has drawn from the sciences and benefitted from a broader understanding of the human psyche. Thus we see an integral relationship between our bodies and our souls. We see the connections between the material and the spiritual realms. This holistic view of human nature, and of our relationship to and interdependence with the whole created order, all of which are of God, pushes us to take very seriously the need for material well-being of our brothers and sisters. As Philip Sheldrake has observed, "Injustice denies the presence of God in the other and is thus a form of practical atheism."[13] The World Council of Churches' focus on "justice, peace, and the integrity of creation" is directly connected to ecumenical spirituality, because it takes seriously the relationship between the material and the spiritual.

This is a challenging mandate. Because much ecumenical work makes hard demands, it is easy to forget the joy. I was reminded of this recently as I reflected on the experience of planning and carrying through four consecutive services of morning prayer held during the Week of Prayer for Christian Unity. The idea of implementing the Week of Prayer in this way occurred to me in the summer, when the press of work was not too intense. My idea was to have morning prayer at 7:45 A.M., inviting a different religious leader to preach each morning, and follow worship with breakfast and conversation with the homilist about ecumenical life as he or she experienced it. Then people could go on to their offices to begin the work day.

It seemed like a good idea at the time, but as the Week of Prayer approached, I began to panic. What if the Cardinal arrived and only two or three people showed up? The first morning, the Episcopal Bishop commended me for my courage in trying this experiment. I responded that I thought it was more foolhardy than courageous!

In fact, between forty-five and eighty-five people participated each morning—many of them for all four mornings—to pray together. In retrospect, we really did become a Christian community during those days. And what a community we were! Protestants, Roman Catholics, and a few Orthodox; some clergy, and many laity; men and women— more men than women; a range of socio-economic classes which included everything from a financial district Brooks Brothers-type to a former prize fighter down on his luck.

Since the services ended, I have found myself thinking affectionately and prayerfully about those people—even the "pro-life" zealot who wore a T-shirt proclaiming his sympathies. The hymns we sang together keep floating through my head. Snippets of breakfast conversation, reflections on sermon highlights, flashes of humor and insights about our ecumenical quest articulated by the church leaders—it all has come together in my mind to produce a kind of interior awareness of the significance of our ecumenical ministries, and with it, a quiet joy.

These occasions are grace-filled gifts. We should not pass over them too quickly, but savor them, because they feed us for the ecumenical journey.

Conclusion

In these waning days of the twentieth century, many of us have become so accustomed to making judicious assessments of the calculated possibilities for measured movements toward unity that we have lost the capacity for Christian hope. We keep trying to trim God's reconciling mandate down to our limited imaginings, but the vision of Christian unity God has put before us is expansive. Big dreams call for big hopes.

This is solid Christian theology. It rests on the promises of God. As Dr. Crow has observed, "the power toward unity comes from living in the presence of God."[14] Our hope for Christian unity is shaped by the very nature of the God we know in Christ Jesus through the Holy Spirit. Our hope is not hemmed in by cautious ambiguities. It is expanded by a liberating God who frees the Israelites from the bonds of slavery, by a reconciling God who overcomes death on a cross.

It is no accident that the theme for the 50th anniversary assembly of the World Council of Churches is "Turn to God—Rejoice in Hope!" If we truly believe, then we must fully hope.

This hope is not naive optimism. It exists in the shadow of the cross. Many people around the world live in the shadows. Together, through the ecumenical movement, in our best moments our churches behave in ways that show we are not naive; but we are in danger of being trapped by our own sophisticated cynicism about what is possible and when it will be accomplished. In the final analysis, this way of coming at the world is spiritually bankrupt.

For this reason, savvy focus is not enough. We also need to get down on our knees in prayer, and we need to be doing it together. Paul Crow quotes the World Council of Churches' Evanston Assembly (1954), when the gathered said: "The measure of our concern for unity is the degree to which we pray for it. We cannot expect God to give us unity unless we prepare ourselves to receive his gift by costly and purifying prayer. To pray **together** is to be drawn together."[15]

When we ground our daily lives as individuals and as churches in the spiritual disciplines, we open ourselves to the transforming work of the Holy Spirit. We create space where we can allow greater coherence between what we say we believe about the church and how we behave as its members. As the early Christians discovered on that Pentecostal day, when the Holy Spirit gets moving, extraordinary things can happen.

The ecumenical movement needs people with a Christlike frame of mind. We are one **in Christ.** We are called to conform ourselves **to Christ.** We seek the mind **of Christ.** We see the church as the **body of Christ.**

Attention to the spiritual dimension of our ecumenical vocation fosters this Christlike frame of mind. It widens our vision. It transforms individuals and churches.

Sometimes we may be overwhelmed by the enormous gap between where we are and where Christ beckons us to be. The problems seem intractable. The pain of our divisions can be overwhelming. Frustrations build.

All such experiences are the raw material of prayer. We should be able to bring our concerns before God—both alone and together. Being faithful ecumenists sometimes means just going on being faithful. God does not necessarily work on our timetable.

This was brought home to me the first time I read Rouse and Neill's sweeping volume, *The History of the Ecumenical Movement*.[16] I was struck by how whole generations of Christians had labored for unity and seen very little fruit. Then another generation came and took a quantum leap forward because of all that had gone on before. Ecumenical progress comes in jerky lunges rather than in a steady forward progression. It entails struggle—a necessary part of authentic discipleship. If this is of God, we should do what we can where we are, and trust that it will bear fruit in God's good time.

Notes

[1] *Encounters for Unity*, ed. By G. R. Evans, Lorelei F. Fuchs S.A. and Diane C. Kessler, Norwich, England, The Canterbury Press, 1995.

[2] See my article, "The Forms of Protestant Spirituality: Reclaiming our Roots," in *Ecumenism*, No. 116, Dec. 1994, Montreal, Canadian Centre for Ecumenism, pp. 30-35.

[3] Committee on Purposes and Goals of Ecumenism, Massachusetts Council of Churches, *Odyssey Toward Unity: Foundations and Functions of Ecumenism and Conciliarism*, Boston, Massachusetts Council of Churches, 1997.

[4] Paul A. Crow, Jr., *Christian Unity: Matrix for Mission*, New York, Friendship Press, 1982, p.78.

[5] Crow, *Christian Unity: Matrix for Mission, op. cit.*, p. 78.

[6] Crow, *Christian Unity: Matrix for Mission, op. cit.*, p. 79.

[7] Philip Sheldrake, *Images of Holiness: Explorations in Contemporary Spirituality*, London, Darton, Longman and Todd, 1987, p. 17.

[8] In an essay called "The Power and Meaning of Love," by Thomas Merton.

[9] "Ecumenical Spirituality," by Emmanuel Sullivan, S.A., in *The Westminster Dictionary of Christian Spirituality*, ed. by Gordon S. Wakefield, Philadelphia, The Westminster Press, 1983, p. 126.

[10] Philip Sheldrake, *Images of Holiness: Explorations in Contemporary Spirituality, op. Cit.*, p. 14.

[11] Sullivan, "Ecumenical Spirituality," *op. cit.*, p. 126.

[12] Crow, *Christian Unity: Matrix for Mission, op. cit.,* pp. 79-80.

[13] Sheldrake, *Images of Holiness: Explorations in Contemporary Spirituality, op. cit.*, p. 17.

[14] Crow, *Christian Unity: Matrix for Mission, op. cit.*, p. 78.

[15] Crow, *Christian Unity: Matrix for Mission, op. cit.*, p. 79.

[16] *A History of the Ecumenical Movement,* ed. by Ruth Rouse and Stephen Charles Neill, Philadelphia, Westminster Press, 1954. 2nd. ed., 1967.

CHAPTER SIX

CONFLICTING WORLDVIEWS AND THE ECUMENICAL QUEST

Michael Kinnamon

Paul Crow's leadership in the ecumenical movement has come during a quarter century of astonishing transition and consequent uncertainty. What does it mean to be "ecumenical"? How is Christian unity to be envisioned and pursued? How are we to understand the relationship between continuity and change in the search for the visible unity of the church?

Throughout the century, leaders in the ecumenical movement have recognized that confessional differences affect the way we answer such questions. More recently, ecumenists have acknowledged that cultural context helps shape one's understanding of the ecumenical task. What I want to suggest is that our pluralistic age is marked by a conflict of worldviews, even among those of the same confession and culture, and that these worldviews dramatically affect the way Christians involved in the ecumenical movement conceive of its purpose and method.

This topic seems particularly appropriate for a *Festschrift* honoring Paul Crow since he has been, in many respects, a mediating figure among divergent worldviews. I will not elaborate on this point in what follows, but it will be obvious to those who know of Dr. Crow's diverse commitments—including his appreciation for Orthodoxy, his long-time advocacy of the Consultation on Church Union, and his leadership in the Faith and Order study on "The Unity of the Church and the Renewal of Human Community."[1]

* * * *

In my judgment, a particularly acute observer of the current cultural and ecclesial situation, especially in Europe and North America, is the theologian, David Tracy. In one of his essays for the journal *Concilium* ("On Naming the Present"), Tracy argues that our era is marked by a "conflict of interpretations" which he labels modern, anti-modern, and post-modern.[2] It is common-place to acknowledge that these competing frameworks for interpreting reality have given rise to different theologies. What I want to suggest, using Tracy as a point of departure, is that they also give rise to distinctive options for understanding the ecumenical movement.

The defining characteristic of the modern (Enlightenment) heritage is probably its confidence in the possibility of obtaining objective truth about ourselves and the world through empirical observation (scientific method) and the use of reason. This ruling assumption has many implications, but I will name only three: 1) The modern worldview assumes it is possible to identify and articulate universal norms for judging among competing truth claims. 2) Those who share this outlook tend to be tolerant (they would likely say "welcoming") of others; but they assume that modern culture is the center into which these others are welcomed. 3) Religion, in this framework, becomes privatized into a "harmless abstraction" (Tracy) that doesn't threaten the dominant, rationalist view of reality.

To put it less polemically, religion, like art, has not been valued in the modern era as a way of knowing truth about reality (it is a matter of privately-held opinion)—which is why, as Tracy notes, both religion and art have been treated as consumer goods.

Reactions to the modern worldview are united in their objection to the way that the modern, with its mechanistic model of the universe, denies even the possibility of a transcendent dimension to experience. One form that such reaction takes is fundamentalism which, generally speaking, returns to some point in the history of the church and makes it absolute. Indeed, as Tracy sees it, this is fundamentalism's great weakness: its inability to recognize the historical relativity of its favored traditions and the consequent need for their continual, critical reappropriation. Christians within this stream of anti-modernism are not involved in ecumenical discussions since unity can only mean others becoming "like us."

There is, however, another form of anti-modernism, one that is well represented in the ecumenical movement and that, as Tracy sees it, merits "full intellectual respect." Its argument runs something like this: The Enlightenment, in its protest against authoritarian tradition, threw the baby out with the bath water. Human beings can't live creatively into the future without a sense of memory (tradition) and authoritative community. It is time to acknowledge that "the modern" has become what it most feared and despised—another tradition. And, thus, it is time for Christians to recover their distinctive, God-centered story.

This approach is also marked by a strong appreciation for the sacramental power of visible forms of Christian life. Religious symbols, doctrines, creeds, and institutions don't just express human experiences of the divine (as Protestant liberalism has maintained); rather, they shape our experiences. Apart from communities of memory and ritual, we lack the language even to name God's presence in our lives.

The anti-modern reaction still assumes a center, a norm by which all else is judged. What it denies is that the Enlightenment provides an adequate center, especially for Christians, but for other human beings as well. This, however, is where the anti-modern is most at odds with the third of Tracy's categories: the post-modern. Post-modernism's defining characteristic is its suspicion of all claims to objectivity. All knowing is contextual. No longer can we speak of a center with margins since there are many centers, many competing worldviews. Others are really *other*, not projections of our assumptions and fears.

The post-modern sensibility may appreciate tradition, but only as long as we recognize that tradition is never innocent. Tradition also includes the memory of oppression (what Tracy calls "the great Christian countermemory to all tales of triumph") and the memory of prophets who challenge any temptation to celebrate unduly our own rituals and confessions.

Another way to get at the contrast between modern and post-modern is to note how the modern worldview speaks of the self as autonomous. For the modern, dialogue is a way of knowing, a way of coming to understand the autonomous other with an eye toward agreement. The post-modern, on the other hand, sees the self as fundamentally relational; and dialogue, as a consequence, is understood as a way of being, not simply as a means to an end. Those who hold a post-modern perspective don't think it is possible to adjudicate theological differences by appeal to universal norms, but this doesn't diminish their enthusiasm for dialogue. They have reconceived its purpose.

The most dramatic contrast with regard to ecumenism, however, has to do with definitions of unity. In the modern paradigm, particularity is subordinate to wholeness. Individuals may be regarded as autonomous and traditional forms of authority may be eschewed, but there is also appreciation for uniformity of structure and transcontextual consensus. As a result, models of unity ("organic union") from a generation ago now feel to many ecumenical participants like corporate merger.

In the post-modern paradigm, particularity is *constitutive* of wholeness, and unity is, thus, defined as a community of unlikeness. Along with this often goes a conviction that the fundamental division in the human family is between rich and poor, oppressor and oppressed, and that the basic divisions within the church have to do with how we respond to, or participate in, these divisions of the world. The language of "unity in solidarity" is increasingly common. The focus is not on common structures or agreed statements, but on a shared willingness (perhaps expressed through some form of covenant) to live and act together in response to need.

The anti-modern seeks unity through a common recovery of biblical and patristic roots and is usually marked by an appreciation for confessional traditions as carriers, at least in part, of this apostolic heritage. Christians don't invent or negotiate the faith; they *receive* it as the only sure foundation for communion in Christ.

It is interesting to note that both anti-modern and post-modern ecumenists have been looking for a word to replace "unity" (since they find it tainted by modern usage), and that both groups have gravitated toward the same Greek term: *koinonia*. At the Fifth World Conference on Faith and Order—held at Santiago de Compostela, Spain, in 1993—several speakers equated koinonia with solidarity, with the sharing among those who remain diverse. Others saw it pointing to the nature of the triune God, a nature definitively presented in the formulations of the early councils. The terminological confusion reached its peak when a bishop from the Church of North India declared his own "church merger" a failure and called on the World Council of Churches (WCC) to abandon its commitment to "visible unity." But his alternative vision of "diverse structures of mutual accountability" sounded exactly like the depictions of unity as koinonia set forth by several other speakers.[3]

*   *   *   *

I hope that the brief preceding discussion has been usefully provocative. Such categories, however, can never do justice to the nuanced positions of actual thinkers. In the following pages, therefore, I want to explore this conflict of interpretations by contrasting the visions of ecumenism held by two of the movement's prominent figures: Konrad Raiser, general secretary of the WCC, and Wolfhart Pannenberg, longtime participant in the work of the WCC's Commission on Faith and Order. Raiser and Pannenberg were among the featured speakers at the Santiago conference referred to above; but their prescriptions for what the ecumenical movement should be and do as it moves into the 21st century were astonishingly divergent.

Some readers may, at first sight, object to my choice of two white, male Protestants from Germany. Their similarity, however, is precisely the point. Their differences, I am trying to demonstrate, are less those of culture and confession than of worldview.

Let's begin with Pannenberg. The great problem, as he sees it, is that the ecumenical churches are surrendering the substance of the Christian faith and are, therefore, in danger of being unable to present an alternative "to the spiritual emptiness of modern life." As he told the delegates in Santiago, "the period of half-hearted compromise with the spirit of modernity that departs more and more from Christianity must come to an end."[4] The church need not fear the lessons of science or modern biblical study (his position has nothing in common with fundamentalism); but "the church must never forget its obligation to proclaim and embody the truth that the triune God is the first and last word on reality." The church, to put it another way, is to be a resistance movement, a counter-witness, in the midst of modern, secularist culture.

George Lindbeck, a well-known American theologian, makes the distinction between what he calls the ecumenism of *aggiornamento* and the ecumenism of *ressourcement*.[5] The former term, as used by John XXIII at Vatican II, calls to mind the image of throwing open the windows of a stuffy church to let in the world. The latter term means a "return to the sources," and it calls to mind the image of roots—exploring one's heritage. This is Pannenberg's approach. If Christianity is to be renewed and united, he argues, then it must recover the voice of scripture as interpreted by the creeds and authoritatively taught in the church. Unity, he contended at Santiago, demands

> communion in one and the same faith. Christians have to hold in common what they believe, at least the core of it . . . from the origins of the church until the parousia of our Lord. The faith of contemporary Christianity cannot be a different faith from that of the apostles and the fathers of the ancient church.[6]

Pannenberg would agree with the Roman Catholic theologian, Avery Dulles, when he writes that the church cannot be properly understood as a "coalition for action."[7] It is, first of all, a community of faith and witness and as such requires shared vision. "Therefore, even today we express our faith in the words of the fathers of the patristic church who in the symbol of Nicea and Constantinople summarized the apostolic faith on behalf of the entire Christian community, with a claim to authority for all Christians in every place, but also for all future times until the return of our Lord."[8]

The great fear behind this, it seems to me, is relativism. Different ways of expressing and interpreting the gospel are inevitable; but Christians should never forget that they are under obligation, even obedience, to proclaim a Word that is not their own. The ecumenical movement is important for Pannenberg precisely because it is a shared struggle to recover the fullness of this Word, a Word which the modern world desperately needs to hear. The search for unity, understood as theological dialogue aimed at consensus, is thus necessary for the very integrity of the faith. Our different perceptions may well help us to flesh out the one faith which was once and for all delivered to the apostles.

Pannenberg also insists, however, that the unity of the church is itself a central element of the apostolic faith. Unity is not just "instrumental"—that is, for some purpose. It is a divine imperative which Christians are bound to obey, even if they are unable to see any practical benefits from it. I have heard Pannenberg assert on several occasions that our identity as members of the universal church takes precedence over all other identity markers, including race, nationality, culture, and class. The fact that Christians war against each other is, thus, nothing less than "a shameful defeat of our faith."

If I read him correctly, Pannenberg would likely agree with Lindbeck's summary of the history of the modern ecumenical movement. The movement, as Lindbeck sees it, began through a confluence of Protestant evangelicalism and theological liberalism, both of which emphasized cooperation, not doctrinal agreement (though they did so for quite different reasons). The entry of the Orthodox churches and, later, the Roman Catholic Church helped forge, however, a new consensus: namely, that the unity of the church involves more than interdenominational cooperation between autonomous bodies that are still divided over the questions of faith and order.[9] It was this press for a visible eucharistic fellowship which has given rise to the scores of ecumenical dialogues around the world.

Today, however, there are plenty of new voices suggesting that visible unity of the churches in faith is secondary, if in fact it is desirable at all. The primary concern is liberation from various forms of political and economic oppression or promotion of human unity through interfaith dialogue or (at the other end of the theological spectrum) the saving of souls through evangelism. In each of these cases, the unity of the church is welcomed if it serves this other goal—and that is precisely what Pannenberg rejects. The church has an "explicit commandment" to be what it is—one eucharist fellowship. "The most important contribution that Christians can make to human unity," he wrote in an earlier essay, "would certainly be to regain their own unity."[10]

The impulse for unity is also weakened, he noted at Santiago, by the current indifference to confessional identity that is so much a part of North American religious life. Ecumenism has had the effect of helping to legitimize the dissolution of denominational loyalties, and, thus, has made "church-hopping" respectable. For Pannenberg this means, ironically, that the search for genuine unity may need to be preceded by a period of re-confessionalization, during which we learn again what particular gifts our traditions have to bring to the table.

Let's turn now to Raiser, who (quite typically) began his address in Santiago by talking not about the state of the church but the state of the world. Raiser, to use traditional categories, thinks in terms of God-world-church (the church as a participant in what God is doing throughout creation) while Pannenberg thinks in terms of God-church-world (the church as a sign and instrument of God's purpose for creation). Pannenberg, in line with the New Testament, sees the Spirit working through the church for the renewal of the world. Raiser, in line with certain strands of Old Testament thought, sees the church as following the Spirit that is always ahead of it at work in creation.

Raiser ended his speech in Santiago (also typically) with a call for "conversion." As he sees it, the patient accumulation of consensus through painstaking theological conversation, which Pannenberg so applauds, ignores the most essential thing needed in the work of the ecumenical movement: namely, repentance for what we have been. Another problem with ecumenical dialogue, says Raiser, is that it simply hasn't worked. For twenty-five years, the major churches have tried in theological discussions to overcome the doctrinal differences that divide them and thus to prepare the way for fellowship. The reports of these discussions now fill several large volumes, but the churches find it difficult to draw the necessary conclusions for their common life and witness from these agreements. Instead of increasing fellowship, there are signs of a new confessionalism.[11]

Karl Rahner once spoke about "the neurotic fear that we might be in agreement" so that whenever we get close to it, the churches "raise the ante." Raiser has a devastating analysis of this in his book, *Ecumenism in Transition*:

> . . . church leaders have a pressing concern to keep their own church together institutionally as an integrated whole . . . . They thus promote the ecumenical movement whenever it benefits their own church; but they remain hesitant, or apply the brakes sharply, when ecumenical initiatives could disturb the inner unity of their own church, or make their own members restive. They speak of the 'scandal' of the division of the church . . . , but when it becomes a matter of re-examining traditional loyalties(national or confessional) so as to strengthen ecumenical friendship and solidarity with other churches, then they often point to their own church members, who (they say) are not yet ready to go along with the steps demanded of them![12]

But while church officials and theologians are trapped in this dilemma, a new ecumenical reality is taking shape around us. Shared liturgies and forms of spirituality, common struggles for justice, cooperative projects involving laity and youth—all of these things, he argued at Santiago, " . . . have helped to create an awareness of solidarity and belonging together to which the old forms no longer correspond."[13] There is no need to create unity or to negotiate it because it already exists in the lived experience of many Christians. These persons are often little interested in theological disputes about the Trinity or the eucharist or ministry, but they are nonetheless the bearers of authentic community which needs only to be celebrated and extended.

Let me suggest how I think Raiser reads the history of the ecumenical movement. Up until the late 1960s, the movement, as he sees it, was basically an effort to unite the shards of a fragmented Christendom, to bring together a church split by Reformation-era disputes. But around that time the world changed, and the fact of cultural and theological diversity—the fact that we are truly, thankfully diverse—began to sink in.[14] To put it another way, the ecumenical movement has always insisted that unity doesn't mean uniformity, but, in fact, past models of unity thought of diversity as a problem to be dealt with and resolved. Particular confessional identities needed to die as part of the cost of church union. Particular ethnic or racial groups needed to be "included"—read "blended in"—for the church to experience wholeness. Theological differences needed to be eliminated through negotiations aimed at reaching consensus. Raiser objects to the whole paradigm. "Fellowship," he writes in his book, "does not come into being as a result of individuals joining together on the basis of common commitment, belief or inclination. The abiding difference of the other is rather a condition for the possibility of relationship and fellowship."[15] I have heard him, more than once, suggest dropping the phrase "unity of the church" from the ecumenical vocabulary altogether because it has so often implied a consensus, a subordination of diversity, based on the preferences of a privileged group.

In a speech delivered in the United States in 1992, Raiser argued that the idea of unity, at least as historically used in the ecumenical movement, is not biblical since the Bible speaks of communion among those who are unlike. Unity rooted in agreement is a Greco-Roman concept that requires hierarchy and "easily leads to the stigmatization of the irregular as heresy. Many of the divisions in Christian history are not so much the result of deliberate separatism as of a rigid understanding of unity which perceived diversity as a threat."[16] Pannenberg talks about how to determine the limits of diversity. Raiser is much more worried about "the limits of tolerable, acceptable unity." Where Pannenberg fears relativism, Raiser fears articulations of the faith that are foisted off as universal by those in power—which helps explain his antagonism to Pannenberg's attempted recovery of the apostolic tradition:

> The message of salvation in Christ does not represent a timeless truth; it needs to become incarnate in the life situation of particular people and communities. The continuity of tradition as a living process can only be maintained by accepting the risk of transformation.[17]

Let me now add my own voice more directly to the conversation. In my opinion, the strength of Pannenberg's vision is that it takes the theological life of the church seriously. My experience in seminary tells me that our churches often don't know what they believe, which makes them easy prey for cultural prejudices coated with the veneer of religiosity. Pannenberg is surely correct that not all diversities are acceptable, no matter how zealously they may be proclaimed in the name of Jesus Christ. How are we to say an emphatic "No!" to Nazis if we are unable to articulate the theological norms by which we live as Christians? Some degree of shared faith is essential if we are to have any chance of preserving our identity in the midst of the idolatries of modern life. There is an anti-intellectualism in modern culture which prefers practice to theory; but it is an artificial separation. Ideas have consequences. What we believe helps shape how we act.

I have already hinted at some of the problems I see with Pannenberg's model of ecumenical growth, including its dependence on reception by official church bodies who have proved generally unwilling to undermine their own prerogatives. But my biggest problem with the vision that Pannenberg represents may be the way that it locates theological work prior to the restoration of communion between now-separated Christians. We need more theology, not less; but we need it in our congregations, not just our church union committees. We need to see theological conversation as the result of deeper fellowship, not simply as a pre-condition for it.

It is probably clear that I have considerable appreciation for Raiser, especially his recognition that all theological formulations are shaped by context and, thus, are inevitably diverse. I agree with him that the church's catholicity is demonstrated by its capacity to adapt to a multiplicity of settings and, thus, that dialogue among cultures is as important to the ecumenical movement as the search for apostolic continuity. Beyond that, Raiser's writings suggest four points that, for me, are crucial as we try to speak authentically about unity.

First, Christian unity, while rooted in a common story, is not synonymous with or dependent upon agreement. The Mennonite scholar, John Howard Yoder, puts it this way in *The Royal Priesthood*:

> The functional meaning of church unity is not that people agree and, therefore, work together but that where they disagree they recognize the need to talk together with a view to reconciliation . . . where people operate on the assumption that unity is the product of agreement, this is the sociological form of works religion, namely, the understanding that the reality of the gospel is the product of human performance. This is to deny the gift quality of the gospel which is precisely that we have been, despite ourselves, by virtue of grace, made one with people with whom we were not one.[18]

This understanding, argues Yoder, would allow us to examine and clarify differences rather than "fuzz them over." My own experience in the church suggests that Christians are often afraid of conflict because, in part, they assume that disagreement means division. As I see it, the ecumenical vision is served neither by minimizing or ignoring genuine disagreements on faith nor by claiming that agreement in faith is a prerequisite for communion. Rather, it is the recognition of our given oneness that compels us to search for ever-deeper common expression of our shared faith. Life together is not the end of theological conversation but its beginning.

Second, unity is always rooted in repentance. There is a kind of schizo-phrenia in the ecumenical movement that was clearly displayed at the Santiago conference. The worship at that meeting was dominated by a haunting refrain: "Tell us Lord. What has happened to us? Where did we go astray?"[19] Most of the speeches, however, including Pannenberg's, focused on the gradual increase of communion through various forms of mutual recognition, as if unity could be achieved without repentance through the patient accumulation of consensus. Like Raiser, I am less and less convinced. Documents such as *Baptism, Eucharist and Ministry* help clear space within which the churches and their members may open themselves to the transforming work of the Spirit. They call us to repentance for our partiality, our own refusal to recognize God at work in our neighbors.

Third, unity must be constantly and deliberately related to the struggle for a more just and peaceful human community. The history of Christianity surely shows us that, if divorced from the search for a renewed human community, Christian unity has often served as a bolster for the powers that be. Thus, as Letty Russell puts it, "a crucial criterion for all forms of unity is whether or not these forms contribute to the whole-ness and well-being of de-humanized and marginalized people in this and other societies."[20] The ecumenical vision, by affirming the inter-dependence of those who are different, is a counter-testimony to all forms of domination.

Fourth, unity is not a static concept but an ever-growing and dynamic process (an idea implied in the term koinonia). Ecumenical documents sometimes sound as if unity were a matter of agreements ratified and structures approved: "Once we do this, then we will be one." But surely there will never be a time in history when we can say that we are the church God wills. Christian unity is, finally, a matter of loving one another as Christ has loved us. Since that will be realized only in the reign of God, we must always be willing to disrupt our present partial expressions of unity for the sake of deeper, more authentic expressions of koinonia.

For all of this, however, Raiser's "post-modern" perspective is under-mined, in my judgment, by a major problem—what might be called "ideology of pluralism."[21] I appreciate his warning that an over-emphasis on unity may lead to forms of community that are bland and/or authoritarian. But an over-emphasis on diversity may also result in communities that are fragmented and provincial. Raiser sometimes sounds as if the evils facing the world fall entirely under the heading "oppression"; but, surely, fragmentation is also one of the great dangers of our age.

The church always holds unity and diversity in dialectical tension. But the ecumenical movement must put the accent on unity. The question is not, "How do we find fellowship among diverse cultures, confessions and agendas?" but, "How do we celebrate and grow from the diverse character of our given oneness?" The church, writes the apostle Paul, is like a single body made up of parts that are wondrously diverse.

I stress this because the ideology of pluralism—that is, putting the accent on diversity rather than unity—has, it seems to me, reinforced the notion that being ecumenical is a matter of tolerant cooperation. The conviction that has given energy to the ecumenical movement, however, is not that Christians should get along but that we need each other, and are given one another, in order that we might grow together, through the mutual sharing of gifts, in knowledge and love of God. In our era, a movement that was intended as an instrument of renewal has often served as an instrument for preserving the status quo. Diversity, understood as constitutive of unity, is a blessing. Diversity, seen as an end in itself, is an expression of the sinful human tendency to organize reality into homogenous enclaves which often end up threatening those who are outside.

Raiser, in my opinion, is simply too sanguine about *current* instances of cooperation and solidarity among diverse Christians. In his Santiago address, for example, he contended that mainstream Protestant churches in Europe and North America are already *de facto* one—a statement which doesn't begin to do justice to the mutual indifference that characterizes ecumenical life.

In short, Pannenberg's vision, as I see it, puts too much weight on our treasures and not enough on a repentant readiness to receive the gifts others share, too much emphasis on continuity and not enough on change in response to the new gifts that God is giving us in our neighbors. Raiser's vision runs the risk of down-playing our particular theological treasures and the need to share them to the point that, at times, it feels more like ecumenism by erosion than by mutual enrichment.

* * * *

While I obviously hope that the preceding discussions of Pannenberg and Raiser have done justice to their positions, the point I really want to make goes beyond their specific arguments. Different approaches to the ecumenical movement, its basic purpose and future direction, cannot be necessarily reduced to differences of culture or confession. Large parts of the world are now marked by a genuine pluralism, by conflicting frameworks within which reality is interpreted. Since this conflict has received little attention in ecumenical circles, participants in ecumenical conversation often talk past one another or, worse, dismiss one another's positions as "unecumenical." We need more analysis of, and dialogue about, these competing worldviews in order to claim one another as partners, however divergent, in a common effort.

Notes

[1] The first phase of the study (1983-1992) culminated in the Faith and Order Study Document *Church and World: The Unity of the Church and the Renewal of Human Community*, Faith and Order Paper No. 151, 2nd, revised printing, Geneva, WCC Publications, 1992.

[2] David Tracy, "On Naming the Present" in *On Naming the Present: Reflections on God, Hermeneutics, and Church*, Maryknoll, NY, Orbis, 1994, pp. 3-24.

[3] S. B. Joshua, "The Future of the Ecumenical Movement From the Perspective of a Member of a United Church," in Thomas F. Best and Gunther Gassmann, eds., *On the Way to Fuller Koinonia: Official Report of the Fifth World Conference on Faith and Order*, Faith and Order Paper No. 171, Geneva, WCC, 1994, pp. 146-52. [Significantly, Bishop Joshua's views were challenged strongly by others from the Church of North India attending the Sixth International Consultation of United and Uniting Churches held in Ocho Rios, Jamaica, in March, 1995.—ed. note]

[4] Wolfhart Pannenberg, "Communion in Faith," in *On the Way*, p. 112.

[5] George Lindbeck, "Ecumenical Theology," in David F. Ford, ed., *The Modern Theologians: An Introduction to Christian Theology in the Twentieth Century*, vol. II, Oxford, Basil Blackwell, 1989, p. 258.

[6] Pannenberg, "Communion in Faith," *op. Cit.*, pp. 112-13.

[7] See Avery Dulles, "Paths to Doctrinal Agreement: Ten Theses" in *Theological Studies* 47, 1986, p. 32.

[8] Pannenberg, "Communion in Faith," *op. Cit.,* pp. 113.

[9] Lindbeck, "Ecumenical Theology," *op. Cit.,* pp. 256-57.

[10] Wolfhart Pannenberg, "The Unity of the Church and the Unity of Mankind" in *The Church*, trans. By Keith Crim, Philadelphia, Westminster, 1983, p. 151.

[11] See Konrad Raiser, "The Future of the World Council of Churches and the Role of Faith and Order Within the Ecumenical Movement," in *On the Way, op. Cit.,* pp. 168-174.

[12] Konrad Raiser, *Ecumenism in Transition: A Paradigm Shift in the Ecumenical Movement?*, Geneva, WCC, 1991, p. 25.

[13] Konrad Raiser, "The Future," p. 170.

[14] See Raiser, *Ecumenism in Transition: A Paradigm Shift in the Ecumenical Movement?, op. Cit.,* chapters 1-3.

[15] *Ibid.,* p. 76.

[16] Konrad Raiser, "Ecumenism in Search of a New Vision," in *The Ecumenical Movement: An Anthology of Key Texts and Voices*, ed. By Michael Kinnamon and Brian E. Cope, eds., Geneva, WCC, 1997, p. 73.

[17] Konrad Raiser, "Beyond Tradition and Context," in *International Review of Mission*, pp. 353-54.

[18] John Howard Yoder, *The Royal Priesthood: Essays Ecclesiological and Ecumenical*, Grand Rapids, Wm. B. Eerdmans, 1994, p. 292.

[19] See the daily worships, *Worship Book: Fifth World Conference on Faith and Order*, Geneva, Commission on Faith and Order, 1993.

[20] Letty Russell, "Unity and Renewal in Feminist Perspective," *Mid-Stream,* No. 1, January, 1988, p. 58.

[21] See Arie Brouwer, *Overcoming the Threat of Death*, Geneva, WCC, 1993, pp. 102ff.

CHAPTER SEVEN

THE REVENGE OF THE SCARLET SATIN PILLOW

DESPERATE REFLECTIONS ON WORSHIP AND THE UNITY OF THE CHURCH

Daniell C. Hamby

There has been a growing awareness and consensus since the Second Vatican Council that the unity of the Church is not a matter left in human hands alone. Unity is, at least theologically, a gift from God. Even among sisters and brothers in the Evangelical and Orthodox traditions—for whom the experience of the *ekklesia Christi* is understood differently than by Roman Catholics, Anglicans, or "Protestants"—there is general agreement that the thing which separates us has more to do with human poverty than God's abundance.

This essay assumes that the church of Jesus Christ is one, and our divisions are a reflection of human frailty and an inability to be obedient (to "hear"). Through the eyes of a liturgist, and from several points of view, this essay will address our separateness. It will reconsider Prosper of Aquitaine's axiom *lex orandi, lex credendi*. It will respond to the call from a 1994 WCC Faith and Order consultation, held in Ditchingham, England on the role of worship in the search for Christian unity, for renewed attention to the *ordo*, the *way* in which we pray together. This call, sparked by Gordon Lathrop's presentation, was adopted and developed at the consultation, as reported in *So We Believe, So We Pray*.[1] My essay will offer a few modest reflections for conversation, conversion, prayer and service. But first, a story to set the context.

The Saga of the Scarlet Satin Pillow

In a parish church, in the high middle ages, somewhere in France (as the story goes), a local priest decided to attempt liturgical innovation. Historically it was the time following the arguments at Corbie about the nature of the Bread and Wine: what *really* happens to the bread and wine, when it happens. It was a time when the cup was denied to the laity for fear they would spill the blood of Christ.

After much critical and careful thinking, the priest in this parish decided that it was theologically and spiritually problematic to deny the cup to the laity. So, he announced to his parish that the cup would be offered for any who wished to receive "in both kinds." As the story unwinds, a bold and faithful member of the parish came forward to receive. When the cup was presented, the parishioner got confused, reached out to assist the priest, and in doing so caused the priest to drop the chalice. All of the sweet wine spilled onto the carpet. A hushed, sudden silence overtook the assembly, and the assisting priests looked on with contemptuous "I told you so" eyes.

The spilled wine is a dilemma. It is, after all, in the mind of the priest and people, the Blood of Christ. Although much of the wine was mopped up with a purificator and other linens, there was still much in the carpet. The Blood of Jesus in the carpet! What to do? As the priest and his cronies pondered the matter, a yet more terrible event took place. The church mice, always on the lookout for a morsel of food, sniffed the carpet, and promptly devoured the parts of the carpet where the wine had soaked in. When the priest discovered the holes in the carpet made by the mice, he was horrified. Now the Blood of Jesus was not only on the floor, but in the bodies of the church's mice. Now what to do?

The answer, of course, was to get a smart cat—which they promptly did—whose job in life would be to catch the mice—which the cat promptly did. But then another dilemma arose. What do you do with a cat, in whose body are mice, in whose body is the Blood of Jesus? The solution, according to the experts in charge, was to incorporate the cat in the ongoing life of the parish. So a scarlet, satin pillow was commissioned, and each Sunday the cat would ride the scarlet satin pillow in the procession into the church. The pillow would be placed in an honorable position near the altar, and the Mass would proceed. The cat lived a long, pampered, and happy life, died at a ripe old age, and was buried (with appropriate funeral rites) in the church yard. Which left the scarlet pillow.

On the Sunday next after the cat's demise, the pillow-bearer took his ordinary place in the procession with the empty scarlet satin pillow. No questions were asked—after all, the pillow had been part of the procession for many years. Many years passed, and the ravages of time took their toll on the satin material of the pillow, until it was so unsightly that something had to be done. By then a new priest had come to the parish. He asked, naturally enough, "why do we have this scarlet, shredded-satin pillow in the first place? It isn't in the *rituale.*" Members of the parish said, "because we've always had it." When the priest did his homework and discovered the story of the pillow, he suggested that the old pillow needed to be laid to rest and promptly dismissed the pillow bearer and the pillow from the procession. The Sunday afternoon following the absence of the pillow and pillow-bearer, the priest was called forth from the rectory, flogged, stoned, and burned at the stake for heresy. And on the following Sunday a new, scarlet, satin pillow was put in place.

It is a true story, with only minor embellishments. Whether canonically accurate or not, the saga of the scarlet, satin pillow offers insight for the divisions of the church. Why are we divided? "Because we always have been divided," at least for as long as anyone can remember. In the words of an Episcopal Bishop, when asked why Episcopalians in the United States are so willing to embrace the Evangelical Lutheran Church in America in the Concordat, and so indifferent to the nine communions in the Consultation on Church Union (COCU): "It is because we can see ourselves in the Lutheran Church, and we do not see ourselves in the COCU Churches." The Bishop tells a profound truth about the poverty of homogeneity, the poverty of wanting always to be with "people who are like us." Like the scarlet satin pillow, living differently is a problem, a threat, and a matter for retrofitted theologies which insist on remaining separate in the face of the abundance of God who calls all of creation into his heart.

Poverty and Brokenness in the Christian Community: A Liturgical Matter

The influence of the liturgical life of the church has been a subject of conversation since the earliest communities of faith. No more profound observation of life together has been made than that of Prosper of Acquatain, a fourth-century theologian, reflecting on God's grace. Prosper wrote: *legem credendi statuit lex supplicanti:*[2] the law (rule) of one's belief or faith (*legem credendi*) establishes (*statuit*) the law (rule) of what one must believe (*lex supplicanti*). For the purpose of this essay, I translate both *legem* and *lex* as a "rule" rather than law. Law implies a casuistry not present in Prosper, while "rule" implies a way of life. A rule is the pale blue line on a sheet of notebook paper which helps one write in legible sentences; it is the set of values, practices, and disciplines which we adopt, and which inform our faith as we keep them regularly, day in and day out, such as morning or evening prayers, regular reception of the Eucharist, making the sign of the Cross, or saying grace before or after meals. A rule is about *praxis*, the way we "do" faith, not in a Pelagian sense of works righteousness—which Prosper deplored—but in the sense of the Letter of James: "faith without works is dead" (2:26).

Prosper's observation about the relationship between prayer and belief is significant for the ecumenical life of the church because it is about baptismal identity. It is "first level" theological construction. We come to understand who God is, what God's gracious doings in our life are about, what God is calling us to do, who God is calling us to be, as we engage in the praise and adoration of God. Our doxology is the living activity of faithfulness, the engaging language of faith, in which we experience God's abundant love, singing God's praise. Our theological insights about God are intrinsically related to our liturgical expressions, related not like a fountain to a stream, but as currents in a single river.[3]

Liturgical life becomes a place of revelation for the *economia* because it is the place where we see and experience the Spirit at work. Liturgy, then, is the place we learn about salvation, not as an individual, but in community. Salvation is for the community of faith, for the sake of the Gospel, not for individuals in isolation. To engage in prayer is to be a part of the whole work of the Gospel. God justifies the community of faith, not one part of the community, for the sake of the Gospel.[4] The *lex supplicanti* is a whirlwind. Our life together is shaped by the experience of redemption; a gathered community praising God learns about God by praising. Our worship is, with Alexander Schmemann, the ontological condition of theology, the way we come to understand the *kerygma*.

Recent scholarship has offered more reflection on Prosper's axiom. Adian Kavanaugh has suggested that the *lex orandi, lex supplicanti* is not simply a linear argument, but it also is a circular argument. The rule of prayer not only establishes the rule of belief; but the rule of belief establishes the rule of prayer. "Belief" in this instance is best understood in the active sense, not in the ordinarily inactive. It is not simply an activity of the mind or heart, but belief which is acted upon: *praxis*. The church has for centuries mistranslated the word "Orthodoxia" as having to do with right belief. Properly, right belief would be *ortho*pistis. *Ortho*doxia, on the other hand, is about right praise, right worship. The antithesis of orthodoxy has often been called heresy. Properly speaking, however, the antithesis of orthodoxy is *heterodoxy*, wrong worship.

Faith is a way of living and belief is always consequent upon the encounter with the Source of the grace of faith. We do not worship simply because we believe, but we believe because the One in whose gift faith has been given is met in worship. A worshipping assembly can never conjure up God (despite the use of the term "invocation"), but a worshipping assembly encounters God because God has promised to be in the midst of them "helping, right early" where two or three are gathered together. To hear, to remember, to reflect, to appropriate, to "sing, pray, swerve not from God's ways," all of these things inform faith.[5] Not only, therefore, does belief shape prayer, but praying together shapes belief and believers. If there is anything ecumenically to be learned from Prosper's axiom, it is that the way the church prays together profoundly affects and influences what the church believes, not only about God, but about itself. It is akin to the story of the scarlet, satin pillow. For generations the pillow (with or without the cat) was so much a part of the liturgical assembly that no one questioned its meaning. It simply was part of the orthodoxy of that place. Similarly, I believe that we continue to experience divisions within the body of Christ because we act like divided Christians: *we simply do not worship together.*

The separation of Christians may once have had to do with significant theological matters, and those differences must never be ignored or given short shrift. On the other hand, our liturgical behavior has significantly eroded the possibility for easy recognition of one another as sisters and brothers in Christ. The Episcopal Bishop who spoke of finding "no identity" in the COCU churches, for example, told the truth. It is difficult to find recognition in a group of strangers. The African-American theologians in the United States remind us that there is no more segregated hour than 11:00 A.M. on Sunday morning. It is a painful truth. I believe, however, that the division of the churches will continue to beset the Body of Christ, and will continue to be a scandal, a stench in the nostrils of God and a confusion to the world, until we find ways to worship together. It is true, finally, that the church not only forms, but is formed by, its worship. Our orthodoxy, finally, must be doxological.

Toward a Common Ordo: The North American Rite

In *So We Believe, So We Pray*, Gordon Lathrop offers an important reflection on the significance of the *Lex Credendi*, calling for attention to the *ordo* common to so much of the worship of our divided churches as a basis for our worshipping together ecumenically. I have noted above how this call has introduced a new stage in the ecumenical discussion of the role of worship in the search for Christian unity.[6] In this section of my essay, I respond to Professor Lathrop and to the Ditchingham consultation in another way, offering an historical account from the early life of the Consultation on Church Union. During the General Secretariat of Paul A. Crow, Jr., in whose honor the essays in this book are written, significant steps were taken which led to what might be called a common North American liturgical rite. This is an ecumenically—and liturgically—hopeful sign.

The Consultation on Church Union came into being in response to a December 4, 1960 sermon by Eugene Carson Blake, at Grace Episcopal Cathedral at San Francisco, in which Blake invited the Episcopal Church, and any others who wished, to join together in forming a church that would be "truly catholic, truly evangelical, and truly reformed." The response to Blake's invitation was electric, and within a few months plans were made to form a consultation of interested communions. By

1962 the Consultation had been formally organized, and soon a full-time General Secretary (a certain Rev. Dr. Paul A. Crow, Jr.) was called. The Consultation immediately organized commissions to lead the work toward unity. Among the first were commissions on Church Order and Theology—and, more importantly, a Worship Commission.

The Worship Commission of the Consultation on Church Union was made up of the worship executives and other significant liturgical architects of the member communions, as well as observers from the Roman Catholic, Lutheran, and Reformed Church in America. The decade of the 1960s saw the work of the Second Vatican Council as well as significant theological documents on Ecumenism and the Constitution on the Sacred Liturgy, the latter of which had a profound influence on liturgical renewal in most churches. It was as if the Roman Church set the stage for liturgical revision and renewal for everyone else. James F. White suggests that the United Methodists were the earliest forerunners in liturgical revision, leading the way for others.[7] However, another source for common liturgical renewal quickly became the Consultation on Church Union Worship Commission.

In the COCU Worship Commission were the pioneers of liturgical renewal in various communions. Massey Shepherd (Episcopal), Horace Allen (Presbyterian), Hoyt Hickman and James White (United Methodist), and Keith Watkins (Disciples) are a few notable names. From the work of the COCU Worship Commission several early liturgical texts emerged. Most significant in their early work was a Lectionary, developed by Jim White and others. From the lectionary work the Consultation on Common Texts (an ecumenical enterprise) continues, producing in the early 1990s a revised "Common Consensus Lectionary." Other work for COCU included a common Baptismal rite, an order for the Lord's Supper, and work on a common ordination liturgy (which was never published).

Apart from the work for the Consultation, however, a significant set of revised liturgical and musical resources were being developed within the communions. These resources, which have many common elements, began appearing in the churches as early as the mid-1970s. The resources were heralded by the *Supplemental Liturgical Resources* of the Presbyterians, the *Prayerbook Studies* of the Episcopal Church, and the *Supplemental Worship Resources* of the United Methodists. Stanley R.

Hall, Professor of Worship and Preaching at Austin Presbyterian Theological Seminary, has identified common numerous elements in the various liturgical traditions, which he calls a North American Rite. They include similar patterns in Sunday worship (e.g. the significance of Sunday as the principal feast day for the church, Service for the Lord's Day, Sunday Service, and The Holy Eucharist), similar patterns for the Eucharistic canon (e.g. including the rites of Hyppolitus and Basil in the Eucharistic Canon), and rites for Daily Worship. Many of the revisions include services for the "Renewal of Baptismal Vows" and, for many for the first time, there are services of Healing. As the liturgical scholars met to hammer out the liturgical contributions of the Consultation on Church Union, they also were involved in significant liturgical renewal in their own churches. So that COCU became not only a bright ecumenical promise, but the fertile seedbed in which ecumenical liturgical consensus took root.

Speaking musically, beginning with the *Hymnal 1982* of the Episcopal Church, there appeared to be a common corpus of hymns available to each of the traditions. New texts and tunes such as *Lift High the Cross*, and *Here I Am, Lord* are present; and, more significantly, beginning with the new Presbyterian Hymnal (which was issued about the same time as the new United Methodist Hymnal) significant attention is given to psalms. The Psalmody represents a diverse collection of metrical, responsorial, and Anglican, as well as traditional plainsong settings. In the newer hymnal revisions, ecumenical contributions from around the world are included, including material from *Taizé* and the *Iona Community* as well as musical selections from Africa, Central and South America, and from the Orthodox. It is probably stretching matters historically to suggest that COCU is responsible for the liturgical revisions in the various communions. However it is more than an accident of history that the liturgical and hymnal revisions of the COCU member churches share so many common texts.

As Gordon Lathrop indicates in his article, paying attention to and using common liturgical patterns and texts will serve to assist in the visible unity of the Church. One is prompted to ask, in the face of eucharistic differences, about the liturgical meaning of texts and their relationship to church-dividing issues. For example, what is the difference between—and what are the implications of—an Episcopal Priest standing at an altar and leading a congregation through Eucharistic Prayer D, which is virtually identical to Prayer II in the Roman Sacramentary? What are the implications, for ecumenical Eucharistic unity, of an ordained woman in the United Church of Christ leading her congregation through the eucharistic Canon of Hyppolitus? What are the implications of a Presbyterian minister doing so, and of a United Methodist minister doing so?

If the intention of the church is Eucharist, if the people who receive the bread and wine, and who say the prayers, expect and believe that they are in some way receiving the mystical body and blood of Jesus, if the texts used are officially approved by the communions . . . . what does that imply for the Communion (koinonia) of the body of Christ? If, as the *lex orandi, lex supplicanti* asserts, prayer and faith shape each other, how long will we continue to say the same texts, sing the same hymns, and profess the same faith *and still remain apart?* Or, to sharpen the point, in the words of Regis Duffy: "Who finally defines the church? The canonists who write the laws, or the worshipping assembly who sing the prayers?"

This section of my essay has been a response to Gordon Lathrop's paper and the results of the Ditchingham consultation, and an encouragement to the churches to draw the consequences from the points made there. And my essay has shown how the common *ordo,* or patterning, which are becoming central to ecumenical reflection on liturgy in relation to unity already exists in a North American Rite which has its roots in the early work of the Worship Commission of the Consultation on Church Union. As in the story of the revenge of the scarlet, satin pillow, the suggestion is that our disunity is not so much a result of theological disagreement but of impoverished, separate liturgical practices.

Wondering Out Loud

The division of the churches raises meddlesome questions, especially in view of a growing theological consensus and, liturgically, the development of a common North American rite. One must not only question the human divisions of the Body of Christ but, in the midst of the confusion, ask about the basic unity of God. In the final section of this essay, I shall "wonder out loud" about unity, conversation and conversion, prayer, and a call to action in the name of Jesus.

From a liturgical point of view, the disunity of the church is a violation of the image of God. Our disunity raises not only the profound ecclesiological questions which, in the past, have held the church apart. It also asks theological questions about our understanding of God. The key question we face every time we worship revolves around who we believe God to be and, more importantly, what we believe God to be about. It becomes a question of intentionality, and so of conversion. What, precisely do we intend when we affirm that "we believe in one, holy, catholic and apostolic Church?" Do we really intend to "believe in" the church of Jesus Christ, or the church of the communion in which we live? "Intent" has to do with eschatological longing. It is intrinsically related to justification. Justification is not an individual, communal or private possession. It is a gift to us in community. More than assisting us with our private lives, justification prods us to ask about God's life. Are we, in our separateness, so full, so complete, that we have no need of what God gives?

With the *Groupe des Dombes* the call to action must be a call for conversion and for conversation. Conversation and conversion emanate from the same word *conversatio,* which means, literally, to "turn around." It is one function of the liturgy to be in "conversation" with God in the worshipping assembly, and to be profoundly and radically shaped by that dialogue. Conversion in an ecumenical context is our willingness to let God be God; it is the reminder that our lives are not the only lives in the universe. Conversion keeps us from the false belief that God is only seen from our individual experience. If I am limited to my subjective understanding of God, my heart is impoverished. Conversation is an encounter with others which turns us around. It is intrinsically linked with conversion because it is about obedience (listening). It offers the possibility that, in the dialogue, we can receive a gift.

Finally, it must be said that disunity, the separateness of the churches, reinforces our isolation. When we worship with a limited salvific awareness, in our separateness, when we continue to celebrate our communal isolation, when we eschew the Christian conversation with others, we deny the unity of God. But! When we gather together in joy and praise, we anticipate the table set for us, set with the cup that overflows.

It is imperative that the church learns again how to pray together. The *lex orandi* is not simply a static axiom. It is a dynamic process which brings humankind to the heart of God. When we pray together our minds and hearts are changed by the work of the holy spirit. We are brought close to the realm and rule of God or, as Antoinette Wire has recently put it, to the "inheritance of God." In the face of the inheritance we are prodded to ask, "Do we wish to receive it?"

And what is the inheritance of God like? It is a gift into which one comes that provides basic resources. By means of this gift God saves and heals people and sets us on our way or, more precisely, on God's way. God's inheritance is an old woman who sweeps her whole house, searching in every nook and cranny for a lost coin. God's inheritance is a shepherd who leaves sheep in the fold to go out into the desert to find one lost lamb. God's inheritance is a father, whose eyes scan the horizon for a son gone to squander life. And when the boy appears on the horizon, the old man runs out to meet him, pulls him close and says to him "I love you, boy."[8] It is prayer that opens to us the realm and rule of God . . . the inheritance of God; it will finally be our prayer which inaugurates the healing of divisions within the body of Christ.

The call to action inherent in a liturgical critique of the divisions of the church is a call to koinonia: to full, conscious, active participation in the life of God. In writing to the Corinthians, St. Paul reminds us that anyone in Christ is a new creation (2 Cor. 2:5). What we must learn and remember is that "new creation" assumes that there is a creation in the first place. God has already created the church as one. The liturgical life of a Christian community delineates its self-understanding as church, and the extent of its discipleship.

The scarlet, satin pillow must be recognized for what it became: the systematic shaping of the faith in a community of God's people. It is, finally, not an accident that the churches remain divided, even though we verbally affirm our unity, when the single most important thing we do as followers of the Christ keeps us apart. There are no longer any good reasons to be separate. Even venerable hurdles like Eucharistic hospitality can be overcome with patience, forbearance, and persistent participation in loving God. We are formed as a community of faith by our liturgy, and the liturgical behavior of our communions. Somehow, I suspect, when the time comes for us to account for our lives before

God, the question we will face will not be about our life, its communal purity and integrity. The question will be about God's life and the way we lived within a gracious reception of God's gift of wholeness.

Notes

[1] See in *So We Believe, So We Pray*, ed. By Thomas F. Best and Dagmar Heller, Faith and Order Paper No. 171, Geneva, WCC Publications, 1995: Gordon Lathrop, "Knowing Something a Little: On the Role of the *Lex Orandi* in the Search for Christian Unity," pp. 38-48; and "Towards Koinonia in Worship: Report of the Consultation," paras. 4-9, pp. 6-8. [The work on *ordo*, together with other aspects of the Ditchingham consultation, has been developed in relation to baptism in a January, 1997 consultation in Faverges, France. The report ("Becoming a Christian: The Ecumenical Implications of our Common Baptism") and papers from the consultation will be published in the second half of 1997.—ed. note.]

[2] *Patrologia Latina*, J. P. Migne, ed., 51:209-210.

[3] Catherine Mowry LaCugna, "Can Liturgy Ever Again Become a Source for Theology?," *Studia Liturgica*, Vol. 19, No.1, 1989, pp. 1-16.

[4] Ernst Käsemann, *Commentary on Romans*, trans. And ed. By Geoffrey W. Bromiley, Grand Rapids, William B. Eerdmans Publishing Co., 1980.

[5] Adian Kavanaugh, *On Liturgical Theology*, New York, Pueblo, 1984, pp. 73—95.

[6] See note 1, above.

[7] James F. White, *Protestant Worship: Traditions in Transition*, Louisville, John Knox Press, 1990, pp. 150-170.

[8] Antoinette Wire, in *Lutheran Reformed Theological Reflections on Full Communion*, Chicago: Department for Ecumenical Affairs, Evangelical Lutheran Church in America, 1997.

CHAPTER EIGHT

MISSION AS ECCLESIOLOGY
CHRISTIAN IDENTITY AND THE BURDEN
OF DENOMINATIONALISM

William J. Nottingham

I t is not generally known that the Three Self Movement in the People's Republic of China takes its name from the slogan in missionary circles of the 19th century: "indigenous churches which are self-governing, self-supporting, and self-propagating." As early as 1855 this expression had entered the discourse of mission strategists, as well as the preaching and teaching of informed clergy and laity in Anglo-Saxon Protestantism.[1]

Although this goal was largely re-directed to "missions"—and eventually to denominational reproductions of the mother church in Europe or North America—by the time of the Edinburgh World Missionary Conference in 1910, it showed an important and necessary emphasis on ecclesiology. Therein lies the inseparable relation between mission and unity, in spite of a history of conflicting "paradigms" and the controversies to which they gave rise and from which they grew.

This theological emphasis on ecclesiology continued to germinate, subversively perhaps, as respect for the church "in each place" until it came to flower in the recognition of fully autonomous churches in mid-20th century, and in cooperation with endeavors towards Christian unity that occurred principally in former "mission fields." Today, it measures unity by commitment to justice and solidarity with the poor across confessional lines and by witness to the unity of humankind in cultural, economic, and environmental well-being. The *orthodoxy* of Christian unity finds its realization in the *orthopraxis* of a liberating participation in the global community, because the Church of Jesus Christ is a bearer of hope to the world. Ecclesiology is determined by mission, just as it engages Christians in mission.

The three-self terminology occurs specifically in the *Survey of Service*, a 700 page report edited by W.R.Warren in 1928 for the "Organizations Represented In International Convention Of Disciples of Christ." Examples of this usage are found on pages 416, 505, and 517; they occur in the 200 pages focussed on the "Foreign Fields" of the United Christian Missionary Society. Ecclesiology, with its inherent presupposition of the unity of Christ's church (e.g. Ephesians 4:4), was already being affirmed at the heart of the missionary project—and in stubborn defiance of sectarian inclinations and constituency pressures for denominational conservatism.

Thomas Campbell had pointed to the irony of trying to preach the Gospel to the Indians or to minister to the families on the frontier, "many of them in little better than a state of heathenism," with the scandalous condition of division which existed in the church.[2] Years later, W.K.Pendleton referred to the Christian Association of Washington, founded in the interests of unity by the elder Campbell in 1809, as itself a "missionary society!"[3]

Alexander Campbell gave a picture of the church universal when he wrote in 1854: "We shall, therefore, regard it as a fixed fact—*that the Church of Jesus Christ is, in her nature, spirit and position, necessarily and essentially a missionary institution.*"[4] In 1860 he wrote: "The church, therefore, of right is and ought to be a great missionary society. Her parish is the whole earth, from sea to sea."[5] Archibald McLean, president of the Foreign Christian Missionary Society, probably exaggerated in saying in his book on Campbell in 1908 that Christian unity was, for Alexander Campbell, "a means to an end", that its purpose was to enable the church to fulfill its mission.[6] It could also be said that the mission enables the church dialectically to fulfill its unity, since mission is part of the spiritual mystery of the church. McLean made the point later that for forty-one years the missionary text Revelation 14:6-7 was on the title page of *The Millennial Harbinger*—something significant where it appears, but which is not true for all the annual volumes.

To this day the "forerunners" are remembered for their unique commitment to church union, and the subsequent struggle to be consistent to that vocation in the area of world mission is remembered with mixed appraisals. I see it as a problem of authentic Christian identity encumbered with denominationalism.

Of course we are told that there is a difference between history and memory, and that the latter often assumes a continuity which the former does not warrant. This might be true especially of the modern missionary movement! For example, is there really anything in common between the founding of the American Christian Missionary Society in 1849 and that of the Christian Woman's Board of Missions in 1874? Everything had changed since the Civil War! Is there really anything in common between mission work in Japan before, and after, World War II and Hiroshima? Nevertheless, some ecclesiological integrity is woven into the texture of the past which does connect with the present ecumenical reality. For Disciples that is due to our original interest in the early church of Scripture and its extended apostolic and catholic tradition. It also includes tempering early 19th century eschatology with the role of community, and emphasizing the unity of Christians in the practice and meaning of the Lord's Supper. Because of the way Disciples see the church, sooner or later mission and unity go together!

Similarly the papal encyclical *Lumen Gentium,* produced by Vatican II in 1964, shows the missionary nature of the church in a way that David J. Bosch describes as a convergence between Catholic and Protestant views.[7] The encyclical of "the servant people" patterns itself along the lines of Karl Barth's theology, thanks to Vatican II theologians like the late Yves Cardinal Congar. Christian mission is seen as ecclesiology, not the "missiology" of a dominant church speaking on behalf of traditional Christendom and the tenacious assumptions of Eurocentrism. It is in this respect that unity and mission belong together concretely, theologically, and mystically.

That is why it is not surprising to find in *Survey of Service* a chapter called "Association For the Promotion of Christian Unity," the ancestor to the present-day Council On Christian Unity. One of the purposes of the Association was "to bear witness for Christian unity, believing that the will of Christ for the unity of his church as expressed in his great intercessory prayer is of equal authority with his great missionary commandment . . . "[8] While this might reveal a mild polemical intent, it was also a challenge to present the missionary movement as essentially ecclesial and to imply that ecclesiology is essentially missionary. Attendance at conferences of both the Faith and Order and the Life and Work movements (the forerunners of the World Council of Churches) was noted.

This report was followed by what is, in effect, the final chapter of the book called "Cooperative and Union Enterprises . . . At Home and Abroad," which shows unreserved participation in national councils of churches from their beginnings in China, Japan, India, Puerto Rico, the Philippines and the Belgian Congo. It is nothing less than a boast, one which includes over thirty interdenominational seminaries, schools and universities of all kinds as well as participation in the International Missionary Council and related bodies. Some hints of apology are evident. On the one hand, it is admitted that Disciples are accused of being "slow and indifferent about practicing their own preaching"—though affirming that, through many agencies, they are "heartily and sympathetically cooperating with other communions in many fields of organized Christian endeavor."[9] On the other hand there is an emphasis on the voluntary character of the councils and commissions, and the notation that the Foreign Missions Conference of North America does not deal with questions relating to "denominational differences."

The depression was still hidden in the future, and although volunteers to "evangelize the world in this generation" had declined significantly since the early twenties, there was an optimistic call for more missionary personnel and for large allocations of funds. Is this the reason the "open membership" controversy is nowhere to be seen in the section on China? Pages tell of China's geography, history, religions and culture as a prelude to the details of the work in Nanking, Wuhu, Luchowfu, and so on; but there is no hint of the debate about receiving Christians who had been baptized by forms other than immersion into the fellowship of Disciples of Christ churches in China.

Is there a clue on the last page of the report under observation seven? There it is noted that "The China mission plans to lay its major emphasis on evangelism *when the mission becomes normal. . .* ?"[10] Possibly this referred to military action. What is certain is that there was a major trauma, both for missionaries and for Chinese Christians, as the report was being written. This followed several years' clash of opinions in North America, resulting in a decisive split in the "brotherhood" and the organizing of a permanent independent convention.[11] Regardless, the 1926 International Convention in Memphis saw the declaration of a policy which did not rescind but superseded the action in Oklahoma

City the previous year, calling for the dismissal of any missionaries who practiced "open membership" and advocated union with pedobaptists. It was agreed, in effect, to let the churches of Asia make their own decisions, not by a positive theological statement but by a positive refusal to take the direction offered by narrow interpretations of the tradition.[12] Freedom of individual interpretation was affirmed and applied to churches overseas: it is in this sense that Joseph M. Smith referred to Memphis as a "decisive turning point".[13] Notwithstanding the criticism of Mark Toulouse, the tension of a progressive orientation toward ecumenical integrity never subsided because of a longing for unity inherent in the ecclesiology which first engaged Disciples in world mission and evangelism.[14] Some would say common sense prevailed— although the Oklahoma directive remained on the books, and was cited in relation to exploratory discussions as late as 1954.[15]

Conflict with the church overseas appeared also in the 1930's, when a spiritual revival transformed the church in Puerto Rico to a strongly autonomous body at odds with missionary leadership. The late Joaquin Vargas includes this painful episode in *Los Discipulos de Cristo en Puerto Rico, "beginnings, growth, and maturity of a pilgrimage of faith, perseverance, and hope 1899-1987"* published in 1988. The singing of *corritos*, speaking in tongues and pentecostal-type worship services were forbidden, locks were put on churches, and financial support was withdrawn. Rev. Vargas also shows the reconciliation, forgiveness, respect and love which resulted later, in part due to the intervention of Samuel Guy Inman, the ministry of Mae Yoho Ward, and the repentance and complete change of attitude of the missionary involved, C. Manly Morton. The issue in this case was not baptism, but deviation from what was considered to be the Disciples tradition in worship and spirituality.

Testing was to come twenty years after the China dispute, when the Disciples of Northern Luzon chose to remain within the United Church of Christ of the Philippines. They had participated in its founding, which grew out of the pre-war union of Presbyterians, Congregationalists and Evangelical United Brethren and the wartime administrative union under the Japanese occupation army. Norwood Tye tells about instructions to missionaries from UCMS, following the April, 1948 Uniting

Assembly, to have no further part in the discussions regarding the UCCP "until certain matters were worked out."[16]

The President of UCMS, H.B. McCormick, and chairman of the Foreign Division, Virgil Sly, visited in February, 1950 and told Filipino leaders that if the Disciples continued in the United Church, support might not be possible from the American and Canadian churches. Sylvestre Morales made it memorably clear that the Ilocano Disciples were staying with the United Church. He said that missionaries had taught the unity of the church in the Philippines since 1901, and that the congregations in North America could keep their money at home if they did not approve![17] There is reason to believe that Virgil Sly welcomed this stance more than his colleague, and that it became part of the motivation leading to an affirmation of ecumenical direction in mission in the years ahead.[18]

A similar problem was presented by Disciples in Japan who were committed to staying as part of the Kyodan. However, it is interesting to note for the record that in the Philippines the unimmersed would have been "affiliated members," while in Japan they would have been rebaptized![19]

Thus, immediately following attendance at the stimulating 1952 Willingen Conference of the International Missionary Council in Germany, Virgil Sly, like many mission leaders of other denominations, began the process for a new statement of policy leading to the document called "Strategy of World Mission." It was the time of decolonization, the taking stock of missions becoming churches in their own right, "rapid social change," the recent creation of the World Council of Churches, and an implicit optimism about the ecumenical future, all in the shadow of the Cold War and apocalyptic dread.

Ira Paternoster was a national director of the UCMS fund-raising Department of Resources at the time. He told me in the early 1970's, when the Disciples' "Restructure" process had confirmed so many of these ecclesiological assertions, that shortly after his return from Willingen, Dr. Sly gave him a document to study. He said, "Take this to your office, close the door, don't let anyone see it, and come back and tell me what you think." It was a first draft of the new *Strategy*. Paternoster said he did as requested—and then told Dr. Sly that it would "tear the brotherhood apart!"

Why were such decisions so difficult all through our history? Not just because of financial pressures, although that must be taken seriously, even understood theologically. It was due to a divided mind caused by what might be called "immersion pietism!" Not only a biblical tradition but also deep sentiment was involved, complicated by fear of more division. And for some, by an honest respect for different opinions in the church! But it was a time when Independents were aggressively taking over congregations from Ohio and Pennsylvania to the Pacific Northwest. Emmanuel School of Religion was founded by former faculty of Butler University. The European Evangelistic Society grew up after World War II, and the Brazil Christian Mission, organized in 1948, carried an ad in the Disciples *Yearbook* with a Martinsburg, West Virginia, address.

It was a theologically ambiguous community. Perry Gresham, president of Bethany College, could put out a paper to satisfy philanthropist Ben Phillips saying that no professor or student was preaching Sundays in an open membership church. National City Christian Church with J. Warren Hastings created "associate membership" to avoid criticism. Jesse Bader, general secretary of the World Convention, kept his membership in lesser-known Flatbush Christian Church in Brooklyn instead of liberal Park Avenue in New York City, where he usually attended.[20]

The separation of congregations at the time of restructure had always been seen as inevitable and was rationalized as long as possible. Almost everyone sought to avoid the polarization which occurred with the decisive ordering of the Christian Church (Disciples of Christ) in the United States and Canada in Kansas City, October 1, 1968. The Consultation On Church Union (COCU), and the partnership with the United Church of Christ, have shown a theological bearing not entirely understood by some younger clergy and many new laity of the congregations, resulting further in the reactionary dissidence of the 1980's and a diminishing number of participating congregations.

The UCMS was indeed a progressive body under these circumstances and it deserves recognition for bringing its own structural life to an end in favor of the ecclesiology which ,at least indirectly, had always been presupposed by its existence. Special credit goes to presidents A. Dale Fiers and Virgil Sly for their vision, which came to realization under the generous leadership of T.J. Liggett. These three represent missionaries, mission executives, UCMS board members, Disciples clergy and laity—especially the Christian Women's Fellowship—who understood mission in terms of the church and its united witness and service in the world.

The *Strategy of World Mission* was adopted by the board of trustees of the UCMS in January, 1955, after discussion at three annual meetings of the Board of Managers (with its 120 members) and their final approval at the Miami International Convention in October, 1954. Copies were sent to all congregations and missionaries and, in 1956, staff visits were made to every overseas location. After final review, the "operational administrative policy" was approved in October, 1958, and implementation begun. Noteworthy is the following statement: "Welcome the emerging and maturing younger churches into full partnership . . . Utilize every resource available for larger participation in cooperative work and become active in the promotion and support of Christian union and federation on the field."[21]

In the 27-page document, pages 14 to 18 are entitled "Mission and Unity." Indeed, it is specifically stated that "no one of the three words *church, unity and missions* can be understood without the other two." More than once "a quickened concern for Christian unity" is mentioned, along with Emil Brunner's expression, "The church exists by mission as fire exists by burning." But clues of reticence or prudence are also to be found, and are understandable in the light of the ambiguities described above: advising that "no commitments [should be] made until the responsible administrative body . . . and the board of trustees are of one mind," noting "problems of doctrine and practice" in plans of union, cautioning to "frankly state our position," and allowing for "the extent to which participation (of UCMS) is possible and desirable."

Still, it is clear: there will be acceptance of united churches without exclusion on baptism, there is the recognition of national autonomous bodies, and the declaration that "Disciples of Christ carry their passion for the union of the church into all of their missionary endeavor. Missionaries should work for the union of all God's people according to the prayer of Christ that his followers be one."[22] A Relationship with the World Council of Churches and councils "on the field" was recommended to all emerging churches.

There were other new directions mapped out such as tactical mobility, the study of priorities, evaluation of institutions, changes in methodology, and so on. A subtle indication appears that control of the denomination's overseas work was being taken out of the hands of missionary parleys, which heretofore even gave the name to "the mission," in favor of more authority being vested in the regional executive secretary and the staff of Missions Building.[23] This was to be the pattern for all the mainline churches for the next thirty years. It was also a means to facilitate administratively the emergence of national church leadership and structures! It must be noted that a very few missionaries who later generated their own funding, projects and beneficiaries were scornful of the new policies from the start.[24]

Serious theological discussion appears in 1958, when UCMS and the Council on Christian Unity sponsored a commission on the theology of mission which corresponded to the process of restructure of the denomination.[25] Other panels followed. Still needed forty years later is a better understanding of Christian identity, and therefore the theology of the church's unity and mission. This includes the existential relevance of the atonement, the new social reality and personal transformation brought into being by the Holy Spirit, the meaning of hope in the eschatological reign of Christ, and the revelation of God's grace in what Karl Barth calls "a second and outer circle." On the threshold of the 21st century, the renewal of authentic spirituality in our church, and others of the Reformed tradition, will call for attention to these biblical and doctrinal issues.

In 1981, at Anaheim, California, the General Assembly of the Christian Church (Disciples of Christ) in the United States and Canada voted approval of the *General Principles and Policies*. This updated the policy of the Division of Overseas Ministries, the general unit of the church which was the successor to the Division of World Mission of UCMS. Following a review of the meaning and origin of the *Strategy*, and changes in the intervening years, the ecclesiological nature of mission is confirmed by the fact that the Division of Overseas Ministries (DOM) clearly exists as a specific unit of the church.

In the opening pages of the *General Principles and Policies* we read: "The *Strategy* declared the church is mission . . . " Therefore the purpose of DOM, as stated in the Articles of Incorporation, is "to enable the Christian Church (Disciples of Christ)" to fulfill its calling. This is described as "to participate faithfully in Christ's ministry to witness, service and reconciliation in the whole world." DOM is to serve as the division through which the Christian Church (Disciples of Christ) relates to overseas communities to: 1) engage in forms of ministry that invite and prepare persons to receive and manifest the new life and relationships offered in Jesus Christ; 2) develop relationships and structures through which persons and resources are shared in a mutual ministry in the world; and 3) respond to or initiate programs which equip people to understand and foster conditions supporting health, justice and peace.[26]

In a theological section the document lists faith principles which include the affirmation that "the church is the community God calls into being and enables to engage in God's mission. It does not exist for itself alone but for the sake of the world." And under a section entitled "Commitment to Church Union" it says, "The Church of Christ is one . . . Commitment to evangelism, mission and justice is inseparable from a commitment to church union." Under "Policy Guidelines" it says: "The primary work of United States and Canadian churches is in their own countries, but no true witness and service is ever merely local. Without global concern. linkages and interaction, U.S. and Canadian churches will lose sight of the nature of the gospel and *the nature of the church*."[27] It gives more than lip service to the ecumenical bodies in saying that executive staff are expected to give the time, energy, and program funds necessary for responsible participation in order to take seriously "the denomination's membership in the World Council of Churches and the National Council of Churches of Christ in the USA and the commitment that represents to the great world, regional and national ecumenical structures."[28]

Under the leadership of the late Robert A. Thomas, and after more than four years' study and discussion in the DOM board of directors, the policy statement said, "The time for western domination of the church's life and witness around the world is past. Partnership and mutuality, servanthood and sharing are the words descriptive of world mission today."[29] Along with sections on transferring all overseas properties to legal entities of the partner churches and institutions, "a dialogical style" with people of other faiths and ideologies—since "God has never in any time or place been without witness"—and the increase in joint funding of overseas personnel with other denominations, the document speaks of multinational economics. Seen from the point of view of churches in the Third World, the management of the earth and its resources is exploitative and oppressive and calls for "solidarity with the poor in their struggle for liberation and justice."[30]

In April, 1996 the first meeting was held of the Common Global Ministries Board, bringing together the administration of the world mission programs of the Christian Church (Disciples of Christ) in the United States and Canada and the United Church of Christ. Through their respective units, the Division of Overseas Ministries and the United Church Board for World Ministries, a single board of 20 members each, plus six from partner churches around the world, oversees the cooperation and interaction of relationships in global mission. According to Patricia Tucker Spier, president of DOM since January 1, 1994, five guiding principles show the continuation of the ecclesiological tradition illustrated above: sharing life in Christ, sharing persons in mission, telling the Gospel story, healing God's continuing creation, and interfaith dialogue and cooperation.

This Common Global Ministries Board was in the making since D.T. Niles, general secretary of the EACC (now the Christian Conference of Asia) challenged UCMS and UCBWM to demonstrate Christian unity—and advance the creation of the Church of North India—by combining their offices for that region. The two boards took seriously the possibility of an even more extensive union. In 1967, Telfer Mook was appointed executive secretary for India and Nepal (later called the Department of Southern Asia) by both UCMS and UCBWM, and I was called to be Latin America secretary for both boards in 1968. Not only was a sign of unity sought through this administrative merger, but the logic of a deeper relationship between the churches—something which the COCU movement had put on hold, and which Disciples restructure had made plausible—was revived. The ecclesial partnership of the two churches was declared as "full communion" in 1989, and included the recognition of a direction already undertaken by calling for "deliberate commitment to engage in mission together wherever and whenever possible."[31] The world ministries of both churches contributed to this churchly partnership, and were encouraged by it, being authorized repeatedly in synods and general assemblies to proceed towards the creation of the Common Global Ministries Board.

All of the Disciples' missionary work in Asia has resulted in united or "post-denominational" churches. Indeed, to a great extent their leadership gave the example. The Disciples Community of the Church of Christ in Zaire has been a leader in united Protestantism in that country, with over 60 member bodies; and Disciples of South Africa have long been part of the United Congregational Church of Southern Africa. The British Churches of Christ became part of the United Reformed Church in the United Kingdom in 1982. Disciples of Christ in Jamaica and the former United Church came together to form the United Church in Jamaica and the Cayman Islands in 1992. In recent years, Disciples of Christ in Argentina and the Methodist Church have formed united congregations at the local level. Many other united churches in Africa are linked through our common ministry with the UCBWM, and an African Independent Church of indigenous origin is a partner: the Christian Apostolic Holy Spirit Church in Zion of Swaziland.

In addition to historically Disciples churches, and UCC sister churches continuing to share concerns in mission, other partner churches are mostly of the Presbyterian or Reformed tradition. These have often come into cooperation through the struggle for human rights beginning in the 1970s (for example in South Korea, Taiwan, Indonesia, Sri Lanka, the Pacific, and Brazil, or with the Lutheran Church in El Salvador and Guatemala). In Latin America there is close cooperation with Pentecostal churches in Cuba, Venezuela, Nicaragua, and Chile. Relations in the Middle East have been notably with the Orthodox churches and with the Middle East Council of Churches. This has included cooperation in funding and personnel since the 1950's, in part through the World Council of Churches' Project List, the World Student Christian Federation, and aid to Palestinian refugees.

In cooperation with the Week of Compassion and One Great Hour of Sharing, service projects conducted through many agencies of the churches and councils of churches show the ecumenical reality which has become second nature to Disciples' world mission in the preceding half-century. Roman Catholic friends have included Maryknollers and

Jesuits and Catholic sisters joining in the struggle against injustice, oppression of the poor, the exploitation of women and children, and the domination of the environment by the economically powerful and the politically corrupt. In many cases the universality of unity and mission in Christ has meant support to people's movements such as the African National Congress of South Africa, the Agrarian Leagues in Paraguay, the Buraku Liberation Center in Japan, and the International Network of Engaged Buddhists based in Thailand.

Understanding mission as ecclesiology is the reason that Disciples of Christ have shaped the kind of global ministries which exist today, ministries based on the spirit of Christian unity. Understanding mission as ecclesiology has been a constant point of reference in the faith which has led to 150 years of involvement in the missionary movement. This has been true even though interpretations of ecclesiology could differ and could perpetuate the tensions of denominationalism. But it has shaped, on the threshold of the 21st century, a church whose vocation is especially identified with Christian unity, and whose mission continues to be described as extending from its "own doorstep to the ends of the earth."[32]

Notes

[1] David J. Bosch, *Transforming Mission*, Maryknoll, Orbis Books, 1991, pp. 331, 450.

[2] Thomas Campbell, *Declaration and Address*, St. Louis, Bethany Press, [1809], 1955, pp. 28, 108-109.

[3] *The Millennial Harbinger*, 1866, p. 503.

[4] Emphasis original.

[5] *Ibid.*, 1854, p. 547; 1860, p. 563.

[6] Archibald McLean, *Alexander Campbell As Preacher*, New York, Fleming H. Revell Co., 1908, p. 34.

[7] Bosch, *op. cit.*, pp. 371-3.

[8] W.R. Warren, editor, *Survey of Service*, St. Louis, Christian Board of Publication, p. 667.

[9] *Ibid.*, pp. 672 ff.

[10] P. 385, emphasis mine.

[11] Mark Toulouse, *Joined in Discipleship*, St. Louis, Chalice Press, 1992, p. 177. See also Toulouse, "Practical Concern and Theological Neglect: The UCMS and the Open Membership Controversy," in D. Newell Williams, editor, *A Case Study of Mainstream Protestantism*, Grand Rapids and St. Louis, Eerdmans and Chalice Press, pp. 205 ff., cf. 230-1, fn. 120.

[12] Joseph M. Smith, "A Strategy of World Mission: The Theory and Practice of Mission as Seen in the Present World Mission Enterprise of the Disciples of Christ", Th.D. dissertation, Union Theological Seminary, New York, 1961, pp. 92-100.

[13] See note 12.

[14] Toulouse in Williams, *op. cit.*, p. 229; cf. Don Pittman and Paul Williams, "Mission and Evangelism: Continuing Debates and Contemporary Interpretations," in *Interpreting Disciples*, ed. Bouchard and Richesin, Fort Worth, Texas Christian University Press, 1987.

[15] Smith, *op. cit.*, p. 203.

[16] Norwood Tye, *Journeying With the United Church of Christ in the Philippines: A History*, Quezon City, Philippines, UCCP, 1994, p. 67.

[17] *Ibid.*, p. 70.

[18] Smith, *op. cit.*, p. 200, where Dr. Sly is quoted as saying on August 8, 1954: "We must utilize the mission union situation to inject a new spirit in the Disciples of Christ which will result in the revitalization of the church in America in the field of Christian unity."

[19] Smith, *op. cit.*, pp. 145, 146; cf. p. 212, Dr. Smith's remark about the irony of sensitivity in the issue of baptism even among those committed to church union!

[20] The declaration from Bethany was widely circulated at the time. Earl Butz, Assistant Secretary of Agriculture under True Morse in the Eisenhower administration, could not be elected elder in the Washington church because he had not been immersed. Records show that Golda Bader transferred her letter of membership to Park Avenue from Flatbush Christian Church on January 17, 1965, more than a year after the death of Dr. Bader.

[21] *Strategy of World Mission: Basic Policy of the Division of World Mission, United Christian Missionary Society*, Indianapolis, UCMS, 1959, p. 10.

[22] *Ibid.*, p. 17.

[23] Ibid., pp. 24-26; Smith, *op. cit.*, p. 387.

[24] Smith, *op. cit.*, pp. 378-382; 384.

[25] cf. Toulouse in Williams, *op. cit.*, p. 233.

[26] *General Principles & Policies* (Indianapolis: Division of Overseas Ministries, 1981), p. 8.

[27] *Ibid.*, p. 22, emphasis mine.

[28] *Loc. cit.*

[29] *Ibid.*, p. 35.

[30] *Ibid.*, p. 39.

[31] Toulouse, *op. cit.*, pp. 101-2.

[32] "Mission Statement," General Assembly of the Christian Church (Disciples of Christ), Pittsburgh, 1995.

CHAPTER NINE

VISIBLE UNITY IN THE WORK OF THE WORLD COUNCIL OF CHURCHES

Mary Tanner

These reflections on the understanding of visible unity in the work of the World Council of Churches are offered in gratitude for the ministry of Paul Crow. Throughout his ministry Paul Crow has embodied the deep commitment of his own church, the Disciples of Christ, to the unity of the Church. He has worked for that tirelessly in the United States of America, not least of all in the leadership he has given to the Consultation on Church Union. Throughout his membership of the Central Committee of the WCC and its Faith and Order Commission, Paul has inspired others with his passionate commitment to visible unity. He has carried a particular concern to communicate a vision of unity to the next generation. I have been fortunate to serve with Paul in the leadership of the Faith and Order Commission for many years. His own concern for unity made me turn to this as a subject for this tribute. Paul's particular concern for the relationship between the unity and renewal of the Church and the unity of humankind, in the perspective of God's Kingdom, has had a significant influence on the work of the Faith and Order Commission and of the World Council of Churches itself.

Lesslie Newbigin once said, "A sincere intention to seek unity is incompatible with an intention to remain permanently uncommitted to any particular form of unity." In the statements of assemblies of the World Council of Churches from New Delhi (1961) onwards, the World

Council has been concerned to call the churches to the goal of visible unity. No one model has been espoused—organic union, "united not absorbed," full communion, reconciled diversity, unity in solidarity, and so on . . . The Assembly statements have, rather, provided pictures of what was understood by visible unity. It is perhaps timely to recall what has been said about visible unity on the eve of the WCC's Eighth Assembly (to be held in Harare, Zimbabwe in September, 1998). For this Assembly has the task of stating the common understanding and vision of the World Council and of asking, "What sort of instrument, at the world level, will best serve the ecumenical pilgrimage in the next millenium?" Whatever instrument is formed must be one that serves the commitment of the churches to search for visible unity. It is, therefore, imperative that the Common Understanding and Vision process grows out of remembering what has already been understood about visible unity so that it can develop a vision consonant with the past.

The Third WCC Assembly in New Delhi (1961) said this about the form of visible unity:

> We believe that the unity which is both God's will and his gift to his Church is made visible as all in each place who are baptised into Jesus Christ and confess him as Lord and Saviour are brought by the Holy Spirit into one fully committed fellowship, holding the one apostolic faith, preaching the one Gospel, breaking the one bread, joining in common prayer, and having a corporate life reaching out in witness and service to all and who at the same time are united with the whole Christian fellowship in all places and all ages in such ways that ministry and members are accepted by all, and that all can act and speak together as occasion requires for the tasks to which God calls his people.[1]

The Fourth Assembly in Uppsala (1968) further developed certain aspects of the earlier description. It understood the unity we seek through the use of the concept of catholicity, showing how the churches in all places belong together and are called to act together. The Assembly said:

The ecumenical movement helps to enlarge this experience of universality, and its regional councils and its World Council may be regarded as a transitional opportunity for eventually actualizing a truly universal, ecumenical, conciliar form of common life and witness. The members of the World Council of Churches, committed to each other, should work for the time when a genuinely universal council may once more speak for all Christians, and lead the way into the future.[2]

As Professor John Deschner, a former Moderator of Faith and Order, has stressed, Uppsala's contribution to the understanding of the goal of visible unity lay both in its emphasis upon "conciliar fellowship" and in its emphasis upon the Church as "sign." "The Church is bold in speaking of itself as the sign of the coming unity of humankind." This may be an indication of the influence of Vatican II upon the WCC. *Lumen Gentium's* famous sentence claimed that "the Church is a kind of sacrament and instrument, a sign of intimate union with God, and of the unity of all mankind." Uppsala's account, with its phrase "the coming unity," was more eschatological. The emphasis in Uppsala on "sign" implied that unity is a quality to be displayed by the Church in each given situation. That quality has its model—more than that, its source—in the life of the Triune God and in the kenotic love of God shown in the incarnation.

In the years between Uppsala and the Fifth Assembly in Nairobi (1975), Uppsala's concept of "conciliar fellowship" was developed in the work of the Faith and Order Commission so that the Nairobi Assembly was able further to unfold the concept:

The one Church is to be envisioned as a conciliar fellowship of local churches which are themselves truly united. In this conciliar fellowship each local church possesses, in communion with the others, the fullness of catholicity, witnesses to the same apostolic faith and therefore recognises the others as belonging to the same Church of Christ and guided by the same Spirit. They are bound together because they have the same baptism, and share in the same eucharist; they recognise each other's members and ministries. They are one in their common commitment to confess the Gospel of Christ by proclamation and service to the world. To this end each church aims at maintaining sustained and sustaining relationships with her sister churches, expressed in conciliar gatherings whenever required for the fulfilment of their common calling.[3]

Nairobi was not setting up an alternative to the model of New Delhi, but drawing out one of its implications. Christians will know that they are truly united in the same Church and are guided by the same Spirit when they realise at least *three* basic marks of "conciliar fellowship": a common commitment to the apostolic faith; one baptism and eucharist and the recognition of each other's members and ministries; and conciliar gatherings for common deliberations and decision-making.

For some, the Nairobi statement was a breakthrough with its enunciation of the essential characteristics for the visible unity of the Church. For others, it was seen as confusing. It used the same term "conciliar" to describe both one of the three structural requirements for realising the visibility of the one Church (conciliar gatherings), and also the very nature of the Church itself, "a conciliar fellowship of local churches which are themselves truly united." The vision of "conciliar fellowship" was difficult to communicate. It was understood by some as *less* than "organic union" and merely an acceptance of the state of "conciliar fellowship" that already exists in councils of churches and in the World Council of Churches itself. In spite of the fact that the Nairobi statement had made quite clear that "conciliar fellowship" does not describe any present reality, as well as the repeated attempts by Faith and Order theologians to insist that "conciliar fellowship" is *not* an alternative to, but rather an explication of, "organic union," the concept never gained the widespread reception that it deserved.

The Vancouver Assembly (1982) recommitted itself to the goal of visible unity. The Report of section 2 underlined once more the three marks of a united Church:

> First, the churches would share a common understanding of the apostolic faith, and be able to confess this message together in ways understandable, reconciling and liberating to their contemporaries. Living this apostolic faith together, the churches help the world to realise God's design for creation.

Second, confessing the apostolic faith together, the churches would share a full mutual recognition of baptism, the eucharist and ministry, and be able through their visible communion to let the healing and uniting power of these gifts become more evident amidst the visions of mankind.

Third, the churches would agree on common ways of decision-making and ways of teaching authoritatively, and be able to demonstrate qualities of communion, participation and corporate responsibility which could shed healing light in a world of conflict.

Such a unity—overcoming church divisions, binding us together in the face of racism, sexism, injustice—would be a witnessing unity, a credible sign of new creation[4]

There is a breakthrough in this statement, one not often recognised: namely, the way in which the "characteristics" or "marks" of the Church—namely faith, sacraments, ministry and structures of decision-making and teaching—are inextricably linked to the service and witness of the Church. So faith is confessed in lives which help the world to realise God's design for creation. Through a life of faith and sacrament served by a ministry, churches would bring healing amidst the divisions of the world. And through common ways of decision-making, light could be shed in a world of conflict. In this short summary statement the agendas of Faith and Order, Life and Work and Mission are bound together in an understanding of visible unity which sees unity in faith, service and mission as indivisible parts of a single ecclesial life.

At the same time the Vancouver Report emphasises the relation between the unity of the Church and the renewal of human community, picking up the Uppsala stress on the Church as "sign." "The Church is called to be a 'prophetic sign,' a prophetic community through which, and by which, the transformation of the world can take place." Behind this emphasis at Vancouver lay the work of the studies on racism, on the "handicapped," and the study on the Community of Women and Men in the Church. These studies had shown clearly that the divisions and brokenness in the human community (divisions between black and white, men and women, differently abled, and so on) are reflected in the life of the Church These divisions affect the way the faith is confessed, the sacraments are celebrated, the ministry is exercised, the use or abuse of power and authority. The Church has constantly to be "re-formed and renewed into unity."

The Canberra Assembly (1991) made a significant contribution with its statement on unity, "The Unity of the Church as Koinonia: Gift and Calling."[5] This was the only statement which the Assembly formally adopted. On the eve of the Harare Assembly, it is worth reflecting at some length on the *Canberra Statement*. The Statement summed up in "a nutshell" the themes of previous Assembly Statements and, at the same time, broke significantly new ground. In the years since Canberra, although the World Council itself (apart from the Commission on Faith and Order) seems to have made little use of the Statement, some churches have taken it seriously as an important and vital contribution from the most representative ecumenical forum which exists. These churches have used it in their bilateral agreements and movements towards unity.

In the preparatory period leading up to the Canberra Assembly the Central Committee invited the Faith and Order Commission to prepare a statement on visible unity. This was the statement that, with significant revisions made by the Assembly, was adopted at the Canberra Assembly as the *Canberra Statement*.

The title of the Statement received an important addition at the Assembly. The original title, *"The Unity of the Church as Gift and Calling,"* was changed to *"The Unity of the Church as Koinonia: Gift and Calling."* The notion of koinonia, or "communion," echoes throughout the Statement, thus reflecting the centrality of this theme in many of the bilateral theological reports of the 1980's. The end or *telos* of all, of the whole of creation, is that it should be brought into communion with God. The divided churches are called, here and now, to "full communion," and to witness and work to bring all into communion with God. In spite of their divisions the churches are recognising today that "a certain degree of communion" already exists between them. Thus the theme of koinonia is fundamental in understanding the reality of the Church and its own calling, as well as the destiny of humanity and of all creation. Moreover, *koinonia* is seen as the gift of God's own trinitarian life: "The grace of our Lord Jesus Christ, the love of God and the communion of the Holy Spirit (2 Cor. 13:13)." The calling of the Church is to reveal God in Christ-like form to the world, through the power and gift of the Holy Spirit.

The "elements" or "characteristics" of visible unity are enumerated as: the common confession of the apostolic faith; a common sacramental life entered by the one baptism and celebrated together in one eucharistic fellowship; a common life in which members and ministries are mutually recognised and reconciled; and a common mission witnessing to all people to the Gospel of God's grace and serving the whole of creation. The Statement goes on, with an important addition. "The goal of the search for full communion is realised when all of the churches are able to recognise in one another the one, holy, catholic and apostolic Church in its fullness. This full communion will be expressed on the local and universal levels through conciliar forms of life and action."[6]

The picture of visible unity, of "full communion," owes much to the earlier unity statements, not least in its emphasis on "conciliar life." However, as some have pointed out in the years since Canberra, there is an ambiguity in the Statement. Does the phrase "all of the churches" (who are to be bound by these characteristics of faith, sacraments, ministry and conciliar life) refer to *local churches*, the "all in each place" of the New Delhi Statement? Or is it to be read as churches in the sense of *denominations*? This is a crucial question for understanding the portrait of unity which the *Canberra Statement* paints, as well as the goal to which the ecumenical movement is oriented.

It is worth noting that the Statement's emphasis on "conciliar life" was a move away from the draft which the Faith and Order Commission itself had offered to the Assembly. The draft spoke of forms of ministry exercised in "personal, collegial and communal ways," picking up the emphasis on this in *Baptism, Eucharist and Ministry*.[7] The development of this theme could prove to be the one of the most promising areas in ecumenical debate in the next phase.

One important further theme contributed by the Assembly itself was the section on diversity. The Assembly was challenged to say something about diversity in view of explorations of the theme of the Holy Spirit which were presented at the Assembly. The Statement is clear that unity entails diversity: diversities rooted in theological traditions, or in cultural, ethnic or historical contexts are integral to the nature of communion.

Nevertheless, the Statement is also clear that there are "tolerable limits" to diversity. And, when challenged to indicate what they might be, a bold but reticent statement is made:

> Diversity is illegitimate when, for instance, it makes impossible the common confession of Jesus Christ as God and Saviour the same yesterday, today and forever (Heb. 13:8); salvation and the final destiny of humanity as proclaimed in the Holy Scripture and preached in the apostolic community[8].

The *Canberra Statement* challenges the divided churches to take steps on the way to visible unity; "towards the realisation of full communion." It encourages the churches to learn from one another and to work together for justice and peace, and to care for God's creation even now.

Two years after the Canberra Assembly the Fifth World Conference on Faith and Order in Santiago de Compostela (1993) expressed in its own conference theme a statement about unity: "Towards Koinonia in Faith, Life and Witness."[9] The Conference was in some senses a commentary upon, and exploration of, the *Canberra Statement* in the light of Faith and Order's work over a thirty-year period. The working document emphasized the theme of koinonia, developing the short paragraphs in the *Canberra Statement*. The visible characteristics of koinonia laid before the Conference were those of a communion in faith, a faith grounded in Scripture and focused in the Nicene Creed; a communion in life focused in the sacraments of baptism and eucharist, nurtured by an ordained ministry within the ministry of the whole people of God; and a communion in witness entailing the renewal of the Church as prophetic sign of the Kingdom. This summed up several of the Faith and Order studies: *Confessing the One Faith, Baptism, Eucharist and Ministry*, and *Church and World*.[10] The latter was the final and culminating text from the Faith and Order study programme "The Unity of the Church and the Renewal of Human Community," of which Paul Crow was the moderator.

But the World Conference did not simply affirm this picture. It added to it by asking for work on *what* structures of mutual accountability, authority and decision making would sustain the unity and communion of the Church. Reference was made to the synodical and primatial structures needed to serve unity. Moreover the Conference strongly emphasised the characteristic of ethical living (referred to in recent ecumenical discussion through the language of the church as "moral community") as an element in understanding visible unity. This theme was present in the second part of the *Canberra Statement* where churches are invited to recommit themselves to work for "justice, peace and the integrity of creation, thus linking more closely the search for sacramental communion of the Church with the struggles for justice and peace."

Behind this new emphasis on the understanding of the relation between the unity of the Church and common moral values and shared action for justice and peace lay the insights of a consultation held in Rønde, Denmark shortly before the Fifth World Conference on Faith and Order. This pathbreaking meeting was the first in the study programme on "Ecclesiology and Ethics" conducted jointly by Faith and Order/WCC Unit I and WCC Unit III. It featured an insightful and stimulating paper by Paul Crow,[11] who guided Faith and Order's involvement in this project through its completion in 1996. In this consultation, and two that followed, the Faith and Order and Life and Work traditions were searching to find a common theological language "in order to formulate a more coherent and vital agenda for church unity and for common action in face of challenges confronting both the church and the world today"[12]

The most recent contribution to the debate on visible unity is offered in the draft statement on the "Common Understanding and Vision" of the WCC. The statement is only now in the preliminary stage but it is perhaps worth noting that the preamble contains a vision of visible unity:

> We are drawn by the vision of a church that brings all people into communion with God; a church that is visibly one, sharing one baptism, celebrating one eucharist, and enjoying the service of a reconciled common ministry.
>
> We are compelled by the vision of a church whose unity is expressed in bonds of conciliar communion which enables us to take decisions together and to interpret and teach the apostolic faith together, with mutual accountability and in love.

We are inspired by the vision of a church that engages in dialogue and cooperation in service with people of other faiths.

We are challenged by the vision of a church that is fully inclusive, mindful of the marginalized, overcoming divisions based on race, gender, age and culture, promoting justice and peace, and respecting the integrity of God's creation.

We aspire to the vision of a church that reaches out to everyone through a life of sharing, proclaiming the good news of God's redemption, being both sign and servant, drawing all ever more deeply into the fellowship of God's own life.[13]

The attempt to extract from the reports of the World Council of Churches, particularly from Assembly Statements, what has been said about the visible unity of the Church has obvious weaknesses. It is necessarily selective and fragmentary. The *Canberra Statement*, however, is different. It was carefully prepared for the Seventh Assembly and is a more complete portraiture of visible unity. Moreover, it was formally adopted by the Assembly.

There is, however, a question of how far the member churches themselves can, or will, affirm and receive these statements. Even an Assembly vote for the adoption of the Canberra Statement cannot be taken as a church's acceptance of it. Nevertheless, it is clear from the use some churches are making of that Statement that there are some who accept it as a summary of where the ecumenical movement is today in its thinking about visible unity. The Statement at least provides some notion of what sort of visibly united Church Christians seek to live together.

Some churches have taken the Canberra Statement, or parts of earlier statements, and used them within bilateral dialogues and agreements. For example, the emphasis of the "all in each place," united to the notion "all in every place," influenced the report of the International Anglican—Reformed dialogue, *God's Reign and Our Unity*.[14] The description of unity in the Meissen Agreement between the Evangelical Church in Germany (involving Lutheran, Reformed and United Churches) and the Church of England use the description of the threefold characteristics of unity from the Vancouver Assembly.[15] The more recent agreement between the Moravian Church and the Church of England in the *Fetter*

Lane Common Statement uses the *Canberra Statement*.[16] These regional bilateral agreements, which have issued in changed relationships in the lives of the churches, show how the attempts of the "broadest ecumenical forum" to give a portrait of visible unity can help to provide a consistency and coherence to bilateral partnerships at an international, regional or local level. Within the present complexity of the ecumenical movement the picture of visible unity held out by the WCC helps churches to assess whether their agreements are moving in the same direction.

However, there are also dangers in these statements if they are taken as a mere list of fundamentals which can be "checked off," as if they were an ecumenical "checklist," a checklist which will be added to again and again. Equally there is a danger if a statement like the *Canberra Statement* is taken as fixed for all time. The truth about visible unity is that as we move together on pilgrimage new possibilities open up in our understanding of that reality.

No single statement, portrait, or model can capture the diversity, dynamism and boundless possibilities of the one, holy, catholic and apostolic Church. But as new steps are taken, new stages reached in relationships between Christian churches, producing an incredibly complex (and increasingly "messy"!) ecumenical movement, some provisional attempts to express the unity we seek are surely needed in order to beckon us on. But it is more than to beckon us on, it is also to make sense of that which experience already tells us is *so*, as we pray and work together for justice and peace with Christians of other traditions. Without some commitment to some shape of unity, some portrait of unity, however dimly seen, our sincere intentions to seek unity are, as Lesslie Newbigin said, likely to be called into question.

Paul Crow has played an important role in keeping alive within the ecumenical movement a commitment to visible unity. The Church of England owes him a debt of gratitude. I know that Dr Robert Runcie, who met Paul Crow on a number of occasions during his time as Archbishop of Canterbury, would wish to be associated with this tribute to a distinguished and committed ecumenist.

Notes

[1] W. A. Visser 't Hooft, ed., *The New Delhi Report: The Third Assembly of the World Council of Churches, 1961*, London, SCM, 1962, p.116.

[2] Norman Goodall, ed., *The Uppsala 1968 Report: Official Report of the Fourth Assembly of the WCC, Uppsala, 1968*, Geneva, WCC, 1968, p. 17.

[3] David M. Paton, ed., *Breaking Barriers: Nairobi 1975*, London and Grand Rapids, SPCK and Wm B. Eerdmans, 1976, p. 60.

[4] David Gill, ed., *Gathered for Life*, Geneva, WCC, 1983, p. 45.

[5] M. Kinnamon, ed., *Signs of the Spirit: Official Report of the Seventh Assembly*, Geneva, WCC, 1991, pp.172 ff.

[6] *Ibid.*, para. 2.1.

[7] *Baptism, Eucharist and Ministry*, "Ministry" section, Faith & Order Paper No. 111, Geneva, WCC, 1982, paras. 26 and 27.

[8] *Canberra Statement, op. Cit.,* para. 2.2.

[9] Thomas F. .Best and Günther Gassmann, eds., *On the Way to Fuller Koinonia: The Fifth World Conference on Faith and Order*, Faith & Order Paper No. 166, Geneva, WCC, 1994.

[10] *Confessing the One Faith*, Faith & Order Paper No. 153, Geneva, WCC, 1991; *Baptism, Eucharist and Ministry, op. Cit.; Church and World: The Unity of the Church and the Renewal of Human Community*, Faith & Order Paper No.152, 2nd, rev. printing, Geneva, WCC, 1992.

[11] Paul A. Crow, Jr., "Ecclesiology: the Intersection Between the Search for Ecclesial Unity and the Struggle for Justice, Peace, and the Integrity of Creation," in Thomas F. Best and Wesley Granberg-Michaelson, *Costly Unity: Koinonia and Justice, Peace and Creation*, Geneva, Faith and Order/ Unit I and Unit III, 1993, pp. 53-58.

[12] "The History of Ecumenical Work on Ecclesiology and Ethics," by Peter Lodberg, in Thomas F. Best and Martin Robra, eds., *Costly Commitment: Ecclesiology and Ethics*, Geneva, Faith and Order/Unit I and Unit III, 1995, pp.1 ff.

[13] "Preamble: Vision Statement of the Member Churches of the WCC," in *Towards a Common Understanding and Vision of the World Council of Churches: A Working Draft for a Policy Statement*, Geneva, World Council of Churches, November, 1996, pp. 5-6.

[14] *God's Reign and Our Unity*, Report of the Anglican-Reformed International Commission, London, 1994.

[15] *The Meissen Common Statement*, Council on Christian Unity, 1992.

[16] *Anglican-Moravian Conversations: The Fetter Lane Common Statement*, Council on Christian Unity, 1996.

CHAPTER TEN

THE DISCIPLES OF CHRIST-ROMAN CATHOLIC INTERNATIONAL DIALOGUE, 1977-1997: HISTORICAL PERSPECTIVES

By David M. Thompson

The year of Dr. Paul Crow Jr.'s retirement, 1998, will be the twenty-first anniversary of the Disciples of Christ-Roman Catholic International Dialogue, a fitting commemoration of one of Paul's most fruitful ecumenical initiatives. For those of us who have been members of the three dialogue teams, it has been a unique experience of theological sharing and personal friendship at the deepest level.

The prospects for such a dialogue can scarcely have looked promising at the outset. Alexander Campbell, the leading spokesman for the first generation of Disciples, shared the conventional Protestant assumptions of his time about the Roman Catholic Church. The Preface to one of his most widely circulated books begins,

> Since the full development of the great apostacy foretold by prophets and apostles, numerous attempts at reformation have been made. Three full centuries, carrying with them the destinies of countless millions, have passed into eternity since the Lutheran effort to dethrone the *Man of Sin* . . . . The Protestant Reformation . . . will long be regarded by the philosopher and the philanthropist as one of the most gracious interpositions in behalf of the whole human race.[1]

Similarly, in his public debate with the Rt Revd John B. Purcell, Bishop of Cincinnati, in 1837, Campbell sought to prove a standard set of protestant polemical points against the Church of Rome.[2] In this Campbell was not unusual, except that he did not approve of contemporary anti-Catholic movements in the U.S.A. and always remained a good friend of Purcell.[3] The changed ecumenical climate since the Second Vatican Council has required all to revise their earlier preconceptions.

Disciples of Christ had been represented at the Second Vatican Council by a series of observers, including the Revd Dr. George Beazley, Dr. Crow's predecessor as President of the Council on Christian Unity of the Christian Church (Disciples of Christ) in the U.S.A. and Canada. So it was natural that, as the Roman Catholic Church began to establish international bilateral dialogues with a series of Christian World Communions in the late 1960s, Disciples of Christ should also wish to be involved. In 1967 a national dialogue within the United States was begun, which culminated in a report in 1974, *An Adventure in Understanding*.[4] This was one of a number of dialogues undertaken by the Committee for Ecumenical and Interreligious Affairs of the National Conference of Catholic Bishops in the U.S.A.

The idea was first conceived by Dr. George Beazley and Monsignor (later Bishop) William Baum at a breakfast during the Triennial Assembly of the National Council of Churches at Miami Beach, Florida in December 1966. Some eight or nine meetings were held over a period of six years, covering many of the major areas of difference. The topics ranged (by chance) over the seven sacraments of the Roman Catholic Church, and in a perceptive analysis at the conclusion, Dr. Beazley pointed out that the basic question requiring further discussion was that of magisterial authority and freedom in the two churches.[5] At the very beginning of this national dialogue Dr. Beazley drew attention to two features which have been of recurring significance in the subsequent history of the international dialogue. The first was that the two churches relied on "a basically catholic concept of the church," shared the conviction that worship should include the eucharist at least weekly, and believed in salvation by faith without insisting that it was "by faith alone." The second was "the fact that the Roman Catholic Church and the Christian Churches (Disciples of Christ) had never gone through anathema and counter-anathema during the Reformation period, nor through a formal separation in which each expressed its dogma in opposition to the other."[6]

After George Beazley's sudden death on a visit to Moscow in October 1973, his successor, Dr. Paul A. Crow Jr., initiated the discussions which were to transform a national dialogue into an international one. Dr. Crow had already attended some of the meetings of the earlier group from 1970, when it considered the concept of the parish in the Plan of Union prepared by the Consultation on Church Union, of which he was General Secretary. In January 1977 a Preparatory Committee met in Indianapolis to consider a program, the composition of the two sides, and the procedure to be adopted. The goal agreed for the dialogue was "so to develop the relation between the Disciples Churches and the Roman Catholic church that the unity willed by Christ may be attained and given visible expression." The topic chosen for the first five-year program was "Apostolicity and Catholicity in the Visible Unity of the Church." It was agreed that the papers presented to the dialogue meetings might be published, together with agreed reports of each annual meeting. This was the first time that such permission for publication had been given. There were to be eight participants on each side; on the Roman Catholic side five were to be appointed by the U.S. Bishops' Committee for Ecumenical and Interreligious Affairs and three by the Secretariat for Promoting Christian Unity; on the Disciples side appointments were to be made by the Council on Christian Unity and the Disciples Ecumenical Consultative Council. Another "first" for this dialogue was that there was a woman member of each team. It was agreed that the co-chairmen would be the Most Revd Francis R. Shea, Bishop of Evansville, and Dr. Crow (though in the event Bishop Shea was unable to act, and was replaced by Bishop Stanley J. Ott of New Orleans).[7]

The first meeting of the new International Commission took place at the Alverna Retreat House in Indianapolis, Indiana from 22 to 27 September 1977. Although not at that stage a member of the Dialogue, I was visiting Indianapolis at the time, and was privileged to attend the opening. Msgr. Basil Meeking in the opening meditation summed up the significance of the dialogue in a way which still rings true twenty years later. "What we begin today," he said, "is a task of study, of theological understanding." But it was more than that. "This meeting is saying in its own way that our two confessions intend not only to study together, not only to discuss together, but intend to walk together." Things would never be the same again between the two partners, "for this very process of the dialogue is an opening up of ourselves to one another, an agreement to help each other to be open to the grace and unifying power of Jesus Christ." That could have far-reaching consequences: "as we try to come to a deeper agreement about faith and its content the more possible it will be to discover a pluralism in the expression of that faith, a diversity in theologies, in cultural forms, in the ways of organizing the Christian community and its life." That involved the tension of being loyal to our own traditions as well as being able to look ahead. "We have been deputed because we can represent where our churches actually are, because we are willing to moderate our pace to them, prepared to help them progress together towards full visible unity."[8]

The work of the Commission was developed through the study of four themes: the nature of the Church and elements of its unity (Indianapolis, 1977), baptism: gift and call in the search for unity (Rome 1978), faith and tradition in the life of the Church (Annapolis, 1979), and the dynamics of unity and of division (New Orleans, 1980).[9] The last meeting at Ardfert in Ireland in September 1981 was devoted to the revision and approval of the Report to the Churches under the title, *Apostolicity and Catholicity*.[10]

Two concepts which were developed at the Indianapolis meeting have remained significant for the dialogue, those of spiritual ecumenism and evangelical space. The idea of spiritual ecumenism derives from the Decree on Ecumenism of the Second Vatican Council, where it is described as the "change of heart and holiness of life, along with public and private prayer for the unity of Christians" which is the "soul of the whole ecumenical movement."[11] The word "spiritual" in this context refers to the work of the Holy Spirit. It is a reminder that grace dominates the structure or means instituted for its transmission. Thus Fr. Jean-Marie Tillard, OP, argued that it was urgent "that we provide a new impulse to spiritual ecumenism in order to create the evangelical space outside of which no authentic unity would be possible." Organic unity could not be achieved simply by doctrinal consensus, however profound: "without what we call 'evangelical space', deriving from the life of grace, the most promising ecumenical dialogues will fritter away."[12] In the final Report the point was developed to include the notions of repentance and renewal. "This *metanoia* thus provides what might be called an 'evangelical space'—an arena for the operation of the Gospel—in which we find God's grace newly available to bind us together in praising, blessing, beseeching the God who makes us one. In this evangelical space, we discover new possibilities for genuine exchange and sharing and for seeing in a new light these affirmations that find historical expression in our still separated communities."[13]

This starting point for the dialogue was significant. From the beginning the search was for principles of unity that spanned churches with separate institutional histories. The significance of institutions was not underestimated—far from it: but it was neither necessary nor possible to begin from some watershed of separation, with the inevitable tendency to make judgements about who was responsible and who was right.

Apostolicity and Catholicity also articulated agreements on baptism and the relation between faith and tradition. The connection between these two is significant. Both Roman Catholics and Disciples affirmed that in baptism we enter a new relationship with God because our sins are forgiven and we become a new creation. "Since God never revokes the new relationship brought about in baptism, rebaptism is contrary to the Gospel and should never be practiced." This agreement prefigured that in *Baptism, Eucharist and Ministry*, which was nearing completion at the same time. Both traditions also affirmed the role of faith in baptism: "incorporation into the Body of Christ and forgiveness of sins are primarily acts of God that presuppose faith and call for a continuing active response of faith for their full development and fruitfulness."[14] The traditional Disciple belief that baptism was for the remission of sins aided agreement at this point. This primary agreement enabled certain continuing differences to be reinterpreted. Disciples continued to affirm that baptism should be preceded by a personal confession of faith and repentance, though they acknowledged an increasing appreciation for the place of infant baptism in the history of the Church. Roman Catholics affirmed the practice of infant baptism for historical, theological and pastoral reasons, but they saw the "fundamental belief of their church regarding baptism as expressed with new clarity in the revised rite for adult baptism, which includes personal confession of faith."

There remained a continuing difference on the mode of baptism, because Disciples practised immersion; but Disciples abandoned the kind of argument originally used by Alexander Campbell that, since the Greek *baptizo* actually meant "immerse," any other mode was not baptism. Instead the discussion turned to the paradox that baptism was both a sign of unity and a reminder of disunity, since the same act incorporated all Christians into Christ but also into their own separated ecclesial communities. The Dialogue therefore distinguished between two affirmations of faith: one, "the fundamental assent of the person to God's gift of grace in Jesus Christ," the other, "the induction into a particular ecclesial community with its own explication of the one faith."[15]

That distinction explained why baptism was linked so immediately with the question of faith and tradition. Faith was God's gift both to the individual and the community; indeed the report affirmed that "each Christian's faith is inseparable from the faith of the community. Personal faith is an appropriation of the Church's faith and depends on it for authenticity as well as for nurture." Believers were called to offer a common witness of faith to the world, so that the world might believe; thus "both the individual believer and the pilgrim Church are ever called to a deeper conversion to Christ, a more authentic faith. Scripture, mediating the Word of God, has a central, normative, and irreplaceable role in this process of personal and ecclesial conversion." So it was possible to see the relationship between faith and tradition in terms of the question of "how Christians from age to age come to the knowledge that Jesus Christ is the Lord of life and the way of salvation for the whole world."[16] Again differences were expressed over the role of creeds and confessions: Roman Catholics believed that such statements were necessary for a more complete expression of the truths that are in Scripture than Scripture alone affords; Disciples believed that "the New Testament is a sufficient expression of the essential faith, doctrine and practice of the individual Christian and the Christian community" and that "freedom and diversity in expressions of belief and worship need not threaten [the Church's] unity."[17]

The Report concluded with some affirmations about "the unity we seek," including the manifestation of the visible community which both believed to belong to the very *esse* of the Church. Whilst the two churches were not asked to make a definitive judgment on the Dialogue's work or to commit themselves to a decision which could have structural consequences, there was a firm belief that interior communion between Christians across divisions had been discovered in the dialogue and that a framework had been established in which further work on unresolved issues could be undertaken.

The meeting at Ardfert which agreed the final text of *Apostolicity and Catholicity* contained some tense moments, which had not been apparent in the dialogue hitherto. But the ecumenical observer, Robin Boyd, Director of the Irish School of Ecumenics in Dublin, made some stimulating observations on the Report. He was not so enthusiastic as the Dialogue members to discuss the questions of Church, eucharist and ministry, and noted the different relationship between the participants in this dialogue from dialogues involving Anglicans or Reformed. "When Roman Catholics recognize baptized Disciples as members of the Body of Christ," he wrote, "they do not mean that they are "anonymous Roman Catholics" (though that idea was discussed at the meeting!). The very fact that these two Churches are so far apart in how they express their faith and how they organize their structures gives hope of a coming unity whose features will be quite different from the features of either Church—an open-ended future known only to God, and with room for much diversity as well as 'radical unity'."[18]

The reception given to *Apostolicity and Catholicty* was sufficiently warm for a second phase of the Dialogue to be authorized in 1982. This phase, however, was sponsored exclusively by the Secretariat for Promoting Christian Unity and the Disciples Ecumenical Consultative Council. This allowed a broadening of the international representation in both teams. The new Roman Catholic Co-chairman was the Most Revd Samuel Carter, SJ, Archbishop of Kingston, Jamaica. Archbishop Carter was an ecumenical pioneer in leading his Roman Catholic regional bishops' conference into full membership of the Caribbean Council of Churches, the first time that this had happened anywhere in the world. His gracious charm and wise leadership contributed greatly to the success of the second phase. The Disciples representation now included Great Britain and Jamaica, as well as Canada, Zaire and the U.S.A., and later included Australia. The Roman Catholic representation included England as well as Ireland, and Jamaica, in addition to Canada and the U.S.A. When Msgr John Mutiso-Mbinda succeeded Basil Meeking as the Vatican staff person in 1986, Kenya was represented as well.

There was also a greater turnover of membership in the dialogue team in the second phase. The most grievous loss was that of the Most Revd Kevin McNamara, who had moved from Killarney to become Archbishop of Dublin in 1984; he died in 1987 of cancer and the Commission lost someone of penetrating mind and absolute charity and integrity.[19] Dr. Efefe Elonda from Zaire also died prematurely in 1990. The insight he brought from Africa was always valuable, and he also reflected the significance of the francophone community. It should perhaps be noted that the Dialogue worked almost entirely in English. So long as Dr. Elonda was a member, some work was done in French, but after his death in 1990, the work was all in English. This facilitated communication and understanding among the members, which was undoubtedly advantageous in drafting; but it also meant that there was not always the same relentless drive towards unambiguous expression which is imposed by the need to ensure that what is said is readily translatable into several languages.

Cardinal Willebrands, speaking in Indianapolis in October 1982 at a meeting to celebrate the first five years of the Dialogue, saw its significance in the common concern for full communion in faith and sacrament; and in calling for a renewed commitment to ecumenism he commented that "the dialogue team was right to stress that only the Holy Spirit can confirm in us the will for visible unity, enabling us to overcome obstacles to grow towards it."[20] In the first Peter Ainslie Lecture in Baltimore a few days later, he returned to the same theme, noting that the dialogue was too little known outside North America. It reflected the need "to focus attention on being one, on the koinonia of faith and of life," because "from the start this dialogue has concerned itself with the visibility of the Church and its unity."[21] This illustrates Rome's hopes for the dialogue and probably explains why the second phase was made fully international.

The second phase occupied the next ten years. By the time its report was completed in 1992, under the title, *The Church as Communion in Christ*,[22] *koinonia* had become a much more prominent theme: indeed it was the main focus of the Fifth World Faith and Order Conference at Santiago da Compostella in Spain in 1993.[23]

The opening meeting in Venice in 1983 considered the significance of the term *koinonia* in the New Testament, and the nature of the Church of God. The 1984 meeting in Nashville was entirely taken up with the nature of *koinonia*, and the 1985 meeting in Mandeville, Jamaica considered the link between *koinonia* and sacrament, and the Church as sacramental community and as community of faith. At Cambridge, England in 1986 the meeting concentrated on the eucharist and the visibility of the Church's *koinonia*, and this was then used as the focus for a discussion of the continuity of the Church with apostolic tradition in 1987 at Duxbury, Massachusetts. That in turn led to a discussion of ministry and apostolic tradition in 1988 at Gethsemani, Kentucky; in the light of that, the topic of the Church and apostolic tradition was revisited at Venice in 1989. The meetings in Toronto, 1990 and Rome, 1991 were used for drafting the Report and it was formally agreed in St. Louis, Missouri in 1992. That meeting also considered the kind of program which might be envisaged for a third phase.[24]

The contribution of the dialogue was assessed by Fr Jean-Marie Tillard, OP, in the tenth Peter Ainslie lecture on Christian unity, given in Louisville in October 1991; it is interesting to compare it with Cardinal Willebrands' assessment ten years before. Tillard's lecture concentrated on the dialogue's contribution to the ecclesiology of the ecumenical movement. Once again emphasis was placed on the lack of any formal separation of Disciples from the Roman Catholic Church. Hence the dialogue was not "an encounter of former parts of the same ecclesiastical group wanting to be reunited, trying to forget the past mistakes, to discover either an explanation of their conflicts or to find the theological justification of their rupture."[25] Their search was for union, not reunion.

Thus in discovering what was common to each other, each had to recognize the action of the Holy Spirit at work in parallel groups without structural or even sacramental communion. Tillard found particular significance in the emphasis Disciples had placed on weekly communion from their origin, just at a time when in other Protestant traditions such an emphasis had virtually disappeared. But the common features discovered by the Commission in their two traditions were not to be regarded simply as "the surviving traces of the former unity the People of God enjoyed during the apostolic times;" rather they were "provocative signs of the Holy Spirit awaking the conscience of the divided communities, calling them to remember the will of Christ for the Church."[26]

Another discovery concerned the relationship between creeds or confessions of faith and the unity of the Church. Traditionally Disciples had rejected creeds as tests of fellowship; but the Commission's discussion had shown that such rejection did not mean rejecting of the necessity for confessing the faith—the emphasis on believer's baptism showed the importance attached to such personal confession. Rather, the Disciples rejection of creeds and confessions of faith was a rejection of the use to which such statements had been put, particularly in consolidating divisions within the Church. By laying such emphasis on regular participation in the eucharist as the demonstration of personal and communal faith, Disciples had approached the Catholic principle of *lex credendi, lex orandi* by a different route; and Tillard suggested that the Latin might be appropriately translated, "truth is always expressed in its liturgical sacramental celebration, especially at the Eucharist."[27] Finally, Tillard returned to an emphasis which had been made in the first report of the Dialogue: the need for "evangelical ecumenical space," a life of prayer and commitment to unity that transcended everything that theologians might achieve and was the condition for the effective reception of those agreements that had been reached.

Tillard's assessment anticipated some of the points which were to be made in the second report. The report had two main sections. The first dealt with the specific nature of the dialogue within the ecumenical movement, reviewing the differences in Christian faith and life between the two communions and sketching out a convergence of vision—to an extent recapitulating the first report. The second moved through five subsections. "New creation and communion" outlined the context of redemption in which communion was experienced. The theme of continuity was treated first in relation to the eucharist, and then in relation to teaching: in both cases the significance of the biblical usage of the word "memory" was highlighted. "Memory, as in biblical usage, is more that a recalling to mind of the past. It is the work of the Holy Spirit linking the past with the present and maintaining the memory of that on which everything depends—the faith itself and the Church which embodies that faith" (para 28).[28] A fourth subsection on "the gifts of the Spirit for the Church" linked the variety of charisms given to the Church and its members by the Spirit with the particular charism of the ordained ministry. The final subsection on "the Church" affirmed three important truths held in common: that a person is saved by being introduced into the communion of believers; that this communion is never given to the believer without the involvement of other believers, some of them being the ministers of the Church; and that this communion is ultimately with the apostolic community, whose memory is constantly kept alive and made present (para 46).[29]

The Commission recognised that they still had much work to do. Four topics were noted in particular: teaching and practice concerning the presence of the Lord in the celebration of the Supper, its sacrificial nature, and the roles of the ordained minister and the community; understanding of the fundamental structure of the Church gathered around the Eucharist, especially in relation to episcopacy; the nature of the rule of faith in a changing history; and the primacy of the Bishop of Rome. But the Commission believed that progress could be made if further work was authorized. Authorization was given and a third phase began in 1993.

The Report received a largely favorable review from Fr William Henn, OFM CAP, of the Pontifical Gregorian University. He drew attention to a number of points upon which clarification would be helpful, and made two general comments. First, he noted that the report demonstrated the value of using the idea of the Church as communion as the basis upon which to seek convergence on several ecclesiological issues. In particular it enabled the place of the Church in God's overall plan of salvation to be considered very positively and also made it possible for both Roman Catholics and Disciples "to acknowledge the language of sign, instrument and sacrament as appropriate categories for describing the Church," without eliminating the concern for continual renewal within the Church. The notion of communion also highlighted the deep connection between the Eucharist and the Church and the unity in faith reaching back to the apostolic community. Secondly, Fr Henn, while noting that the notion of a Catholic or Protestant ethos was less threatening in certain respects than the notion of different or conflicting beliefs, suggested that the relation between ethos and faith needed to be clarified. Acknowledging the emphasis the Report laid on the reception of agreements by the faithful, he suggested that this could lead to a softening of ethos and a coming together in a common mind, "a fact which both underscores the importance of the process of reception of the results of ecumenical dialogue and counsels patience to take the time necessary for growing together in faith."[30]

It is too early to comment on the work of the third phase. At its meeting in Rome in 1993 the Commission discussed the best way of setting the agenda for the next period. Of the four topics noted for further work in the report on the second phase, the third was picked out for attention: the nature of the rule of faith in a changing history. It was decided to pursue the question of the transmission of the faith in such a way that its significance for both the individual and the community was recognised. Thus in 1994 in Indianapolis, the topic was "the individual and the Church," in 1995 in Bose, Italy, it was "the Gospel and the Church" and in 1996 in Bethany, W. Virginia, it was "the content and authority of the early Ecumenical Councils."[31] In 1997 the topic is the nature of the canon. Whilst this might seem like a deliberate turning away from the hard questions of eucharist, episcopacy and Roman primacy, a careful handling of those questions depends upon an agreed basis for understanding the continuity of faith. This is particularly important where there is no common institutional history.

The Disciples/Roman Catholic Dialogue has a particular importance in the wider ecumenical scene. Dialogue is possible because both sides recognize in the other a common concern for the visible unity of the Church, and believe this to be expressed uniquely in the regular celebration of the eucharist. The fact of this mutual recognition of a common concern has opened up new perspectives on traditional issues such as the question of what happens in the eucharist, and the nature of the ministry of the one who presides at the Lord's table.

Both sides have also been forced to reflect on the nature of the continuity of the Church. Disciples have had to recognize that scripture alone is not sufficient: to be effective the good news declared in scripture has to come alive in each generation, indeed for each person. This requires living people to hand it on, which is the essence of tradition. Roman Catholics have had to recognize that ministerial continuity alone does not give a sufficient account of the many and various ways in which God's good news is passed on from generation to generation. The recognition that a common faith, despite diversity of expression, has been passed on in both communions has focussed attention once more upon the work of the Holy Spirit, not least the way in which Spirit always exceeds our expectations and transcends the limits to God's action which we often assume to exist. That in turn requires a rethinking of the justifications which are offered for the continuing disunity of the Church. Of course, as Fr Tillard never tires of reminding us, there is no "cheap ecumenism": we cannot simply say that things will now be different and forget the past. But neither can the past, simply because it is past, dictate the form of the future. What is required most of all is a change of heart, a *metanoia*—but that is something we have to receive by grace; it cannot be achieved by good resolutions. In a unique way, Paul Crow has seen the wider importance of this dialogue, carrying forward the vision first glimpsed by George Beazley; and his determination to keep it in the forefront of Disciples' ecumenical agenda has been rewarded in the agreements that have been reached.

Notes

[1] A. Campbell, *Christianity Restored: A connected view of the principles and rules by which the living oracles may be intelligibly and certainly interpreted: of the foundation on which all Christians may form one communion: and of the capital positions sustained in the attempt to restore the original gospel and order of things*, Bethany, Va. 1835, p. 3. The second edition, under the title *The Christian System* (1839), was more widely published.

[2] *A Debate on the Roman Catholic Religion between Alexander Campbell and the Rt Rev John B. Purcell*, Cincinnati 1852, pp. vii-viii. These included denial of apostolic succession, purgatory, indulgences, auricular confession, transubstantiation etc. and the suggestion that "the Roman Catholic

religion, if infallible and unsusceptible of reformation, as alleged, is essentially anti-American."

[3] Eva Jean Wrather, "A Nineteenth-Century Disciples-Catholic Dialogue," *Mid-Stream*, xxv, 4 (1986), pp 368-74.

[4] Wm. Jackson Jarman & Philip D. Norris, *An Adventure in Understanding*, U.S. Catholic Conference Publications Office, 1974, also reprinted in *Mid-Stream*, xii, 2-3-4 (1973), pp 5-15; cf. P.D. Morris, "Roman Catholic/ Disciple Dialogue, 1967-1973" in *New Catholic World*, July-August 1977.

[5] G. Beazley, "Catholic-Disciple Bilateral Conversations: an analysis of agreements and areas of difference," *Mid-Stream*, xi, 2-3-4 (1973), pp 192-3, 205. These two themes were echoed in the international report of 1992: see below. The papers presented at the Conversations were reprinted in *Mid-Stream*, vii, 2 (1967-68) and xi, 2-3-4 (1973).

[6] G. Beazley, "Editorial Introduction," *Mid-Stream*, vii, 2 (1967-68).

[7] "Joint Report of the Preparatory Meeting," *Mid-Stream*, xvi, 2 (1977), pp 242-4.

[8] B. Meeking, "To the Eye of Faith: Opening Meditation," *Mid-Stream*, xviii, 4 (1979), pp 343-4.

[9] The papers and agreed accounts of these meetings were published in *Mid-Stream* as follows: Indianapolis 1977 and Rome 1978: xviii, 4 (1979); Annapolis 1979 and New Orleans 1980: xx, 3 (1981).

[10] *Apostolicity and Catholicity*, Indianapolis 1982; reprinted in *Mid-Stream*, xxi, 4 (1982), pp 555-70. See also the valuable assessment of the Report by the Revd Dr. Robin Boyd, an ecumenical observer for the last meeting, which is also in *Mid-Stream*, xxi, 4 (1982), pp 571-7.

[11] Decree on Ecumenism, 8 in N. Tanner (ed), *Decrees of the Ecumenical Councils*, ii (London 1990), p. 913.

[12] J.M.R. Tillard, "Elements of Unity in recent Ecumenical Discussion: a Roman Catholic View," *Mid-Stream*, xviii, 4 (1979), p. 393.

[13] *Apostolicity and Catholicity*, pp 4-5.

[14] *Ibid*, p. 6.

[15] *Ibid*, pp 7-8.

[16] *Ibid*, p. 9.

[17] *Ibid*, p. 10.

[18] R. Boyd, "Disciples of Christ-Roman Catholic Dialogue: 5th Session in Ireland," *Mid-Stream*, xxi, 4 (1982), p. 577.

[19] See B. Meeking, "Homily in Memory of the Most Rev Kevin McNamara," *Mid-Stream*, xxvii, 4 (1988), pp 411-3.

[20] J. Willebrands, "The Significance of the Roman Catholic-Disciples of Christ International Dialogue," *Mid-Stream*, xxii, 1 (1983), pp 117-8.

[21] J. Willebrands, "Called to Unity and Wholeness," *Mid-Stream*, xxii, 1 (1983), p. 3.

[22] *The Church as Communion in Christ: Report of the Disciples of Christ/ Roman Catholic International Commission for Dialogue, 1983-1992*, Indianapolis 1994; also published in the *Information Service* of the Pontifical Council for Christian Unity, iii/iv 1993, pp 162-9.

[23] See T.F. Best & G. Gassmann, *On the way to Fuller Koinonia*, World Council of Churches, Geneva 1994.

[24] The papers and agreed accounts of the meetings of the second phases are contained in issues of *Mid-Stream* as follows: Venice 1983: xxiii, 4 (1984); Nashville 1984 and Mandeville 1985: xxv, 4 (1986); Cambridge 1986 and Duxbury 1987: xxvii, 4 (1988); Gethsemani 1988 and Venice 1989: xxix, 3 (1990).

[25] J.M.R. Tillard, 'The Contribution of the Disciples of Christ/Roman Catholic Dialogue to the Ecclesiology of the Ecumenical Movement', *Mid-Stream*, xxxi, 1 (1992), p. 16.

[26] *Ibid*, p. 18.

[27] *Ibid*, p. 22.

[28] *Church as Communion in Christ*, p. 10.

[29] *Ibid*, p. 17.

[30] W. Henn, :An evaluation of the 'Church as Communion in Christ'," *Information Service*, Pontifical Council for Promoting Christian Unity, iii/ iv (1993), pp 170-5 (quotations from pp 174 and 175).

[31] The reports and papers of these meetings may be found in *Mid-Stream* as follows: 1994 (Indianapolis): xxxiv, 1 (1995); 1995 (Bose) and 1996 (Bethany): xxxv, 4 (1996).

CHAPTER ELEVEN

THE ROMAN CATHOLIC CHURCH AND ECUMENISM

J. M. R. Tillard, O.P.

I t is usual to say that "the Roman Catholic church started to be involved in the ecumenical movement only after Vatican II." Recently, during an important meeting, John XXIII was praised as "the real father of Roman Catholic ecumenism" and Cardinal Bea was described as "the first Catholic official figure" in this field. Such affirmations are wrong. They manifest—especially when those who speak this way are Roman Catholic teachers—an unforgivable ignorance of the struggles of the Catholic church to be faithful to the Lord's supreme demand to the Father: that all of the disciples "may be one." Vatican II was not a beginning but a turning point in the Catholic ecumenical concern for the visible koinonia of all the Christian communities.

I-1 After the break between East and West—a break which started already during the struggles of Photius with Pope Nicholas—the Roman Catholic church *as such* never resigned itself to the inevitability of this rupture. It constantly tried to find a solution to overcome or at least repair it. Indeed it is true that because of its strong desire to preserve its own *exousia* (authority) and to guarantee its privileges of *potentior principalitas*,[1] and because of its affirmation that *ecclesia romana semper habuit primatus*,[2] its proposals always seemed so alien to the mind of the other churches that they were not "received." Moreover, the political complexity of the times made impossible a clear understanding of the goals of the unity for which people were looking. Nevertheless, even under the most intransigent declarations, it is generally possible to discover an authentic longing for the reconstitution of an authentic koinonia.

For instance, in the network of political, religious, and ecclesiastical reasons which led to the convocation of the councils of Lyon II and

Ferrare-Florence, we cannot deny that the reason for the Roman See's commitment to this enterprise was the genuine longing for unity. Gregory X (d. 1276) was certainly sincere when he laboured to make possible a union with the Eastern churches, whereas the Emperor Michael Paleologus was inspired by more political ambitions. One year before the convocation of the famous council of Basle (1431-1449), plans for a council which would gather representatives of Eastern and Western churches were accepted by Martin V. The dealings of Eugenius IV (d. 1447) with the delegates of Constantinople are well known, and no one can ignore how great was their impact on the decisions made there. In one of his letters to the arrogant Fathers of Basle, Eugenius affirms that union is the goal and that he is ready, for the sake of union, to yield even to their own arrangements.[3]

I-2 One of the most significant works manifesting the genuine intention of the Catholic church in this complex situation is certainly the treatise *Opus tripartitum*[4] which Humbert of Romans (d. 1277) wrote at the invitation of Gregory X in preparation of the Council of Union (the 2nd Council of Lyon), in the preparation of which Thomas Aquinas was also asked to collaborate. Humbert, who had been the Master of the Dominican Order, stresses the huge responsibility of the Western part of the church in the slow evolution towards the schism of East and West. He also shows how, mainly because of its ignorance of foreign languages, the Catholic church, and especially the Roman Curia, was unprepared really to understand the mentality and anxieties of the Greek church. Unity will always be fragile if it is based on many misunderstandings, since these lead to false judgments and wrong criticisms. The Bishop of Rome himself has had to take the initiative of offering the Eastern bishops "the right hand of koinonia" as Peter, together with James and John, did for Paul and Barnabas. Moreover he has to offer them the help of the Western church whenever they need it. If necessary he has even to go to Greece to encounter, in their own church, the Christians of the East with their bishops.[5] Unity is a necessity: the Roman See, Humbert says, cannot cease working for it.

Barlaam (d. 1348) was not the "bad theologian" some Orthodox writers depicted.[6] When, after joining the Roman church, he was sent to Constantinople to discuss plans "of reunification," he was not speaking in his own name. The Bishop of Rome wanted the reunion of East and West, *not only* for political reasons and *not only* for the consolidation of his own power. The separation of East from Wast was, for the Church of God, a tragedy he wanted to repair. The more we know the complicated history of this period, the more it becomes evident that many of our judgments need to be modified. One can no longer write, without nuances, that "the Holy See had put aside any authentic love for the other part of the Church," or that "the Roman Pontiff considered that real cooperation with the Orthodox church was no longer part of his mission," or that "only political motivations led the Roman church to seek communion with the Byzantine leaders." On the contrary, the majority of those who considered themselves as legitimate *vicars of Peter*,[7] occupying his apostolic *cathedra*, never forgot that their obedience to the Will of Christ, *ut unum sint*, was part of their apostolic mandate.

I-3 In his book *De Ecclesiae occidentalis atque orientalis perpetua consensione, libri tres*,[8] Leo *Allatius* (1587-1669) explained beautifully why a fundamental consensus on faith and sacramental life continues to keep East and West in unity. He made clear that, in spite of the official excommunications, a large practice of sacramental sharing never ceased to exist at the popular level. Even after the failure of Florence, in the mind of a great number of Catholic theologians, bishops, leaders and lay people, the Orthodox churches continued to be regarded as real churches.[9] To be sure, these positive views were quite often marked by the "superiority complex" of the Latin church, and by a wrong understanding of the authentic *exousia* of the Patriarchs. The history of the first centuries was not always rightly interpreted, and the authority of the bishop of Rome was for many theological circles so absolute that no room was left for real "fraternal" relations. Nevertheless, when Pope Pius IX invited the Orthodox church to take part at Vatican I, an invitation strongly refused, [10] it was presumably "not simply to submit." In spite of the tone of his letter, he expected more. The constant declaration by Leo XIII of his love for the Eastern traditions, and his will to give them the place and role they deserve in the life of Christianity as a whole, was not a "game," even if it reinforced so-called "uniatism." There is an essential link which runs from his encyclicals to the crucially important presence of Orthodox observers at Vatican II and their warm reception by John XXIII and Paul VI. Even when relations were at their worst,[11] the Roman Catholic church remained sure that Christ was asking to offer the Orthodox churches the right hand of koinonia. It would be illuminating to *quote* the encyclical letter *Praeclara gratulationis* of Leo XIII (20 June, 1891).

II-1 it is evident that the attitude of the Roman Catholic church could not be the same towards the Western Churches which had broken *communion* at the time of the Reformation. They were "part of its own flesh" and their departure took them out of the Catholic church's life, mission, and internal love. Quite often this resulted in hostility, hard confrontations, and mutual condemnations. Nevertheless, already at the beginning of this sad history, important Catholic persons tried to understand the problems at stake and to make re-union possible.

Probably the best-known of these "apostles of Christian unity" is Gasparo Contarini (d. 1542), whose name is associated with the famous *consilium de emendanda Ecclesia*, convened in order to prepare the Council of Trent. In 1541 he was sent to Regensburg as papal delegate. He felt it was right to declare that the Lutheran article on justification, as amended after the discussion, was fully consonant with Catholic faith. An agreement on this issue—the most controversial— was possible.[12] In France, Du Pin and Girardin, two theologians of the Sorbonne, discussed in a very rich correspondence[13] with William Wake, Archbishop of Canterbury (from 1716), the conditions for a reunion of Anglican and Gallican churches. Was this unity a mere dream? Did not Bossuet and *L'Assemblée du clergé* warmly the approve the work of George Bull? In English Catholicism, a quite interesting reaction against the too-rigid views of the Counter-Reformation created a climate of Catholic irenism.[14] During the following century people like Ambrose Phillipps de Lisle (who from 1825 was Roman Catholic[15]), James Warren Doyle (1786-1826), the Irish bishop of Kildare and Leighlin,[16] John England (1786-1842), bishop of Charleston in the United States of America, Désiré Mercier (1851-1926), Fernand Portal (1855-1926), and Paul Couturier (1881-1953) constantly put the concern for Christian unity in the front rank of their pastoral duties.

Thanks to the long and well-informed exchange of letters between Bossuet (1627-1704) and the philosopher Leibnitz (1646-1716) we know that not only were eminent thinkers deeply involved in this search for the restoration of communion, but the Holy See itself was working in this direction. In his long preface to the publication of the Bossuet-Leibnitz correspondence, Louis Alexandre Foucher de Careil recalls the efforts of Popes Clement IX and Innocent XI, asking the collaboration of some cardinals (Spinola, Spada, Cibo, Albritii), and of Dominicans or Jesuit theologians.[17]

II-2 Therefore the encyclical letter *Mortalium animos* of Pius XI (which is quite negative in its estimation of the ecumenical movement), the refusal by the Holy Office of Catholic collaboration with other denominations, and the cold reception accorded to the founders of the *Faith and Order movement,* cannot be considered as the only signs of Roman Catholic attitude about this matter before Vatican II.[18] The situation is more balanced. The Catholic hierarchy, the theologians, and some lay people were, on no rare occasions, passionate defenders of the unity which God wills. In 1949 the Holy Office writes:

> The Catholic Church takes no part in "Ecumenical" conferences or meetings. But, as may be seen from many papal documents, she has never ceased, nor ever will, from following with deepest interest and furthering with fervent prayer every attempt to attain that end which Christ our Lord had so much at heart, namely, that all who believe in Him "may become perfectly one" (*Jn 17.23*) . . . The present time has witnessed in different parts of the world a growing desire amongst many persons outside the Church for the reunion of all who believe in Christ. This may be attributed, under the inspiration of the Holy Spirit, to external factors and the changing attitude of men's minds, but above all to the united prayers of the faithful. To all children of the true Church this is a cause for holy joy in the Lord; it urges them to extend a helping hand to all those sincerely seeking after the truth by praying fervently that God may enlighten them and give them strength . . .

So the Catholic church has never ceased to consider the restoration of Christian unity as one of its main tasks. The difficulty was the way in which it understood the unity for which it was looking. For its lay people, theologians (even Humbert of Romans), bishops (even Bossuet), legates (even Contarini), Popes (John XXIII at the beginning of Vatican II will be the last one to use this language), the re-unification of the

Church was seen mainly as the return of the "dissidents" to where they had been "before their departure." But then they were in what Catholic documents called "the only one house of God, the Catholic church" itself. In this church, indeed under the supreme authority of Christ and his divine Father, the Bishop of Rome was said to act as the "ministerial" *pater familias*. Even if this church had, especially since the Council of Trent, recognized the need for a deep "renovation" and the necessity of a fresh re-thinking of its exercise of authority, it nevertheless continued to affirm that outside its frontiers the real Church of God was not present.

> The union of Christians cannot be fostered otherwise than by promoting the return of the dissidents to the one true Church of Christ, which in the past they so unfortunately abandoned; return, we say to the one true Church of Christ which is plainly visible to all and which by the will of her Founder forever remains what He Himself destined her to be for the common salvation of men. For the mystical Spouse of Christ has in the course of the centuries remained unspotted, nor can it ever be contaminated, and no one remains in it, unless he acknowledges and accepts with obedience the authority and power of Peter and his legitimate successors . . . Therefore, to this apostolic See, founded in the City which Peter and Paul, the Princes of the apostles, consecrated with their blood, to this See which is the "root and matrix of the Catholic Church," may our dissident sons return; let them do so, not with the thought and hope that "the Church of the living God, the pillar and ground of the truth," will sacrifice the integrity of the faith, but, on the contrary, with the intention of submitting to her authority and government . . . [19]

Consequently—given this point of view—the *ecumenical endeavour* of the Catholic church has consisted firstly in opening its arms and its heart to other Christians, with mercifulness and full generosity, and secondly in reforming itself in such a way that these "returning" Christians will find themselves at ease within its institutions and its style of evangelical life.

II-3 It is important to understand the difference in the way in which the Catholic Church looked at the separated Eastern Churches. Western communities which broke the *communion* with Rome were not considered to be sister Churches angry with their "elder sisters," but daughters leaving the home of their mother. They were compared with the Prodigal Son, repudiating the family and wasting the inheritance of centuries of faithful koinonia within the Tradition of the Church of God. This is why the only solution for them was to *return* to the "House of God" which they had left, to the father whom they had outraged by their departure but who was still waiting for them. The 19th century became the theatre of new agressive expressions, oppositions, and divisions between the groups and Catholics. This happened not only due to the definitions of Vatican I but also because of the missionary expansion of all the Western churches, an expansion which was the source of difficult conflicts. Nevertheless Leo XIII and John XXIII never ceased to proclaim: "Your common father is still waiting for you. Please . . . come back."

It is very significant that whilst the general councils of Latran, Lyon, Florence (dealing with the Eastern churches) were dreaming of a corporate "return" to koinonia, the official Catholic documents alluding to Protestant Christianity were, generally, looking for individual conversions. For the official Catholic mind, the communities of the Protestant *ethos* went so far in refusing essential elements of the Tradition that it was illusory to hope for a corporate return. Only with the Anglican church it might perhaps be possible to establish some links, since it had preserved the Catholic structure of the church. Nevertheless, even in this case the official Roman position was for the return to the Holy See by individual conversions. The reactions provoked by the Malines conversations (1921-1926) made that quite clear.[20]

III-1 The turning point in this history of Catholic ecumenism is certainly the pontificate of Leo XIII. Indeed, Leo continues to share the official Catholic position: unity means return to the See of Rome. For him this unity is so radical a necessity that all the local churches have to be involved in the search for it, and Holy See itself needs to take initiatives to "promote" this most necessary task. But something is changing. He first considers all the other churches with sympathy, discovering the gifts and beauty of their traditions; he stresses the crucial distinction between the attitude of those who, in the past, broke relations with Rome and the sincerity of Christians who, here and now, do their best to be faithful to Christ within their own communities, separated from Rome as they may be. Moreover Leo XIII does not think only in terms of individual conversions. Indeed, like the father of the Prodigal Son, he is still waiting, with his heart full of compassion. But what he expects is not only the "return" of individuals; he desires, above all, the coming back of confessional families *as such*, and in such a way that they keep all their gifts, their richness. This is a great change.

III-2 After the cold winds of the Pontificate of Pius X (1903-1914), the Pontificate of Benedict XV (1914-1922) coincides with the famous Anglican Lambeth Call (or Appeal) for Unity (1920). Benedict XV, aware of the ecumenical problems and faithful to the policy of Leo XIII, is not insensitive to this appeal. Through the influence of the Cardinal of Malines, Mercier, he looks with sympathy at the re-opening of the discussions between Anglicans and Roman Catholics (in 1921).

However his successor Pius XI (1922-1939), reacting strangely to the challenges of the various ecumenical activities, published the disappointing encyclical letter *Mortalium animos* (1928). This document seems to identify the ecumenical movement—then in full blossom through the conferences in Edinburgh (on missions, 1910), Stockholm (1925), Lausanne (Faith and Order, 1927)—with a kind of Protestant indifferentism, which proposed a false vision of the Church. The document concludes that it is, therefore, impossible for Roman Catholics to share this conception of unity, and even to take part in the activities of the so-called "ecumenical movement." The only way to realize the will of Christ (*"ut unum sint"*) is to enable the "return" of all the "dissidents" to the Roman See. Discussion with other Christians is useless, even dangerous. The Roman Catholic Church has its own way of working for unity: namely, conversion *to* Rome. After the creative initiatives of Leo XIII . . . we have returned to past centuries.

This letter surprised those within the Catholic Church who were involved in ecumenical discussions and reflexion. For at the beginning of his Pontificate Pius XI had, by his positive and constructive attitude, made possible a handful of initiatives whose consequences on the Roman Catholic mind would prove to be enormous. In fact they proved to be the seed or source of important declarations and decisions of the Second Vatican Council. But these initiatives were taken neither by the Holy See, nor by the local bishop. They all came from what is described today as the "grassroots." It is crucial ecclesiologically to stress this short remark. The *sensus fidelium* has been the main agent of the Holy Spirit for the move of the Catholic church towards a more authentic ecumenism. In this process the *episkopé* of the hierarchy has been more permissive than creative.

One of the most important amongst the promoters of a new spirit in local communities was certainly Father Paul Couturier (1881-1953), a French priest from Lyon. He is probably the father of what is now called *spiritual ecumenism*. His name must be remembered. But in the theological field, Paul Couturier was not the first. Theologians of great stature had already, in spite of suspicions levyed against them, played a crucial role in this opening of the doors. After the declarations of Vatican I, and in the turmoils of the modernist crisis, many outstanding scholars in the fields of church history, Patristic theology, Biblical literature, and liturgical sources explored the Tradition and studied the causes of the great divisions. Moreover they did not work in isolation, but in a genuine trans-confessional scholarship. Thus in addition to the experience of prayer, the field of theological research became a place for an authentic ecumenical sharing. The insights of Leo XIII were not forgotten. A broader ecumenical spirit now enabled them—through a process of osmosis, as it were—to be more widely absorbed.

It is thus clear that what was to be the cradle of a new Roman Catholic ecumenism was woven from serious and concerted threads. Furthermore these threads, as well as those which gave birth to the liturgical renewal, were woven into the *sensus fidelium* of the people of God.

III-3 In this cradle a Catholic ecumenical *ethos* will take form. In the Catholic theological faculties a movement of sympathy, of strong interest in what is at work in the other churches will grow. The names are well known. They will be at the root of the declarations of Vatican II. The World War of 1939-1945 will have a strange ecumenical influence—for it will make possible interconfessional encounters and interconfessional friendships, principally in the rude solidarity of prisons, military groups, "movements of resistance," concentration camps. After the war, this kind of solidarity will meet with the theological efforts I have just described. The confluence of these two streams, together with the impact of the newly-constituted *World Council of Churches* (founded in Amsterdam in 1948), the influence of eminent ecumenical personalities, the persistent attraction exercised by Anglicanism on persons like Montini, the presence of some important Orthodox theological centers in the Orthodox diaspora—all this will create in the Catholic Church a new spirit, a new way to look at "the others": they are not the enemies of Christ! They are not working against the Church! They are not false Christians! What they keep saying about the Roman Catholic church is not necessarily wrong! And theologians will confirm many of these views by serious and objective researches. Thus, in 1950, Father Yves Congar will publish *Vraie ou Fausse Réforme dans l'Église*—truly a prophetic book!

Pius XII, Bishop of Rome from 1939, did not agree with the invitation in 1948 to make the Roman Catholic church a member of the *World Council of Churches*. Nevertheless in 1950 the important *Instructio* of the Holy Office which I have already quoted recognized, for the first time, in the ecumenical movement a fruit of the action of the Holy Spirit—even if it continued to affirm that an authentic unity requires the "return" of the dissidents to the Holy See. It agreed that Roman Catholics may take part in joint meetings with other Christians, provided questions concerning Christian dogmas are not discussed. Indeed the encyclical *Mystici corporis* of the same Bishop of Rome continued to identify the whole church of God with the Roman Catholic Church.

However its main development was a significant step forward in Catholic ecclesiology, even if another encyclical letter, *Humani generis*, repeated some of the traditional negative views. The word "ecumenism" was avoided because it was not considered as a theologically-valid notion. Unity meant return to "the Church," that is, the Roman Catholic church (although other churches deserve consideration). At the end of this pontificate the theological vision and position of the Roman See was thus unclear. Theologians diffusing strong opinions about the necessity of a "new look" on the ecumenical endeavour of the Catholic church were silenced. Nevertheless windows were opened, and the fresh air of a new ecumenism was, slowly, entering. For instance, since the foundation of the World Council of Churches some groups were working—without any official repudiation of the Vatican's policy—to maintain a permanent and active relationship with this organization. In Holland, a priest called John Willebrands (a friend of Visser 't Hooft, who was a chief architect of the World Council of Churches and its first general secretary) was creating the *International Catholic Conference on Ecumenical Affairs*. Many theologians were attracted by this Conference, and the activities of the World Council were seriously discussed, and quite often praised, in theological circles.

IV-1 John XXIII, elected Bishop of Rome in 1958, continued to repeat the warm invitation addressed since Leo XIII to the other churches: "Come to Rome, we are ready to receive you with love and to give you the place you deserve, without any rancour!" When in 1959, at the end of the Week of Prayer for Christian Unity, he revealed his intention to gather a general council, and when in 1961, at Christmas, he officially convoked the Second Vatican Council, the question of the unity of the Church was explicitly among his first goals. Furthermore in 1960, one year before this official convocation, he had created, in order to prepare the Council, a *Secretariat for Christian Unity*. Its activities were to be—now at the supreme official level—nearly those of the *International Catholic Conference on Ecumenical Affairs* created by John Willebrands many years earlier. Yet John Willebrands was chosen as the Secretary of the *Secretariat for Christian Unity*, of which the President was Father Augustin Bea (a Jesuit and a friend of Pius XII). From now on, Roman Catholic ecumenism will leave its cradle. It will walk steadily, and in a friendly way, on all the main ecumenical roads, and with the strong support of the Roman See.

Probably the most important decision of Bea, Willebrands and the first members of the Secretariat for Christian Unity was the invitation of non-Catholic theologians and pastors as observers at the four official sessions of the Second Vatican Council (1962-1965). These observers were not passive guests. Moreover they were treated by the Secretariat as real brothers. They were consulted. Sometimes they were asked to criticize the first drafts of the documents. They were invited to speak to the bishops. It is evident that they contributed to the understanding and discussion of the main questions which were subjected to close scrutiny. Without this group—which they slowly learned to trust—some bishops would have been afraid to accept, for instance, many affirmations of the *Decree on Ecumenism,* one of the most decisive documents of the Second Vatican Council. I remember how on a cold December morning, before an important vote, I asked Nikos Nissiotis to explain to a group of hesitant Canadian bishops the Orthodox theology of the *epiclesis.*

IV-2 Ecumenical challenge and even ecumenical infiltration can be detected in all the main documents produced by the Council. This is true not only for the Decree on Ecumenism. The main dogmatic constitutions are certainly actualizing, in many of the statements, the consciousness of the action of the Holy Spirit outside the visible borders of the Catholic church. During the discussions of the central declarations of *Lumen Gentium* concerning the *"subsistit in"* of the Church of God in the Roman Catholic church, the ecumenical argument played an important role. It is also clear that the conclusions on Scripture, Tradition and traditions of the *Fourth World Conference on Faith and Order* (Montreal, 1963) were present in the minds of those who discussed the document on Revelation.

Speaking of my own experience, I may affirm that the Decree on Religious Life was influenced by the study of Eastern monasticism and an open discussion with some Reformed religious communities. One may say that Vatican II "received" many of the wishes of the Eastern churches (the *epiclesis,* the meaning of *episkopé*) and of the Reformed churches (the use of the vernacular, "communion in both kinds" . . .). This "reception" was highly significant ecclesiologically: the Roman Catholic church was now living, like other churches, within the new ecumenical age. This is why Vatican II was followed by important decisions concerning collaboration between the Roman Catholic church and the World Council of Churches, leading to the Joint Working Group between the two, to partnership in *Faith and Order,* to the presence of individuals in some departments of the World Council. During the final session of the Council, Paul VI and the Ecumenical Patriarch Athenagoras restored officially the official mutual love of their two sister churches, and initiated a common path towards full sacramental unity. This was the first official "actualization" of the Council. And this is a sign . . .

No one will deny that, since Vatican II, the Roman Catholic church remains deeply involved in the ecumenical task. The encyclical letter of

John Paul II, *Ut Unum Sint*, is a solemn and explicit reaffirmation of the Catholic ecumenical concern. This concern is grounded in the "recognition" of the action of the Holy Spirit in all the communities of baptized believers. It is because of this "recognition" that, through the voice of the Bishop of Rome himself in this encyclical letter, the Roman Catholic church invites the other traditions to study honestly, and to discuss with the Roman Catholic church, the divisive issues in order to *find together* the authentic way of resolving them. Why? Because at this point of its conversion to an ecumenism very different to that described earlier in this paper—the ecumenism of "return"—it understands that it needs not only to "consult" others but also to work *with them*, even when such specific elements as the Roman primacy are at stake. It not only wants to hear other churches, but to "receive" from them. For this purpose it needs to discuss their own views, not in an apologetic manner, but in an authentic "frankness." The goal of this process is to find, through the *sensus fidei* of all the Christian traditions, the will of Christ.

The ecclesiological turning point

I-1 It is crucial to state that the turning point in this long and complex Catholic evolution is not at all a mere product of ecclesiastical politics. The resistances, hesitations, and steps backwards of the Roman See show also that it is not the fruit of a capitulation before pressures coming from outside. The more one thinks about this cautious attitude of Rome, the more it becomes clear how it is the guarantee that the new official actualization of the Roman Catholic obedience to the *ut sint unum* of Christ is the result of a renewed way of looking at the reality of the Church of God.

The first and probably the most essential ecclesiological perception commanding the new Roman Catholic understanding of the ecumenical task is the experience of the action of the Holy Spirit in communities which broke their with the See of Rome. The discovery that a real holy life, sometimes leading to martyrdom, was existing outside the canonical borders of the Catholic church, the awareness that the teaching of the Gospel was faithfully kept in communities not in communion with the Roman *magisterium*, the experience that the activities of ministers in many of these groups were in harmony with what the Catholic tradition sees as the task of the *episcopé*—all this obliged Catholic theologians to recognize that there the Holy Spirit was at work. The field of the Spirit's genuinely Christian efficacity was, juridically speaking, broader than the totality of Catholic local churches. Moreover in these Catholic local churches the Spirit's action was sometimes less warmly "received" than in many non-Catholic assemblies. This was true not only of the Orthodox liturgies and spirituality which the Catholics had never ceased to admire, even before the letters of Leo XIII, but also of some Protestant churches. For instance, the fashion in which the Word of God had been kept and proclaimed in Lutheran churches was challenging the way the Bible was neglected in many Catholic circles, and the manner in which the Holy Scriptures were read and explained in not a few Catholic celebrations. And the tone of the Anglican association of lay persons in the discussion of the central affairs of the church inspired Catholic theologians and church-leaders who were struggling with the clericalism which was too much at home in Catholic practise.

I-2 Many Roman Catholic thinkers were also discovering—especially through the great voices of the ecumenical movement—how much an authentic love for the Church of God was inspiring, also outside the Catholic church, the search for the unity of the people of God. Thus the Church of God was really the "house" of these Christians, even if it was possible to discern in their teaching some points not entirely in tune with the Catholic doctrine. For many theologians it became impossible to deal with the relation of the Holy Spirit to the Body of Christ without including the reality of this dedication by "other" Christians to the visible unity of the Church.

Moreover, re-reading the history of the last centuries with non-polemical eyes, it appeared that amongst the reactions of the Reformers which led to schisms were some which were, *perhaps*, a warning. God wanted—*perhaps*—to awaken, to alert, the Catholic leaders to the situation of Christian faith and practice in their local churches.

II-1 What was the basis of this faithfulness of communities outside the canonical frontiers of the (Roman) Catholic community? It was not only their good will, their good intention, or (as some writers thought) their desire to repair the damage done in the past. This faithfulness and loyalty to Christ had a sacramental foundation: their baptism.[21] The Augustinian theology, contrasting with the rigid views of

Cyprian, helped to grasp the difficult but crucial issues of the consequences of baptism. By a "valid" baptism—celebrated in the name of the Trinity—a community whose faith in the Trinity is the right faith accepts the salvation which God offers. Since God is faithful to his promise, this community is inserted in the Body of Christ. It may err. It may break communion with other Christian groups. It may be gravely unfaithful to the *martyria* and mission of the Church. Nevertheless the baptismal "character" of all its members keeps them and their whole internal solidarity in what Irenaeus calls the two hands of the Father: the Son and the Spirit. And these two hands are the hands of God's faithfulness. This is why in all the baptised communities there is always a work of divine grace, always a fruit of koinonia with God.

II-2 Hence the relation of the Catholic Church with these other churches remains, because of this fundamental baptismal relation with God, a relation of koinonia. It is, indeed, an imperfect *communion*, not only because the fraternal relations are broken but because quite often important truths are not understood and lived out the same way. But nevertheless it is not only a communion based on friendship, on good human relations. It is a communion which is *genuinely grounded* in the baptismal grace God himself offers to all. Moreover, this communion is communion in the one and indivisible Christ Jesus. In the Body of the Risen Lord, in spite of their division on the understanding of basic points of faith and in spite of their lack of fraternal love, all the Christian communities nevertheless remain bound together by the power of the Spirit, and thus united *en Christô*. These *en Christô* communities are not, therefore, only a collection of loose *vestigia* remaining "after the wreckage." In them the Spirit of God is at work.

III-1 It is this ecclesiological awareness of "the Church outside the canonical limits" which changed the ecumenical orientation of the bishops during the discussions of Vatican II. Even the warm and moving invitations of John XXIII were no longer in tune with this new understanding of the *locus Ecclesiae*. One of the best results of Vatican II is that the Catholic church is now in the midst of a new ecumenical dynamism. It is no longer working for the return of "the prodigal communities" to the family home where the "common father" (the Bishop of Rome) is waiting for them, happy to offer them "the place they desire and deserve." With all the other churches, it now works to make the fulness of the Church of God (with all the essential elements necessary for the full blossoming of an authentic visible koinonia) present in the whole *locus Ecclesiae.*

III-2 It is important to conclude this rapid study by an observation that will probably seem strange for some Catholic readers. Reading again the main theological studies which inspired this crucial ecumenical shift within the Catholic communities one becomes sure that it is, in great part, a fruit of the ecumenical initiatives taken outside the borders of the (Roman) Catholic church. The famous Anglican Lambeth call of 1920, the constituting of the movement on *Faith and Order* (even if Benedict XV received politely, but without any enthusiasm, the delegates who in 1919 desired the collaboration of the Catholic church,[22]) the Malines Conversations of 1921-1926[23] with the famous "united, not absorbed" of Dom Lambert Beauduin,[24] the growth of the *Life and Work* movement, the formation of *The World Council of Churches*,[25] the persistence of the ecumenical leaders in appealing for Catholic participation—all this challenged the classical, official position of the Roman See. It became clear that this ecumenical movement was not foreign to the work of the Holy Spirit who, like the wind, "blows wherever it pleases." Vatican II declared:

> the Lord of the Ages wisely and patiently follows out the plan of his grace on behalf of us sinners. In recent times he has begun to bestow more generously upon divided Christians remorse over their divisions and a longing for unity. Everywhere, large numbers have felt the impulse of this grace, and among our separated bretheren also *there increases from day to day a movement*, fostered by the grace of the Holy Spirit, *for the restoration of unity among all Christians.* Taking part in this movement, which is called ecumenical, are those who invoke the Triune God and confess Jesus as Lord and Saviour. They join in not merely as individuals but also as members of the corporate groups in which they have heard the Gospel, and which each regards as his Church and, indeed, God's. And yet almost everyone, though in different ways, *longs that there may be one visible Church of God*, a Church truly universal and sent forth to the whole world that the world may be converted to the Gospel and so be saved, to the glory of God.[26]

Jean-Paul II will comment:

> The Catholic Church embraces with hope the commitment to
> ecumenism as a duty of the Christian conscience enlightened
> by faith and guided by love. Here too we can apply the words of
> Saint Paul to the first Christians of Rome: "God's love has been
> poured into our hearts through the Holy Spirit"; thus our "hope
> does not disappoint us" (Romans 5:5). This is the hope of Chris-
> tian unity, which has its divine source in the Trinitarian unity of
> the Father, the Son and the Holy Spirit.[27]

Notes

[1] The expression comes from Irenaeus, *Adv. Haer.*, III, 3, 1-3 ("it is with
this church, on account of its more powerful origin—*propter potentiorem
principalitatem*—that it is necessary that every church should agree, that it,
the faithful from all sides").

[2] According to the Latin translation of the 6th Canon of Nicea. See H.
Chadwick, "Faith and Order at the Council of Nicea, a Note on the
Background of the Sixth Canon," *Harvard Theological Review*, 53, 1960,
180-189. This version will be used at Chalcedon by the legate of the
Roman See.

[3] *Epistolae Pontificiae ad Concilium Florentinum spectantes*, ed. G.
Hoffmann, in *Concilium Florentinum*, Rome, 1940-1946, No. 45.

[4] See MANSI, XXIV, 125B-132D: P. Crabbe, *Secundus Tomus Conciliorum
omnium*, Cologne, 1551, 967-1003 (N.B.: MANSI does not give the whole
text); K. Michel, *Das opus tripartitum des Humbertus de Romanis*, Graz,
1926; R. Browne, *Appendix ad fasciculum rerum expetendarum et
fugiendarum*, London, 1690, 185-220 (Anglican).

[5] On Humbert see A. Mortier, *Histoire des Maîtres généraux de l'Ordre des
Frères Prêcheurs*, T.I., Paris, 1903, 415-664; M. H. Vicaire, "Humbert de
Romans," *Dictde Spir.*, VII/1, 1969, 1108-1116; A. Duval, "Humbert de
Romans," in *Catholocisme*, V, 1959, 1093-1096; H. J. Omez, "À propos de
l'unité chrétienne de l'Orient et de l'Occident. Un opuscule du Bx
Humbert de Romans," in *Vie intellectuelle*, 1, 1929, 196-211; M. J. Le

Guillou, *Mission et Unité*, T. 2, coll. *Unam Sanctum* 34, Paris, 1960, 55-58, and "Une voix de l'Occident, Humbert de Romans," in *Découverte de l'oecuménisme*, 34-338; E. Soueges, *Année dominicaine ou les vies des saints de l'Order des Frères Prêcheurs*, T. VII, Amiens, 1893, 519-590.

[6] On Barlaam see M. Viller, "La question de l'union des Églises entre Grecs et Latins depuis le concile de Lyon jusqu'à celui de Florence (1247-1438)," in *Revue d'Histoire Ecclésiastique*, 17, 1921, 260-305, 515-532; 18, 1922, 20-60 (esp. 18, 1922, 21-35); Ciro Giannelli, "Un Progetto di Barlaam Calabro per l'Unione delle Chiese," in *Miscellanea Giovanni Mercati*, T.3, coll. *Studi e Testi*, 123, Rome, Vaticano, 1946, 157-208; M. Jugie, art. "Barlaam de Seminara, théologien et savant du XIVe siècle," in *Dictionnaire d'Histoire et de Géographie Ecclésiastiques*, T. IV, 817-834; Jean Meyendorff, "Un mauvais théologien de l'Unité au XIVe siècle: Barlaam le Calabrais," in *1054-1954 L'Église et les Églises*, T. II, Chevetogne, 1955, 47-64; J. Bois, "Les débuts de la controverse hésychaste," in *Les Echos d'Orient*, 5, 1902, 353-362. The works of Barlaam are in *PG*, 151; see also *Ibid.*, 1247-1256.

[7] The expression *Vicarius Petri* is, until Innocent III (1198-1216), the traditional way to designate the Bishop of Rome. He is not yet called *Vicarius Christi* in an exclusive way. This title was used for all bishops, and even for kings.

[8] Read L. Bréhier, "Allatius," in *DHGE*, T.2, 479-484; L Petit, "Allatius," in *DACL*, T.1, 1220-1226.

[9] See Yves Congar, *Neuf cents ans après, Notes sur le schisme oriental*, coll. *Irenikon*, Chevetogne, 1954, 5-8; A. Battandier, *Le Cardinal J. B. Pitra*, Paris, 1893, 374-377, 435-438; see also in *Irenikon*, 1, 1926, 181-182; 7, 1930, 270, 13, 1936, 561.

[10] See MANSI, XL, 377-418. See also Wanoff Trimadtzaty, *L'Église russe*, Paris, 1978.

[11] As it happened after the Crusades.

[12] See William P. Anderson, "Gasparo Contarini: Sixteenth Century Ecumenist," in *Ecumenical Trends*, October, 1984, pp. 140-142.

[13] The correspondence has been published by J. Grès-Gayer, *Paris-Cantorbéry (1717-1720). Le dossier d'un premier oecuménism*, coll. Textes, dossiers, documents 13, Paris, 1989.

[14] See J. B. Dockery, *Christopher Davenport, Friar and Diplomat*, London, 1960. For the context see Thomas H. Clancy, "Ecumenism and Irenics in

17th Century English Catholic Apologetics," in *Theological Studies*, 58, 1997, 85-89.

[15] See E. S. Purcell, *Life and Letters of Ambrose Phillipps de Lisle*, 2 vol., London, 1900.

[16] See G. Tavard, *Petite histoire de l'oecuménisme*, Paris, 1960, p. 54.

[17] Leibnitz, *Oeuvres publiées pour la première fois d'après les manuscrits originaux avec notes et introductions par Louis Alexandre Foucher de Careil*, 2ᵉ ed., Paris, 1867 (repr. 1969, OLMS, Hildesheim), T-I, Préface, XVIII-XXII.

[18] See the beautiful book of E. Fouilloux, *Les catholiques et l'unité chrétienne du XIXe au XXe siècle: itinéraires européens d'expression française*, Paris, 1982.

[19] Pius XI, *Mortalium animos.*

[20] English Catholics were refusing the Malines conversations because of the reduced number of personal conversions. See J. A. Dick, *The Malines Conversations Revisited*, Leuven, 1989, pp. 45, 91, 107, 145, 149.

[21] See J. M. R. Tillard, "Conversion, oecuménisme," in *Cristianesimo nella storia. Saggi in onore di Giuseppe Alberigo*, Bologna, 1996, 517-536.

[22] See O. Rousseau, "Le grand voyage oecuménique des fondateurs de Foi et Constitution," in *Irenikon*, 43, 1970, 325-361 (340-341).

[23] See J. A. Dick, *The Malines Conversations Revisited, op. Cit.*

[24] See *Ibid.*, 217-225.

[25] See W. A. Visser 't Hooft, *The Genesis and Formation of the World Council of Churches*, Geneva, World Council of Churches, 1982.

[26] *Unitatis redintegratio*, 1.

[27] *Ut unum sint*, 8.

CHAPTER TWELVE

CAN ONE BE UNAPOLOGETICALLY AN AFRICAN AMERICAN CHRISTIAN AND AN AUTHENTICALLY COMMITTED ECUMENIST?

William D. Watley

A t the dawn of the twentieth century, Dr. W. E. B. Dubois wrote the following words in his classic work *The Souls of Black Folk*:

> After the Egyptian and Indian, the Greek and Roman, the Teuton and Mongolian, the Negro is a sort of seventh son, born with a veil, and gifted with second-sight in this American world,—a world which yields him no true self-consciousness, but only lets him see himself through the revelation of the other world. It is a peculiar sensation, this double-consciousness, this sense of always looking at one's self through the eyes of others, of measuring one's soul by the tape of a world that looks on in amused contempt and pity. One ever feels his two-ness,—an American, a Negro; two souls, two thoughts, two unreconciled strivings; two warring ideals in one dark body whose dogged strength alone keeps it from being torn asunder.

The history of the American Negro is the history of this strife,—this longing to attain self-conscious manhood, to merge his double self into a better and truer self. In this merging he wished neither of the old selves to be lost. He would not Africanize America, for America has too much to teach the world and Africa. He would not bleach his Negro soul in a flood of white Americanism, for he knows that Negro blood has a message for the world. He simply wishes to make it possible for a man to be both a Negro and an American, without being cursed and spit upon by his fellows, without having the doors of Opportunity closed roughly in his face.[1]

The poignant and passionate writing of Dr. DuBois raises the question for me, "Can one simultaneously be unapologetically an African American Christian and authentically committed to ecumenism which involves white Americans or persons of Eurocentric ancestry?" The obvious answer to this question is "Yes, since I am such a person." The not-so-obvious answer to this question is, "Yes, but not without difficulty, struggle and soul-searching that is so ongoing that one is constantly bowing before internal altars of recommitment and renewal."

I should observe that African Americans have no difficulty with ecumenism *per se*. From such historic precedents as the Fraternal Council of Negro Churches, and Partners in Ecumenism, to the Congress of National Black Churches and the Black Church Liaison Committee of the World and National Councils of Churches, African Americans and their historic churches have long swum in ecumenical waters of faith and order as well as life and work issues, and have long debated such historic church-dividing issues as baptism, eucharist and ministry, as well as such so-called "current" church-dividing issues as racism, sexism, classism and a myriad of justice concerns. Of course what some others may regard as newer church-dividing issues have been the major traditional and historic existential realities which have ruptured the body of Christ. Historic African American churches have engaged for decades in bilateral and trilateral discussions with the possibility of union or transformation. There have always been those who have asked if ecumenical discussions among black denominational bodies is real or genuine ecumenism. Of course very few, if any, raise that question when white churches talk among themselves.

What then makes participation by African Americans in the ecumenical movement involving those of Eurocentric ethnicity such a challenge? Let me answer this question in several ways and then explain why African Americans should still do it. First, when we as African

Americans participate in ecumenism with whites we are forever outsiders. We constantly feel the "double-consciousness, this sense of being always looking at one's self through the eyes of others, of measuring one's soul by the tape of a world that looks on in amused contempt and pity," that Dr. DuBois talks about. The culture which gives rise to the ecumenical movement fostered and developed by the majority culture is white. The agenda is white. The style of doing business is white, formal and stiff. The worship and liturgy are white and, for the most part, from a traditional black perspective—lifeless. The theologians and primary references are white. The mind-set and *Weltanschauung* are white. The language patterns are white.

This white reality is to be expected and is unavoidable because the churches themselves are white. And even with a Damascus Road experience we still carry the baggage of who we are historically, culturally and mentally. There is nothing wrong in being white if one is white. However if you are black and in a white context, then sometimes even the minimal theological and ecclesiological assumptions of those around you are not necessarily yours. When you are black in a white context you feel your otherness most keenly and most painfully. You are constantly trying to walk in someone else's armour. You are constantly trying to fit in, to understand and adjust. When the standard is other than what you are, you can't help but ask yourself sometimes, "What am I doing here?" and "Why am I putting myself through all of these changes?"

The reaction to your presence also makes you question the feasibility of your participation. Those reactions range from genuine attempts to accept you as an equal and fellow believer to outright efforts at avoidance. Some try to look through you as if you don't exist. Others look at you with hesitation or distrust based upon years of conditioning. To others you are a curiosity, while still others view you with an attitude of disdain and condescension. Still others approach you with a snide racism that masks itself with an inappropriate familiarity and with jokes that reveal their own prejudice. While there are whites whose smile is genuine, whose handshakes and hugs are sincere, and whose friendships are real and lifelong, you still feel a "two-ness" in the context—"two souls, two thoughts, two unreconciled strivings, two warring ideals in one dark body, whose dogged strength alone keeps it from being torn asunder."

Another factor that makes ecumenical involvement with whites difficult is the state of race relations in this country. As early as 1903 DuBois wrote, "The problem of the twentieth century is the color line,—the relation of the darker to the lighter races of men in Asia and Africa, in America and the islands of the sea."[2] What is tragic is that as we approach the end of the twentieth century, we have made so little progress in resolving the color line problem. Over the past several decades those of us in black America have seen a consistent and systematic effort to turn back the clock on the progress of ethnic minorities. The Reagan period was a season of mean-spiritedness and the Bush administration was a time of retrenchment. Government in all of its branches has made overt racism acceptable and in vogue. The burning of the black churches is just another indication of the hate and sickness that has reproduced itself in another generation because of the current milieu of cultural accommodation and political retrogression. Someday the framers of the new Rutherford B. Hayes era will get the message that, as blacks, "we ain't going back." We do not know when this period of heightening tensions will end, or what the future portends, but this much we know—"we ain't going back."

When one views the frightening direction in which this country is headed, with the rise of the religious right and the conservative mood in the pews of many of the so-called "liberal" or ecumenical churches, one questions one's participation as an African American with white Christians. Thus I submit again the question that some may regard as cynical, and others as an oxymoron: "Can one simultaneously be unapologetically an African American Christian and authentically committed to ecumenism which involves white Americans or persons or Eurocentric ancestry?" I submit the bold proposition that one can indeed be unapologetically an African American Christian *and* authentically committed to ecumenism even when white Americans or persons of Eurocentric ancestry are involved, and this for two reasons.

First, the Bible directs such a course of action and involvement. "That they may be one" (John 17:21) is not just a rhetorical phrase, it is the word of Christ. Unity is not the wish of Christ, but the work of Christ. Unity is not the want of Christ, it is the way of Christ. Unity is the will of Christ for the Church. As believers in the Lord Jesus Christ, the great head of the church, ecumenical engagement, participation, confrontation, dialogue, and debate with a view toward rapprochement and reconciliation is not an option. No matter what difficulties and encumbrances are involved, no matter what historic tensions and present trends work against such, no matter what bridges of distrust and alienation must be crossed, ecumenism which seeks to bring healing and reconciliation to a desperate creation and a broken church, is the will of Christ.

Secondly, one can be simultaneously unapologetically an African American Christian and committed to ecumenism involving those of lighter hues ethnically because every now and then one meets a person who is serious about the unity of the church and the unity of humanity. When Dr. Benjamin Mays bestowed upon his young colleague, Martin Luther King, Jr., an honorary degree from Morehouse College, the Sage of Atlanta said: "See how the masses of men work themselves into graves of anonymity, while here and there comes a great soul that forgets himself into immortality." In the ecumenical movement there can seem to be no end to papers, speeches, rhetoric, hypocrisy and discussions that seem to go around and around in circles, making no progress and going nowhere.

However we receive hope because every now and then we meet an individual who really believes in ecumenism—who breathes it and lives it, whose life is dedicated to it, who has a passion for it and who loves it with their entire being. When you are with them and hear them there is such a refreshing quality about them that it causes you to sit up and say with surprise and glee, "Wow, they really believe this stuff!" Such rare individuals by their presence and participation, their image and inspiration, their work as well as their words, encourage us to stay when we are inclined to leave, and to remain steadfast when we are inclined to waver. Paul Crow is such an individual.

Notes

[1] W. E. B. DuBois, *The Souls of Black Folks*, New York, Vintage Books, [1896], 1990, pp. 8-9.

[2] *Ibid.*, p. 16.

CHAPTER THIRTEEN

ON ECUMENICAL FORMATION

Peggy Way

Introduction and Thesis

To look at issues of formation from an ecumenical point of view is to make a contribution to the contemporary dialogue in theological education about the goals and processes of shaping ordained and lay leadership for the Church's ministries.

At the same time, to look at definitional issues of ecumenism from a formational point of view is to press toward greater intentionality in grounding present and future generations in what ecumenical perspectives and ways of living are, and are not.

More simply phrased: Denominations and faith groups seek to form leaders and members who understand, interiorize and embody their histories and claims that they might re-present the Promises of the Christian Faith. It is past time for those with ecumenical histories and claims to be intentional about shaping persons with the ecumenical knowledges of history, theological issues and praxis as those persons humbly live their lives toward the realization of Jesus' prayer that All might be One.

History—An "Accidental Formation"

Insofar as there has been "ecumenical formation" in the 20th century, it has been that of the leaders of the contemporary ecumenical movements. That is, "formation" occurred as ecumenical leadership *created* 20th century ecumenism's experiences and structures. Thus, when I began my ecumenical experiencings on the Executive Committee of the Consultation on Church Union (COCU) (the first Executive Committee that included women), a "self-evident" ecumenical culture existed that spoke of Evanston and Uppsala and later of Naiobi, Bangalore, Lima, Vancouver, etc.) as if everyone had been there. There was a language used and experiences remembered that were, however unintentionally, exclusive. The participants in this culture were, by and large, its creators whose experience *was* the formation—or whose formation lay within these particular experiencings. There was no intentional formation for newcomers such as myself. I quite literally "picked it up" as I went along, experiencing its processes, listening to dialogue about the issues, intrigued by its conflicts, somewhat intimidated by its leadership, and exalting in its worship. But I was not intentionally nurtured in its concepts or histories. Nor, as I myself was "formed" by it, did I take on or participate in educational processes with seminaries or "newcomers" to the movement or with the ever-changing representatives from the denominations who were to serve as our interpreters "back home."

This style of self-evident participatory formation was, indeed, exhilarating for those of us experiencing it. Unfortunately, despite our passion, we did not work intentionally toward the education of future generations by a systemic connecting with seminaries, lay educational programs, Sunday School curriculums, and so on that would either teach about the ecumenical movement or include persons in it in ways that would involve them in the experiences of "life meeting life" that so deeply undergird persistent ecumenical commitments.

In this sense, we did not accept the responsibility to "pass it on"; ironically, we did not seem to notice this even though our concern was for "the whole inhabited earth" and our value was inclusion! Thus the "formation by experience" model (if we can call such a non-intentional shaping a model!) has probably grounded two generations of ecumenists. An older generation of primarily male leaders was a dynamic and insistent force establishing structures and shaping visions. Their creative engagement was its own "formation," so to speak. Similarly, the present generation of "elders" (including staff persons) has been "formed" by participatory experiences, mentorship, specific committee assignments, and so on but has not been the recipient of any intentional educational processes.

Such "accidental formation" has probably served ecumenicity well. It had its own dynamic of involvement in visions, mixing of cultures, intriguing liturgical options, inordinate challenges and engaging times of "narrative meeting narrative" that carried its own appeal. But it is my thesis that *that* "moment" has passed. Except on individual levels, we have failed structurally to "pass it on," at the same time as we enter into a period of history that finds ecumenicity and inter-faith dialogue challenged on all fronts. The "battles" may have shifted—from matters of polity to issues of human sexuality to social fragmentation to intra-denominational divisions—but the urgencies for dialoguing through competing narratives and persistently celebrating our way toward God's One Church are as high as they have ever been.

Yet we do not seem to realize either the profound theological praxis contributions the ecumenical movement has to offer to the Church, or to recognize how desperately we are in need of interpreters throughout church "systems" to keep open the possibility of our contributions. At our worst, our participation in "an ecumenical culture" blinded us to how different our experiences together were from those who had not been with us. With some, we lost connection without even naming what was going on. Some we disdained—not recognizing how powerfully we had been shaped at plenaries and on committees as "life met with life." "Its" became "Thous," strangers became friends, and we ourselves glimpsed insight into how strange we were to others. And even at our best, our limited resources went toward simple survival and minimal funding of staff and offices, plenary sessions and committee meetings, publications and mailings. Always low on the budgetary priorities of every supporter's agenda, priorities did not include intentional programs and processes of ecumenical formation in relation to the structures of theological education, a variety of organizations such as Church Women United, and, perhaps most important, curriculum and other resources to be included imaginatively in the educational programs of local churches. Quite simply, we took our "ecumenical culture" for granted, forgetting that its truly precious experiences had not been shared or interpreted beyond our own praxis. No wonder that we are still not clear about what it means "to teach with an ecumenical point of view," or what should be included in a seminary course on the ecumenical movement, or how mentorships for seminarians and internships for college students and ecumenical experiences for junior and senior highs are needed in order "to pass it on."

No matter how personally invigorating, "accidental formation" is no longer sufficient. Intentional discourse about intentional formation must now become invigorating and embodied.

Examples of Connections *Not* Made

A. The Seminary. A Case Study.

The seminary in which I teach, Eden Theological Seminary of the United Church of Christ, identifies itself as Evangelical, committed to Excellence, and Ecumenical. Yet no intentional or focused experiences of ecumenical formation exist, although the seminary itself is the child of an ecumenically-formed denomination, inclusive of Evangelical, Reformed, Congregational and Christian histories and narratives, and the UCC is engaged in serious conversations about partnership with the Christian Church (Disciples of Christ). We celebrate the diverse traditions from which our students come, but seldom share them in the classroom, or uncover the depth and texture of the affect which lies beneath the ways that they are "used to" matters of both worship and thought. As a "liberal" seminary, we are not always sure what to do with our "conservative" students, and we frequently assume a consensus that simply does not exist.

We offer separate polity courses to members of each faith group, taught by one of their own, and with the exception of my one elective course in the structures and dynamics of ecumenism, which attracts 10-15 students every other year, there are no intentional goals or processes by which we seek to form (or even define) "an ecumenical perspective." I share this not as a confessional (and certainly not to be unjustly critical of my Beloved Eden seminary!) but to stress that we are in transitional times between the "participating and accidental formation styles" of generations past and the urgency to be intentional about the formation of the current and future generations of ordained church leadership. For even my own work here is "accidental," that is, we do not have a policy that concern for ecumenism should appear in all our courses as, for example, we have with issues of racism and multiculturalism. We do not intentionally seek to teach every course with "an ecumenical point of view," and even though we may assume we do so, our oral examinations of first and second level students do not check out their "ecumenical knowledges" or perspectives.

How is ecumenical discussion to be advanced without priority given to the formation of the ordained leadership of the churches? I invite you to reflect upon this in your own context, as I use my situation at Eden as a micro-case study.

1. I find that almost none of our entering students has even rudimentary familiarity with the existing structures of ecumenical discourse and programming. Not even the initials are familiar, aconymns that are thrown around with ease in an ecumenical culture: COCU, NCC, WCC, BEM, bilaterals, conciliar movement. Ecumenical and interfaith dialogue are understood to be identical; ecumenical is often not understood to be Christian! Surely this tells us something about the influential power of ecumenical experiences as the source of a call to ministry, as well as witnessing to the success of the educational programs in the local churches from which our students come!

2. Nevertheless, a strange kind of consensus seems to have occurred around verbalizations that, after all, we worship the same God. Yet behind this weak and uncritical point of view, no matter how well-intentioned, lurks the reality that real differences have not been engaged, that differing expectations of worship have not been discussed, that people baptize in different ways (!)—and that the differences carry affective meanings which are not readily changed. The consensus is especially fragile when racial, ethnic and sexual dynamics enter in and, not having experienced patient and enduring ecumenical dialogue around real differences, the students are without method, knowledges or personal power to name what is occurring. For unlike the best of ecumenical discourse, consensus *follows* hard dialogue, and our students, coming out of COCU churches, are surprised both by how long it takes (BEM took *fifty* years?), and how passionate their own perspec-

tives are when dialoguing with someone who is *demonstrably wrong*!

3. While the seminary system itself witnesses to a complex ecumenism, what this *means* is neither reflected upon nor subject to our complex assessment tools, required by the Association of Theological Schools. Yet each spring our students graduate to offer ordained leadership within local churches struggling with issues of the mutual recognition of ministries, the Reformed-Lutheran dialogue, the UCC-CCDC covenant, "backlash" from conservatives about COCU, and budgets that don't even want to send money to the national offices of one's own denomination! In my own teaching in adult education classes in churches that should know better (!!), fears of some gigantic structural union with a Protestant-type Pope persist, along with concern that the mutual recognition of ministries means that they will get a gay or lesbian pastor from one of those "COCU Churches."

4. The "ecumenical experience" has not been one highly valued in issues of academic promotion and tenure, and except for the few scholars who have worked on ecumenical committees and task forces, current professors may not be adequately prepared to teach in an ecumenical context, that is, to carry "an ecumenical perspective" into the denominational study of history, doctrine, Biblical hermeneutics, theology, etc. This was not as true in an earlier generation, but the vigor of their "accidental formation" did not get "passed on." In some of my academic settings the feeling was that this "ecumenical work" was somehow another of Peggy's peculiar interests . . . Why didn't she publish instead?

Surely it is time for a serious study of what should be the ecumenical formation process for the ordained clergy. Who carries that agenda into the Association of Theological Schools? Where do we even begin with formulating an understanding of the goals and requisites of an ecumenically literate ordained ministry?

B. Church Women United—A Place of Unrecognized Lively Formation

The "official" ecumenical culture has not been intentional in nurturing and connecting with national lay movements such as Church Women United, which for most participants provides their only structural, experiential and innovative contact with ecumenism. Here ordinary women gather from different faith traditions and racial/ethnic identities, worship together, celebrate ecumenical ministries, and serve as significant expressions of various "life and work" agendas. Yet they are not generally rooted in "faith and order" perspectives, and the intentionality of an ecumenical formation has not been perceived.

Perhaps because this is an organization of lay women, it has not been recognized as the powerful ecumenical shaping experience that it offers. In rural communities and major urban areas, in churches which are "predominantly white" and those which are "predominantly black," the participants are stretched toward inclusivity of faith and action. Yet connection to an ecumenical agenda being worked on through "official" ecumenical structures is generally missing.

This implicit ecumenical culture of lay women carries an alternative authenticity to the historic structures primarily developed by ordained men. It is also an alternative to the "accidental" formation that occurs as lay persons serve as denominational representatives to COCU, NCC, WCC plenaries. Yet these participants in Church Women United are the lay persons who are experienced and can be helped to become more substantively knowledgeable about the biblical and theological groundings of the *oikoumene*. They are the ones who actually "pass it on" in local places. CWU should be one of the hallowed acronyms of ecumenical culture!

C. Local Churches

As one who does a lot of teaching in adult educational programs in local churches, I cannot overstate the appalling lack of knowledge about the ecumenical movements, its agenda and history, its structures and visions, the decisions currently being made at national levels and the "official" dialogues going on in bilaterals between their own denomination and another, for example, the Reformed-Lutheran dialogue. As ecumenism has not connected with structures of theological education, so it has not become integrally connected with Christian-church educators, especially those committed to adult education in the local church. Thus, there are few supportive or interpretive voices present when the Readers Digest critiques the World Council; when newsletters present the catastrophic effects of the mutual recognition of ministries; when there continue to be expectations that the ecumenical movement means a Protestant Pope, the "watering down" of Scripture to allow for the ordination of persons who are women or homosexual, and having to give up whatever is most central to "our historic identity" (whatever that may be).

For the ecumenical culture has consistently been disconnected from the local churches for which it cares so deeply. Identified with pronouncements from "the national church" (already enough to be suspicious about!) and primarily worked at by paid staff and seconded professors, the marvelous rich diversities of local churches and their various contexts may have been formally celebrated by ecumenists—but not experienced in local settings. Thus in a period of suspicion toward national church organizations and bureaucrats, the ecumenical movement suffers, and its true base—laity in their own places celebrating One God and being in ministry and mission with the whole inhabited earth—withers away.

Toward An Intentional Ecumenical Formation

What marvelous times for the ecumenical movement! Its needs, and those of the churches and cultures which it loves and seeks to serve, come together in challenging new ways. Whether these times are referred to as "ecumenical winter" or "ecumenism: its second century," it is time for taking inventory of how formation occurs, what new steps might be taken within the primary style of dialogue and invitation, and what the fruits of an ecumenical formation process are considered to be.

For some time now, "main line" seminaries have celebrated the growing numbers of second career persons claiming a call to the ordained ministry. Unrecognized has been the lack of intentionality in nurturing/forming younger persons for ordained church vocations. Similarly, the ecumenical movement celebrates its dedicated participants, but seldom ponders where they came from, how they got there, and what bases should be nurtured for leadership and knowledgeable participation in futures. Within the best of ecumenical "styles," a simple beginning could be made by each context "taking inventory" in its own place: where do our participants come from? How did they get here? With what structures are we connected where persons are invited toward participation, made knowledgeable about ecumenical substance and process? How are we nurturing a younger generation and touching into a new base? Such questions will find differing responses in various cultures—another dialogical learning opportunity.

Hopefully, from such a simple but seriously intentional inventory, a few committed folk would make connection with institutions of theological education within their context. At Eden I am working toward arranging a field education placement with an interfaith organization. Perhaps a council of churches might seek an intern, or a middle judicatory staff person would develop a placement for a seminarian to experience and "cover" ecumenical matters and events. Few seminaries would refuse the offer of a "free course," and its professor (properly qualified, of course) would herself or himself establish new connections with other faculty. A seminary might invite Church Women United to present its programs and purposes to the student body, or its worship services might be held in the seminary chapel.

These modest ventures not only fit ecumenical budgets and personnel, but are also real possibilities. In the past, the best "energies of ecumenism" have been in reaching out to new possibilities—or even impossible possibilities!—and such energies need revitalization for the processes of "passing it on." Thus, it is important that ministries with young persons are intentionally connected to existing ecumenical structures, movements and themes. We ecumenists "missed" their parents' generation; surely there lies within that generation some of the energy and vitality that the first generation of young men experienced in their co-creation of the ecumenical movement itself.

Advancing the Ecumenical Dialogue—
and its Major Contributions

What I call "ecumenical modesty" has been one of the virtues of ecumenicity. We have *not* celebrated big budgets or enjoyed being power brokers; indeed, the concern for ecumenical formation arises not from a desire for "self-preservation," but rather as a continuing offering to the churches. Perhaps the ecumenical gift to the churches has yet to be received. But at this period of history where the ecumenical movement itself has become an antagonist as denominations do battle over their primary identities, it may be the knowledges that lie resident in ecumenism that will be helpful in this period of denominational and cultural fragmentation. What, then, are these primary gifts—an "ecumenical epistemology," if you will?

Beneath ecumenical documents and dramas lie insights into theological method, a theology of change, and the nature of Christian faithfulness that are not routinely recognized and celebrated. Surely these should be the fruits of an intentional ecumenical formation.

First: Ecumenism's dialogical style is itself an expression of a theological method that is so grounded in the nature of God (*one God, one humankind*) that it can "stand differentness." The ecumenical celebration of diversity is *not* a collapse into relativism. Rather it embodies both a perspective on "the one and the many" and a process that is fully congruent with it. Seminarians need this perspective.

Second: Ecumenism's primary method carries within it deep perceptions on the nature of historical change and the nature of Christian faithfulness. The rich and creative work that has been done on issues of faith and order—and on BEM—has tended to mask the kind of contributions summarized below.

Third: In a world where "receiving the Other" is viewed by many ethicists as the highest ethical imperative, only the ecumenical movement is grounded on an epistemology where experience in receiving the stranger is corollary with recognizing that one must also come to terms with the reality that oneself is a stranger to others. It is this commitment to "radical partnership" that holds the ecumenical world together. For it is not, for example, a Protestant world graciously welcoming

Catholics to a world already defined; or a white world condescending to receive persons of color; or a liberal world allowing for conservatives, or an ordained world deigning to receive lay. The ecumenical world is one of full partnership where separate horizons meet and, with the grace of the One God, receive and transform each other. What a gift to Church, Culture, World!

Fourth: An ecumenical epistemology understands the virtues of persistence and endurance in an historical existence that is "already but not yet." Ecumenists may go away from one another in sadness, but, hopefully, don't run out on each other in anger. There may be times when *"He is Risen!"* appears to be the only thing we can say with one another, but that grounding allows for a patience to live "this side of justice" while resisting injustice in one's own places. The ecumenical gift allows continuing embodiment of the vision (the oikoumene) without either giving up in despair or castigating its possibility with disdain.

Ecumenical epistemology is grounded in the knowledge of God and the worship experience. I invite us to pray this prayer, written by one of my former Jesuit students as an invitation to his ordination. He has given permission for it to be used freely.

> We are simply asked
> to make gentle our bruised world
> to tame its savageness
> to be compassionate of all
> (including ourselves)
> then
> in the times left over
> from our ministries
> of Justice and of Care
> to repeat the Ancient Tales
> and go the Way
> of God's Foolish Ones.
>
> — *Peter Byrne, S.J.*

Praise God that ecumenical formation raises up so many Foolish Ones! Pray to God that there may be an ever-increasing number.

CHAPTER FOURTEEN

AN "ECUMENICAL CONSPIRACY"
SOME THOUGHTS ON THE FUTURE OF THE ECUMENICAL INSTITUTE AT BOSSEY

Hans-Ruedi Weber

"Now you have become part of an ecumenical conspiracy!"

Willem A. Visser't Hooft used to say this to students who had participated in courses at the Ecumenical Institute at Bossey. There they had received a common spirit and vision. Many of them felt committed to a struggle: an involvement for the renewal of the churches' worship, mission and service in the world; therefore also for an involvement in prophetic protest and action against injustice and oppression as well as against divided and self-sufficient church life.

What happened at Bossey has been near Paul A. Crow, Jr.'s heart. From the beginning of the Institute in 1946 and throughout its 50 years of work the Disciples of Christ in the United States were faithful supporters of this venture, providing both leadership and finance. From 1975 to 1983 Paul chaired the Bossey board and did much advocacy, helping to safeguard and reorient the program of the Institute. He also prefaced the first small publication about its history, leading to further studies on the origins, development and vocation of Bossey.[1]

In connection with the 1996 Bossey Jubilee much reflection was done on the Institute's present and future role in the field of "ecumenical formation." A colloquium on this theme, the actual jubilee celebrations and the feedback from groups of former Bossey participants from around the world - notably from the USA, Sri Lanka and Germany— provide much material and proposals for future decisions and action by the Institute's board and the WCC governing bodies.[2] The following comments are only a few personal reflections committing none but the present writer.

Is There a Future for Bossey?

This is not a rhetorical question. Partly due to finance and partly because of new developments in the WCC the question of survival had to be faced more than twenty years ago. Already at that time much of the pioneering work of Bossey was gradually being taken over by different WCC program units, other ecumenical agencies, by lay training and study centres in different continents.

With the—probably long-term—financial crisis now faced by the WCC, a continuing work at Bossey is justified only if it serves the future of ecumenical movement in an essential way, and if the Institute is uniquely equipped for it. In this respect the feedback from former participants in the summer courses and the annual semesters of the Graduate School of Ecumenical Studies is significant.

Almost all indicate that, for them, the unique and deepest learning experience at Bossey was the living, studying and worshipping together in a temporary residential group where all continents, many cultures and Christian confessions were represented. At first most participants feel like strangers, having to communicate in foreign languages or through simultaneous translation. Their conscious or unconscious assumptions of faith, their cultural patterns, their ways of worshipping and doing theology are being challenged. The abstract "world" and "church universal" suddenly become a group of concrete women and men of different races with recognizable faces, with often tragic and deeply moving destinies, all marked by their own particular convictions of faith, doubts, hopes and joys. Only by questioning and being questioned, by the readiness to become vulnerable, through confrontations, crisis and reconciliation can a learning community gradually be built up. Thereby trans-cultural and trans-confessional friendships grow, new insights are won and the "ecumenical conspiracy" develops. This is not merely a group dynamics exercise; the learning experience happens as the participants attempt to explore together a subject on which Christians need more clarity, and insight leading to faithful obedience, for their vocation in today's world. Moreover, such community-building and study is done within the framework of common worship. This takes time, more time than the usual ecumenical gatherings and study conferences allow.

Former participants also mention the present location of the Institute near Geneva as an important asset for their learning experience. Both proximity to, and a certain distance from, the headquarters of the WCC and other ecumenical organizations is felt to be needed. Bossey's location also makes available the resources of specialists and documentation in the World Health Organization, the International Labour Office and other international bodies in Geneva, as well as those of the University of Geneva (with which Bossey has an official working relationship).

Obviously there are important ecumenical learning experiences which can be better gained in settings other than Bossey. A multi-religious environment is, for instance, needed for interfaith dialogue. Action-reflection on concrete local and regional issues can be better done through exposure visits, by action groups or in a living local congregation. However, the kind of worldwide learning community gathered for a few months, as mentioned above, and the location near Geneva, make Bossey a unique place for discovering and equipping ecumenical leaders on the local, regional and world level.

There is another reason why, *for the health of ecumenism*, the work of the Institute should continue. Bossey has grown out of a particular vision of the ecumenical movement, one in which both the demands of the gospel, and the urgent questions and needs posed by the inhabitants of this earth, are given priority over "inner-church" affairs. At Bossey the worship, life and testimony of the churches are viewed in the light of God's design for the history and destiny of this cosmos. Church unity is seen in the light of the unity of humankind, and based on the biblical promise of a new heaven and a new earth. Such a passion for the gospel and for the world is of course not unique to Bossey; but the work of the Institute helps to counterbalance a too-narrow, and often too- cautious, bureaucratic ecumenism.

Program emphases

With the above comments only the desirability—and not yet the possibility—for continuing work at Bossey have been stated. The hard fact of having insufficient funds still has to be faced. And even if adequate funds became available, decisions have to be made about what kind of program best serves the advance of the ecumenical movement through the special, partly- unique work possibilities available at the Institute.

During the Bossey Jubilee celebrations Konrad Raiser suggested in his keynote address the following three emphases for the future:

1. Continuation of the annual semesters of the Graduate School for Ecumenical Studies "in which the living memory of the ecumenical movement worldwide and the accumulated common tradition of the churches are appropriated and deepened in processes of common learning."

2. Development of Bossey as "a space where people from different backgrounds and with different experiences can begin to explore together how to reconstruct and strengthen the moral, social and cultural fabric of human community through processes of education and learning."

3. Work at new frontier issues of a common moral and ethical reflection. As an instance he pointed to the following fact: "Whereas the methods of dialogue have been refined in the field of theology and doctrine, the churches seem to lack even the basic elements of a common language where the ethics of life and procreation or of human sexuality are concerned."[3]

These three emphases were always already present in the Bossey program; indeed they were often mixed together, especially during the graduate school. For the participants, this mixture of foci led to a richness of experience but also to many frustrations, and to a certain superficiality and dispersion of work. In the future it might be necessary, in each gathering at Bossey, to concentrate mainly on one of the three suggested emphases. Thus over time more intensive and continuous work could be done on each one of them.

What would this imply for shaping the future Bossey program?

1. The graduate school would continue to be geared mainly to theologically-trained participants, and it would have to work in closer cooperation with other ecumenical Institutes than is the case now. Its program should no longer concentrate on

a theme chosen afresh each year, but on a constantly-refined core curriculum of ecumenical studies.

2. For the second emphasis a 2-3 months course, possibly called a "Summer School for Ecumenical Life," would have to be organized together with partners. It would address itself especially to lay leaders and young people from different walks of life. It should replace the former short and too-diverse Bossey summer courses and conferences. Only through living, studying and worshipping together in a worldwide group for a fairly long period can what K. Raiser asks for be achieved: "The understanding and praxis of ecumenical formation in the direction of education for peace and human rights, for democracy and citizenship, for environmental responsibility and intercultural living."[4]

3. The reflection on moral and ethical issues needs short interdisciplinary seminars like the few Visser't Hooft memorial consultations which took place at Bossey in the course of the last years. There the majority of participants would have to be persons involved in the fields of science and the humanities, with theologians forming only a minority. Work relationships with all the faculties of Geneva university, and with the various international organizations, would have to be further developed for this to realize its full potential.

For all three types of gatherings, a welcoming place and an atmosphere of study, worship and community-building are needed. The needs are many, diverse and demanding: bringing together each year groups of well-chosen women and men from all continents and many confessions presupposes a large amount of scholarship—i.e. financial—aid. An excellent administrative staff is required which can deal with (for example) complicated visa arrangements. Simultaneous interpretation among several languages is absolutely necessary, as is a basic reference library. Also needed, of course, is a small resident teaching staff whose members remain full-time with the learning community, and the work of preparation and follow-up: short-time visiting lecturers and tutors can complement—but never replace—this resident staff. The budget for a program as outlined above would be large, whether the Institute is situated in the relatively-expensive area near Geneva, or elsewhere in the world. One must ask: can the WCC afford this?

The Cost of survival

It was due to a generous gift from John D. Rockefeller, Jr., that in 1946 the work of the Institute could begin. The domain of Château de Bossey, an early 18th century three-floor mansion and its beautiful surrounding park, could be rented for a period of five years. Only one year later the WCC purchased the nearby 18th century country house "Petit Bossey," in order to deal with the increasing number of participants in the courses. The barn which belongs to it is still unused. A further Rockefeller grant made it possible to buy the château in 1950 and to make the necessary transformations. Through the reserves from these grants, and an ensured working budget provided by the WCC, the work of the Institute could proceed and develop until the 1970s without too many financial worries. Gifts especially from Germany and Switzerland made it possible also to build the needed lecture hall and library.

With the financial crisis in the mid-1970s the operating budget of the Institute was severely cut, and the WCC officers even decided that Bossey would have to be closed in 1976 unless new sources of financing were found. Indeed, no centre with some 80 beds and a permanent house staff can survive if for long periods many of these beds are not occupied by paying guests. No educational institution with a full-time teaching staff and participants coming from all over the world can for many years continue to function unless it has assured income and a large endowment and scholarship fund. Adjustments had to be made.

From 1977 onwards a guest house section was developed besides the Institute's own reduced program. Visiting groups were attracted in order to create self-generated income and to increase the low occupancy rate of the château. From 1978-1983 an associate director was appointed for this guest house, improving facilities for the guests and slightly rising the rate of occupancy. It soon appeared, however, that the primary purpose of Bossey - to enable ever-new worldwide and inter-confessional learning communities—came into conflict with the needs and dynamics of the developing guest house section.

This section was never meant to become a streamlined "hotel operation" simply for increasing income. It attempts to introduce the guests to the ecumenical movement. The many groups who came and still are coming—mainly pastors and local church members from Germany—have indeed not just helped the Institute to survive. Through their visits to Bossey and the WCC headquarters, they have received basic ecumenical information—indeed sometimes a basic ecumenical *formation*. Yet the whole Bossey experience has shown that deep ecumenical learning does not happen through lectures—however informative—for people who come only for a few days, and where the multi-cultural, multi-confessional and multilingual interchange and challenge remains minimal. Attempts to widen the geographical and confessional background of such visiting groups have been made, but so far have not been very successful. It must also be recognized that through its mainly Western-European guest house activity Bossey loses part of its essential worldwide intercultural and interracial character. Moreover, providing a program for visiting groups requires much time from both Bossey and WCC headquarters staff.

Even with a reduced budget and program the Institute has done much valuable work, especially through its graduate school. It is quite clear however that financial considerations have, necessarily, increasingly dominated its whole policy. In order to receive travel subsidies and financial assistance from WCC units, and from other ecumenical organizations, the themes of Bossey meetings now usually take up studies and work already planned and initiated by these partners. This has fostered needed collaboration, but at the same time limited Bossey's freedom to pioneer. Staff appointments were, at times, influenced by the degree to which the salary of the appointee would be paid from sources outside the budget of the WCC. The impossible merger from 1989 to 1995 of Bossey and the WCC's Program on Theological Education - an "arranged marriage" which never worked and cost dearly in terms of human energy and relationships - was at least partly dictated by finance.

All the above-mentioned developments have meant that during the last decades the potential and unique possibilities of the ecumenical Institute could not be fully used. A symptomatic example is the fact that, because of the cost involved, several meetings have had to be conducted only in English—although this excludes people who do not speak English, thus contradicting the fundamental purpose of Bossey, and although the simultaneous translation equipment is available.

Could not former participants in courses and graduate schools help in financing the Institute? Already in 1986, on the occasion of Bossey's 40th year, and in a more intensive way during the jubilee year of 1996, the attempt was made to renew contact with former participants. This is important for them because many presently live and work in great isolation, often remaining involved in the "ecumenical conspiracy" against prevailing trends in their own regions and churches. The feedback showed the former participants' thankfulness and emotional attachment to Bossey, confirmed also by moving financial gifts. In a long-term perspective, bequests and such gifts will help to increase the Institute's endowment and scholarship funds. Yet the needed large contributions will hardly come from this source. Participants stay at Bossey only for a week or a few months. They may maintain a strong emotional link with the Institute, but now they are spread all over the world, often in economically very poor areas, and only a very few have the occasion to revisit Bossey. They are not "alumni/ae" in the same sense as for the educational institutions where they have studied for several years. Their primary involvement is now, and rightly, with institutions and work in their own region.

Bossey with or without the chateau?

There is no doubt that the beauty of the domain of Bossey, and its interesting history going back to the 12th century, have made an important impact on the last fifty years of work at the Institute. Old houses, their gardens and trees, the views they offer and the traditions they convey have a "soul" and transmit an atmosphere which functional modern buildings never possess. In recent years much needed restoration work on the roof and the outside walls of the château could be made and, together with the house of "Petit Bossey" and the lecture hall/library complex, the Institute has now adequate facilities for the tasks it is called to fulfill. It would therefore be a great loss for the WCC and the ecumenical movement if, due to the lack of scholarships and further cuts in the program budget, this place would have to become principally a guest house or would even have to be sold.

Nevertheless, the continuation of the distinctive worldwide work of an Ecumenical Institute near Geneva is not absolutely dependent on the château and the buildings on its grounds. From 1930-1939 the former owner of Bossey leased the château to Smith College, a United States women's college. Its students came for a year of studies overseas, focussing on European culture and the work of the League of Nations. For the WCC's "lean years" could a similar arrangement be made with an outside educational institution? "Petit Bossey" would then become the home of the Ecumenical Institute. With the rent received for the château, the WCC might provide scholarships for participants, and make possible the long-planned transformations of the barn and outlying buildings of "Petit Bossey." With a limited number of 20-25 partici-pants the graduate school could continue. A summer school for ecu-menical life be organized and a few interdisciplinary seminars be held. This would be far from ideal, but better than the disappearance of the Ecumenical Institute.

A similar alternative was envisaged already in 1949 when the deci-sion had to be made whether the château should be bought or not. Suzanne de Diétrich, then very much the heart of the early ecumenical Institute, was not convinced of the wisdom of buying the place. She had been involved in the restoration and transformation of two old mansions into conference centres, one at Mouterhouse in northern Alsace and one at Bièvres near Paris. From this she knew how costly is the upkeep of such mansions, and how precarious the situation be-comes when the occupancy rate remains low. In an unpublished memo-randum she explained her reservations and made alternative proposals.

Obviously the situation is now different. Together with many friends of Bossey, Suzanne de Diétrich would today probably hope that a size-able grant could be found soon to ensure that the present facilities are fully used for the purpose for which they are so well suited. But as that grant is not yet in view, it becomes important to look for alternatives. These personal reflections can, therefore, best end with a summary and some quotations from the 1949 memorandum mentioned above.

With regard to finance, Suzanne de Diétrich thought that the neces-sary funds for buying and transforming the château could be found. However she wondered whether in the future the churches would be able to pay the running costs and upkeep for such a large centre. (At that time there was only the château and "Petit Bossey"; now there are, in addition, the upkeep and heating costs of new buildings to the main house as well as the whole complex of the lecture hall and library buildings). What she feared most was that circumstances might arise which would lead to a reduction of necessary scholarships and staff appointments in order to hold on to the buildings. According to her, a reserve of at least two million Swiss franks would be needed besides the cost of purchasing and transforming the château. (Today, of course, the amount would be much larger.)

In addition to financial considerations she felt that "the château, by its style and atmosphere, is of another age. Young people who come do not really feel at home in this house: it is too luxurious without being really welcoming." "We speak to our students about 'a new style of life', but this style is difficult to achieve in such an environment . . . A simpler environment would allow a more fraternal living together and make the break less deep with the conditions from where the students come." Moreover, "we are not a European but a worldwide Institute." For serving the world and not just Europe, another way of working was needed and therefore she asked: Could not "Petit Bossey" be transformed to become the centre of the Ecumenical Institute? It would then be possible to invest more money for scholarships and to appoint a larger, mobile staff, available also for the work of Bossey different regions. Having been trained as an electrical engineer she summed up her vision in this way: "The Institute would become like an electrical power station supplying regional factories."[5]

This memorandum was written as a partly affirmative—and partly questioning—comment on a paper of W.A. Visser't Hooft. He there argued in favor of buying the château and strongly stated the reasons for further developing the work of the Institute:

> Precisely at a time when the World Council takes on its definite character as an organ of the churches themselves, there is the great need for a body which, while directly related to the World Council, has nevertheless considerable freedom of action and can thus enter into new fields of thought and action with which the churches are as yet unfamiliar. It might thus be said that the Ecumenical Institute is the most important energizing centre of the World Council of Churches.[6]

The affirmation of the last sentence may no longer be as true as it was in 1949. However, with or without the château, the special vocation envisaged for the Institute by the pioneers is today as urgent as ever.

Notes

[1] See Paul A. Crow, Jr., "Introduction," *Bossey: Two Vignettes from the Early Years*, Céligny 1981; Arnold Mobbs, *Les origines et les premières années de l'Institut oecuménéque de Bossey*, Bossey, 1983; and H. R. Weber, *A Laboratory for Ecumenical Life: The Story of Bossey 1946-1996*, Geneva, WCC, 1996.

[2] For the keynote address of the Bossey Jubilee year celebrations see Konrad Raiser, "Fifty Years of Ecumenical Formation: Where are we? Where are we going?," *The Ecumenical Review*, Vol. 48, No. 4, October 1996, pp. 440-451. In the same number are printed some of the addresses at the Nikos Nissiotis Memorial Colloquium on "Looking Beyond Fifty Years of Ecumenical Education At Bossey (July 28-August 2, 1996)," as well as feedback from former participants from Sri Lanka and the USA. See further the photocopied documents: "Report of the Nissiotis Colloquium," Bossey, 1996; "Ten Theses: Association of Bossey Friends in the EKD," Bossey, 1996; Madeleine Strub, "50 years Ecumenical Formation in Bossey," Bossey, 1997.

[3] For the full text of these proposed emphases see K. Raiser, "Fifty Years of Ecumenical Formation: Where are we? Where are we going?," *op. cit.,* pp. 450 ff.

[4] *Ibid.*, p. 450.

[5] Suzanne de Diétrich, "Mémoire sur l'avenir de Bossey," August 1949, mimeographed, Bossey Archives.

[6] Willem A. Visser't Hooft, "Memorandum on the Future of the Ecumenical Institute," May 1949, mimeographed, Bossey Archives.

CHAPTER FIFTEEN

• *Pictorial History* •

School Days
1942 - 43

University of Alabama, 1954

**Family Portrait,
1970**

With George G. Beazley, Jr., second president of the Council on Christian Unity

Lecturing to U.S. Conference, World Council of Churches

Disciples delegation to Upsala Assembly of World Council of Churches, 1968

Crow and Beazley with Metropolitan Meliton of Chalcedon, Constantinople

Disciples delegation to WCC headquarters, Geneva, 1995

Russian Orthodox service, Patriarchal Cathedral, Moscow

Private Audience with Pope Paul VI

Meditation at ancient Delphi, Greece

Disciples–Russian Orthodox Dialogue, Odessa, USSR

Top left: With Archbishop of Canterbury, Robert Runcie at Lambeth Conference, 1988

Top right: Metropolitan Daniel of Moldavia and Bukovina (Romanian Orthodox Church), WCC Canberra Assembly, 1991

With Archbishop Desmond Tutu at WCC Central Committee, Johannesburg, SouthAfrica

With COCU's first Secretariat: W. Clyde William, Christian Methodist Episcopal Church, Princeton, New Jersey

With Pope John Paul II at the Disciples of Christ–Roman Catholic International Dialogue, Vatican City, 1991

Mildred Slack (Disciples), Karl Hartz, Director of Ecumenical Institute Bossey, and mentor, Dr. Howard E. Short

Bible Study Lecture to WCC Central Committee, Geneva

Family Portrait, 1994

With Metropolitan Philaret of Minsk, Russian Orthodox Church

Honorary Degree from Yale University with Robert Runcie (center), shown here with Dean Leander Keck, 1986

With friends at the Fifth World Conference on Faith and Order, Santiago de Compostela, Spain, 1993

Mary, Stephen, Susan, Paul, and Carol Ann

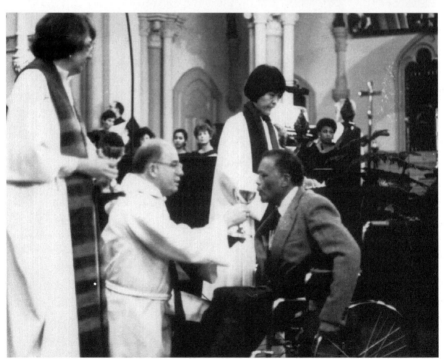

Plenary of the Consultation on Church Union, New Orleans, Louisiana, 1988. Serving Eucharist to dear friend, Richard Highbaugh.

CHAPTER SIXTEEN

A Life in the Service of Christian Unity

TRIBUTES TO PAUL A. CROW, JR.

THE ECUMENICAL PATRIARCH

T he Esteemed Thomas F. Best, The World Council of Churches, Programme Unit I—Unity and Renewal, Ecclesial Unity—Commission on Faith and Order, beloved in the Lord: Grace and peace from God.

It is with great pleasure and joy that we respond to your invitation to contribute to the Festschrift honouring our beloved co-worker in Christ the Reverend Dr. Paul A. Crow, Jr., which will be launched at the forthcoming General Assembly of the Disciples of Christ in July 1997.

Our encounter with Dr. Crow was in the context of Faith and Order, particularly in the context of its Standing and Plenary Commissions, where for many years we collaborated and struggled together in order to promote the mutual understanding of the Churches and their unity in the same faith and one sacramental communion.

In the course of this long association and ecumenical pilgrimage, our Modesty had many opportunities to witness and appreciate the particular attention and reverence Dr. Crow manifested towards the Orthodox Church.

As he himself confesses, his first encounter with Orthodox came through his friend, the late Nikos Nissiotis, during the Third World Conference on Faith and Order held in 1963, in Montreal, Canada. Their friendship and common ecumenical engagement enabled Dr. Crow to become acquainted with the Orthodox theological thinking, to appreciate Orthodox piety and to discover the richness of the Orthodox liturgical tradition.

As the Orthodox contribution to Faith and Order debates and in discussions within the wider framework of the World Council of Churches became substantial and even decisive in many circumstances, Dr. Crow came to the conclusion that the ecumenical vocation of the Orthodox Church is critical because nowadays all Churches, particularly the Orthodox, live in a world radically different from the past. Today's society, he believes, is marked by a deep spiritual crisis with universal dimensions, which cannot be addressed without the Orthodox vision of the Church and the world.

In a recent publication Paul Crow, highlighting the "proleptic" character of ecumenism, underlined that "wherever Churches overcome their past alienation and find a reconciled life, the purposes of God are served."[1] And it is so indeed! From our viewpoint it is precisely the deeper sense of the Orthodox participation in the World Council of Churches and the ecumenical movement in general. The Orthodox participate actively in this movement, because they believe that in doing so they respond to the call of God and they fulfill Christ's will that "all may be one."

It is a generally acknowledged fact that in our days the ecumenical movement passes through critical moments. As our Modesty has stressed on the occasion of the Fifth World Conference on Faith and Order held at Santiago de Compostela, our faith and experience of the ecumenical movement do not permit us to be pessimistic; rather they prompt us to continue and intensify our efforts to find ways in support of the ecumenical movement, simply because the unity of the Church is more than ever necessary.

May Almighty God, Father, Son and Holy Spirit, grant our brother Paul Crow health and long life in order to continue his God-pleasing ministry for the well-being of the Church and the further progress of the ecumenical movement of which he has always been a tireless and devoted servant.

With our paternal blessings and every good wish,
At the Phanar, February 21, 1997
Your fervent intercessor before God,
THE ECUMENICAL PATRIARCH

Bartholomew of Constantinople

[1] In his article "Ecumenical Partnership: Emerging Unity Between the Disciples of Christ and the United Church of Christ," in *Built Together: The Sixth International Consultation of United and Uniting Churches*, ed. By Thomas F. Best, Faith and Order Paper No. 174, Geneva, Faith and Order Commission, 1996, p. 119.

ALEXY II, PATRIARCH OF MOSCOW AND ALL RUSSIA

I t is with a feeling of profound satisfaction that I take part in the *Festschrift* dedicated to our beloved brother in Christ Professor Rev. Dr. Paul A. Crow, Jr., who has been President of the Council on Christian Unity and General Secretary of the world-wide Disciples Ecumenical Consultative Council for many years.

The Revd. Paul A. Crow, Jr. and his colleagues from the Christian Church (Disciples of Christ) have cooperated in a fraternal way with representatives of the Russian Orthodox Church in ecumenical and peacemaking work for over thirty years.

First of all, there has been our cooperation with Rev. Dr. Paul A. Crow, Jr. in the World Council of Churches, which began at the Fourth WCC Assembly in Uppsala in 1968 and has developed in a special way since the Fifth WCC Assembly in Nairobi in 1975, at which he was elected a member of the WCC Central Committee.

Our cooperation has also included the field of common intensive programs of The National Council of the Churches of Christ in the USA, the Christian Church (Disciples of Christ) being among its members, and the Russian Orthodox Church in the 1970s and 1980s, aimed at the overcoming of the "cold war," which alienated and opposed the nations, and the normalization of relations between the two great powers.

This wholesome process has been stimulated and supported by fraternal bilateral relations abounding in mutual understanding. These relations have found their vivid expression in the official visit of a delegation of the Christian Church (Disciples of Christ) headed by Rev. Dr. Paul A. Crow, Jr. to the Russian Orthodox Church in April 1987, and in its impressive results.

At that time I was the Metropolitan of Leningrad and God appointed me to meet our dear guests on Palm Sunday in my cathedral city. I cherish the good memory of this occasion.

Rev. Dr. Paul A. Crow, Jr. has repeatedly testified that dogmatic principles and traditions of his church, which have defined the direction of her ministry and witness, were based first and foremost on the commandment of Christ the Saviour, Who calls all those who believe in Him to become perfectly one, thus bringing the knowledge of God's love to all humanity to the world (cf. John 17:20-23). This, undoubtedly, explains the deep involvement of the Christian Church (Disciples of Christ) in the formation and development of the organized ecumenical movement of the 20th century, which has led to the establishment of the World Council of Churches and, on the regional level, of the National Council of the Churches of Christ in the USA. Thus the spiritual nature of the personality of our dear brother in Christ has been shaped by, and his life has been devoted to, the restoration of the unity in faith in the Christian world, "a sacrifice acceptable and pleasing to God" (Phil. 4:18) which, in human terms, is often a thankless and sometimes an excruciating task.

The experience of our cooperation with Rev. Dr. Paul A. Crow, Jr. of many years' standing is rich with great events in the fields of ecumenism and peacemaking. It allows us to testify to his gift of the fraternal love to which all of us are called by the Apostles Saints Peter and Paul (1 Pet. 3:8, Rom. 12:10), to his openness to fraternal dialogue with the bearers of dogmas and traditions of the One Undivided Church of the first millennium, and to his learning of the historical experience and present ecumenical thought of Orthodoxy, as well as to his profound involvement in the fulfilment of the commandment of Christ the Saviour on peacemaking (Mt. 5:9) and the ministry of reconciliation (2 Cor. 5:18-20).

These virtues of Rev. Dr. Paul A. Crow, Jr. have been convincingly proven during the last decades by cooperation with representatives of our church in implementing many programs of the World Council of Churches, including the elaboration of the Lima documents on Baptism, Eucharist, and Ministry. Likewise, we have had mutual understanding in the solution of common peacemaking tasks of the Russian Orthodox Church and the National Council of the Churches of Christ in the USA, most vividly expressed in the statement "Choose Life" (Deut. 30:19) which was adopted in 1979, and which has become a concrete programme of actions for the Churches of the USSR and the USA for the sake of bringing the relations between the two nations into a healthy state.

It goes without saying that the ecumenical and peacemaking activities of Rev. Dr. Paul A. Crow, Jr. deserve every expression of approval. At the same time they testify most convincingly to the great opportunities for the development of cooperation, and for the deepening of mutual understanding, between the Orthodox and the Protestants as we steadfastly fulfill the commandments of Christ the Saviour on Unity and Peacemaking.

Let us wish our dear brother in Christ Rev. Dr. Paul A. Crow, Jr. the inexhaustible help of God throughout the time of his earthly pilgrimage (cf. 1 Pet. 1:17) and many blessed years of life.

Patriarch of Moscow and All Russia
March 1, 1997

EDWARD IDRIS CARDINAL CASSIDY

A leading ecumenist

For quite a number of years now The Pontifical Council for Promoting Christian Unity has had the honour of being associated with Reverend Dr. Paul A. Crow, Jr., a leading ecumenist and a person with an authentic passion for ecumenism.

In fact the relations go back to the period 1974-1977, soon after Dr. Crow had become the President of the Council on Christian Unity of the Christian Church (Disciples of Christ). He was convinced that if the Disciples were truly committed to the ecumenical movement, it was time to engage in international dialogue with the Roman Catholic Church. Driven by his deep conviction, Dr. Crow persuaded his own constituency of the need for such dialogue, and then travelled three times to Rome to meet Cardinal Willebrands and discuss with him the prospect for an international bilateral dialogue between their two Communions. Dr. Crow was determined to convince the Pontifical Council for Promoting Christian Unity that the Christian Church (Disciples of Christ) was actually international and not simply a local phenomenon limited to the United States. This international character of the Christian Church was important in helping to make a decision on the part of our office. At the final meeting in Rome when Dr. Crow pressed for an answer, Cardinal Willebrands responded: "We must say yes, if for no other reasons that you have asked in charity and we must respond in charity." By the end of these discussions, it was clear to all that Dr. Crow was a person truly committed to the work of promoting Christian unity.

This conviction has been present in every activity in which members of our office have worked with Dr. Crow, as for example in the Faith and Order Commission of the World Council of Churches, where he has made an important contribution as a member and currently as Vice-moderator. His wide-ranging experience and excellent background have enabled him to render valuable service to the work of this fundamental ecumenical organisation ever since 1973 at the Salamanca Consultation, which served as a prelude to clarifying the meaning of "The Unity We Seek" adopted by the WCC Nairobi Assembly in 1975. I am pleased to have this opportunity of paying tribute to him for his contribution to Faith and Order during subsequent years, and in particular for the role he played in getting his own constituency so deeply involved in the BEM process.

His writings bear witness to a firm conviction as a serious ecumenist, who knows that the search for visible unity is willed by the Lord. These qualities are expressed not only in an openness and desire to dialogue with partners, but also to learn from the other. This is a quality in Dr. Crow that has surprised us many times at meetings of the International Commission for Dialogue between the Roman Catholic Church and the Disciples of Christ, where he has demonstrated that doctrinal differences can be overcome through a real change of heart and attitudes, a process that makes it possible to see the positive side of one's partner.

It is in this dialogue in particular, which began its work in 1977, that we have come to admire Dr. Crow's passion for ecumenism. His commitment has been a great inspiration and encouragement to the members of the Commission, and indeed provides real hope for the future. As Co-Chair of this Commission over the years, his deep appreciation for the dialogue and a clear understanding of what ecumenical dialogue means have been for us a true blessing. Much progress has been achieved over the last twenty years, thanks to his leadership and the co-operation of the Commission members. The manner in which Dr. Crow has continually made this dialogue known in his own constituency, and even among Roman Catholics, is a sign of this deep commitment, one for which the Pontifical Council for Promoting Christian Unity is deeply grateful.

Those who gave been associated with Dr. Crow have been most inspired by his optimism even in difficult moments. We recall that in 1982, after completing the first phase of the dialogue between our two Communions, Dr. Crow stated, "There are many areas of disagreement"—and immediately added, "that is positive." His optimism had taught him that the purpose of identifying serious disagreements was indeed to lay them out and to work on them together. Another good example of Dr. Crow's optimism has been his response when asked about the achievements of the bilateral dialogue with the Roman Catholic

Church. His reply has always been that there has been much progress since 1977; and while he was aware of the doctrinal issues that divide the two Communions, he often added that "on our side we are prepared to stay in this dialogue as long as it takes to achieve visible unity."

Appreciation for the traditions of others

A genuine ecumenist is one who first of all knows and appreciates one's own tradition. This is not only an essential quality for entering into theological dialogue, but also creates an interest in understanding and respecting the traditions of others, which in turn helps the enquirer to understand more fully his or her own tradition. Dr. Crow's appreciation and respect for our tradition is indeed based on his being deeply grounded in his own tradition. He has a wonderful gift of being fascinated by other traditions, and an interest to know more about them. We have come to know Dr. Crow as a person who feels at home in our tradition, yet he has not been complacent about the search for unity between our two Communions. On the contrary, his passion for unity has always charged him to explore every possible way to take a step further on the way towards unity.

A distinguished scholar

Several books and nearly three hundred articles bear testimony to Dr. Crow's firm commitment to the ecumenical search, while at the same time illustrating the author's scholarship in the field of ecumenism. At times Dr. Crow has been critical in some of his writings of what he has described as "selective ecumenism" or "selective models of ecumenism," which play one approach off against another. In an article of 1979, Dr. Crow wrote that "this selectivity diminishes and power of ecumenism in the churches . . . "[1]

A friend and a brother in Christ

This tribute from the Pontifical Council for Promoting Christian Unity is to a friend and a brother in Christ, the Rev. Dr. Paul Crow, Jr. We end with this remark because of the warmth with which we have been received each time by Dr. Crow and his wife Mary. We greatly appreciate such friendship which is surely a gift from the Lord and indeed an essential part of dialogue.

Edward Idris Cardinal Cassidy
President
Pontifical Council for Promoting Christian Unity

[1] "Elements of Unity in Recent Ecumenical Discussion: A Disciples View", in *Mid-Stream*, Vol. 18, No. 4, October 1979, p. 404.

KONRAD RAISER

The World Council of Churches is presently developing a new understanding of the ecumenical movement as a whole, and a fresh vision of its role within that movement, through the process towards a "Common Understanding and Vision" of the WCC. As is widely known, that process will come to fulfilment at the eighth WCC Assembly in Harare, Zimbabwe in September 1998, where the churches will be asked both to recommit themselves to the ecumenical quest, and to agree upon a new structure for the WCC.

But even as we respond to new impulses and emphases within the churches and among the people of God, and as we seek new structures which better correspond to the reality of the ecumenical situation today, it is important to honour colleagues who have been a faithful part of the ecumenical journey up to this point. And it is doubly important to honor those who not only have been central to ecumenical history, but who also have a vision of the ecumenical future, who have a deep commitment and a fresh contribution to make as we move toward a new ecumenical vision and new structures for the years ahead.

Thus I am pleased to contribute to this *Festschrift* for Rev. Dr. Paul Crow, who has been involved throughout so many years in the life of the World Council of Churches. Paul Crow and I have several *personal* links through parallel personal and professional engagements. I mention here only one: we have both been active in the academic world, and understand the contribution which that special context can make to the ecumenical movement. Paul Crow taught especially in the fields of church history and theology, while I have been primarily engaged in systematic theology and Christian social-ethical reflection; but we have both introduced several generations of students to the ecumenical movement, its history as well as its central issues and challenges for today. And neither of us approached this as an abstract exercise. Rather we have shown a common commitment for the ecumenical future, by bringing our own students and other young persons into the world of ecumenical reflection and common action.

But as General Secretary of the World Council of Churches I want especially to refer to Paul Crow's contributions to that body, focussing on two areas in particular. The first is *the Ecumenical Institute, Bossey* for which Paul Crow worked tirelessly in the 1970s and beyond, serving during a crucial period as the Moderator of its board and helping to find ways of overcoming a deep financial crisis which then threatened the institution. Understanding well the original vision of Bossey, Paul encouraged its role as a laboratory for ecumenical experience and learning by the whole church—laity as well as religious professionals. But he understood also the importance of Bossey's as an academic center, with contacts to other academic institutions. Indeed I recall the moment in the 1970s when I signed, together with Paul, an agreement with the University of Geneva which established the formal conditions of the relationship between the University and the Ecumenical Institute, Bossey.

The second area is Paul Crow's commitment to the movement on *Faith and Order* and its continuing life within the framework of the World Council of Churches. Serving for many years on the Standing Commission (now Board) of Faith and Order, Paul was instrumental in broadening its work beyond the traditional concerns favored by some as the "legitimate" agenda of Faith and Order. Especially as Moderator of Faith and Order's "Unity and Renewal" study (1984-1992) he sought to ensure some dialogue between different theological perspectives, and to relate the churches' traditional search for unity to the churches' engagement in the world. This commitment continued in his strong support within Faith and Order of the study programme on "Ecclesiology and Ethics" (1992—1996) conducted jointly with Unit III. I remain convinced that this study is of strategic importance for the WCC as a whole. One other aspect of Paul Crow's commitment to Faith and Order and the WCC should be mentioned, namely his policy over many years of seconding staff from the Disciples of Christ. This has been an important support for the work of Faith and Order, and for the WCC as a whole.

Within the ecumenical movement serious convictions are brought to the table, and difficult decisions must be taken. Much is at stake as we reflect on how the WCC and the churches—and the wider ecumenical movement—can be faithful to the ecumenical calling in the world today. In this context it is not to be expected that colleagues always agree with one another, and indeed Paul Crow and I have sometimes differed. What counts is the recognition of one another's commitment, and the willingness to continue dialoguing and working together for the sake of the ecumenical movement as a whole. In this I count Paul Crow as a valued colleague, and express my appreciation for his long and faithful years of service to the WCC and to the wider ecumenical movement.

[signature]

Konrad Raiser
General Secretary
World Council of Churches

RICHARD L. HAMM

Reflections on Paul Crow's Leadership
and the Future of the Council on Christian Unity

This reflection will not be as personal as some of those that will be a part of this *Festschrift* because I have not had the opportunity to work with Paul Crow over many years, as have others. I have worked with Paul closely and know him well only through the last seven years (as a regional minister and now as general minister of our church). However, as we approach a change in leadership within the Council on Christian Unity, a general unit of the Christian Church (Disciples of Christ), there are a number of qualities and commitments that Paul Crow has embodied that I would like to see continued and built upon by his successor. I would like to address these briefly as a way of both honoring Paul and pointing toward the future.

Dr. Crow has given leadership in the
worldwide ecumenical movement

It is hard to imagine that anyone in the world has seen more of the development of the modern ecumenical movement than Paul Crow. In fact, he has been present and has participated in so many of the essential decisions and policy developments of the great ecumenical councils of the church. It is a source of pride for Disciples to know that, through Dr. Crow, as well as other important leaders, we Disciples have contributed to the life of the ecumenical movement to a degree far beyond our size as a denomination. It is my hope that the person following Dr. Crow as President of the Council on Christian Unity will likewise make it a point to be available for significant service to the World and National (USA) Councils of Churches.

This service must, of course, be balanced with commitment and energy given to nurturing the flame of ecumenical vocation within the hearts of Disciples. We were born on the American frontier with an ideological commitment to freedom of the individual. In the late 20th century, radical individualism has continued to increase within American culture to the point that common commitment to a particular expression of the church (a denomination) is threatened, to say nothing of common commitment to the ecumenical vision. As the generation that gave us the modern ecumenical movement is passing from the scene of daily denominational and congregational leadership, it is crucial that the ecumenical vision be intentionally nurtured and tended among us. This is a primary challenge facing Dr. Crow's successor.

Dr. Crow has mentored a host of Disciples leaders toward commitment to the ecumenical vision

Nowhere is Dr. Crow's influence within the denomination more ubiquitous than here. As one looks about at who among younger Disciples leaders has the greatest commitment to the ecumenical vision and to the institutions of ecumenism, one nearly always discovers Dr. Crow's guiding hand. So many of these persons have been identified and intentionally nurtured by Dr. Crow. For example, they have been given the opportunity to take part in great conciliar meetings (as well as nitty-gritty institutional work), to participate in the Ecumenical Institute at Bossey, and to develop the relationships with ecumenical leaders that are so crucial to the formation of committed ecumenical spirits.

Mentoring is itself an "endangered species." All of us in leadership today can point to persons who nurtured us through the difficult passages of ministry and life and helped us prepare for greater responsibility. Unfortunately, few of us can point to as many persons whom we ourselves have similarly mentored. We must recover this art. We can learn much from Dr. Crow at this point, and his successor must be similarly inclined.

Dr. Crow has shared the insights he has gained in his ecumenical experience through writing, teaching and speaking

The journal of ecumenical thought, *Mid-Stream*, receives and deserves wide readership within the Christian Church (Disciples of Christ) and beyond. Dr. Crow has also taught seminary classes, served as guest lecturer in Disciples seminaries (and the seminaries of other denominations), has spoken widely in regional assemblies and congregations, written for a host of publications, authored books, and otherwise disseminated a great deal of accumulated learnings and wisdom. This has greatly enriched Disciples' understanding of the wider Christian world and helped to open up our own perspectives and commitments. Certainly Dr. Crow's successor should seek to continue this teaching tradition.

The Christian Church (Disciples of Christ) has a wide streak of naivete at the heart of its tradition. Though we Disciples has always affirmed the unity of all Christians, we have also taken a minimalist approach to worship and church life. In rejecting the abuses that were common in the denominationalism of the 1800s, we also rejected much of church tradition. The fact is, the church universal did learn much between the time of the Apostle Paul and 1800, and much of this learning is found in church tradition. To ignore history is, indeed, to have to repeat it, and many of the problems we Disciples have experienced in our church life over these past two hundred years could have been avoided had we more fully appreciated the collective wisdom of church history and tradition. Through we have recovered some appreciation for church tradition through our ecumenical involvements, most Disciples are still woefully lacking in their understanding of the wider tradition of the church. The President of the Council on Christian Unity must continue to help us overcome this paucity.

* * *

On this special occasion, I wish to congratulate Paul A. Crow, Jr. upon the completion of so many years of service as President of the Council on Christian Unity, as General Secretary of The Consultation on Church Union, and as a seminary professor. The church owes him a great debt of gratitude. It is my prayer that his retirement years will be filled with good health, much happiness, and continued productivity. In addition, it is my sincere hope that he will write a book—or books—giving account of the many events he has witnessed during his years of service, helping those of us who have come after him to understand this century of prolific ecumenical development.

Richard L. Hamm
General Minister and President
Christian Church (Disciples of Christ)
in the U.S. and Canada

VINTON R. ANDERSON

It has been more than a generation since Paul Crow became the budding legend to which he has now matured in the ecumenical scene. During the late sixties I was being introduced to the Consultation on Church Union, and Paul was busily engaged as a primary mover in the goal toward organic union. While he diplomatically conceded to the numerous nuances and variations in the Consultation on Church Union process, he would remain engaged over the years and never budged in his conviction that visible unity must be the central force which drives the ecumenical movement.

Paul has been steadfast at the cutting edge in the pilgrimage of church unity, and has clearly staked his reputation and scholarship squarely on faith and order issues as the bedrock for faithful ecumenical ministry. His penchant to ecumenical theology has motivated many others to venture beyond the politeness of Christian felicity to substantive engagement and unfettered trust. Paul has never jettisoned his quest for organic union because in his heart of hearts he desires that common expression of visible unity to be achieved.

Whether in the context of the Consultation on Church Union, the National Council of the Churches of Christ in the USA, or the World Council of Churches, there were always opportunities to dialogue and often to partnership with Paul Crow in matters concerning God's kingdom of righteousness, peace and equity.

I have appreciated Paul's friendship for more than a quarter century, and have valued his opinions and applauded his dedication. At whatever table Paul sits, whether for debate or for a meal, his central focus is the unity of the church. This *Festschrift* should be an exciting occasion to salute Paul, and I hope it will bring great joy to him and to his family.

Thanks, Paul, for your unstinted devotion to ecumenism, and for the part you've played in helping to clarify the vision and point the way to a common understanding. May you experience for the rest of your earthly journey the koinonia you greatly cherish.

I don't remember exactly when, but I do remember, Paul, how you brought a fresh testimony of your faith following your father's home going. It was during a sharing time at the Executive Committee meeting of the Consultation on Church Union when you told us that losing your Dad had made the reality of the resurrection a living hope for you. It is that same hope we share with you for the ecumenical movement. No matter how painful the pilgrimage, we have the assurance that in God's eternity, "we *shall* all be one."

Your Brother in Christ,

Vinton R. Anderson
Bishop, Second Episcopal District
African Methodist Episcopal Church
Washington, D.C.

JOAN BROWN CAMPBELL

I t seems entirely impossible to me that Paul Crow is now moving toward that transition in career and calling that we generally refer to as "retirement." Because Paul has long since internalized his labors on behalf of Christian unity and its ever-more-visible expression as a part of his own self-identity, it is difficult to separate Paul's professional achievements from his personal identity and attributes. In both life and career, persistence and determination have been the hallmarks of Paul's ministry.

My own acquaintance with Paul Crow now extends through nearly three decades and involves the quest for Christian unity at the local, state, national and international levels. In my own early days of ecumenical formation Paul Crow, as a leader in my own denomination, identified me as a potential ecumenical enthusiast and identified the ecumenical movement to me as every Christian's true home. Soon I was off to the Caribbean on an occasion of dialogue and encounter. The specifics of that visit have now grown dim in my memory, but its impact upon my soul and psyche remain vivid. Reflecting upon this episode today I salute Paul Crow for that which has been so central to his own teaching ministry—the capacity to bring evangelistic fervor to the identification and mentoring of new recruits to the ecumenical movement he so loves.

I have long admired and treasured Paul's largely unparalleled contribution to the ecumenical movement through his ceaseless determination to bring that movement to an ever-widening circle of people, and to see to the training and preparation of new leadership for ecumenism. Paul has, in the main, operated from a denominational base rather than as an employee of an ecumenical agency. (His service as General Secretary of the Consultation on Church Union is the one chapter of Paul's ministry which is an exception to this). The Christian Church (Disciples of Christ) will long have a broad ecumenical base since Paul has actively recruited young church men and women and provided for their ecumenical instruction, thus preparing them for a future of leadership. Today in the United States, with its pattern of local and state ecumenical agencies, the Disciples have a disproportionate number of executives in the leadership of such local councils. This is, of course, due in part to the broadly ecumenical basis and self-understanding of that denomination. Yet it is also true that such leadership emerges only where it is nurtured and encouraged. In his own homeland and abroad Paul Crow is able to call the names of a dizzying array of ecumenical servants, including this General Secretary, whom he first introduced to their ecumenical callings.

In keeping with this commitment to leadership development Paul has naturally been a steadfast friend of the World Council of Churches' Ecumenical Institute at Bossey, near Geneva, Switzerland. Paul has studied, taught, served on the Board, raised funds, and recruited students and faculty for Bossey, knowing well the difference such a place of study, preparation and discernment can mean for individuals and ultimately for the Church.

For many years Paul has served as a representative of the Christian Church (Disciples of Christ) on the delegation representing that church at the General Assembly of The National Council of the Churches of Christ in the USA (NCCCUSA). In the ever-evolving scene of ecumenical relationships Paul now serves on "my" board—even as I once served on "his," as a member of the Disciples' Council on Christian Unity. Paul was not the first Ecumenical officer for his communion. That distinction belongs to George Beasley, who saw to it that the Disciples were among the earliest churches to place sufficient importance upon ecumenical matters to assign specific staff to these responsibilities. Paul came to that office determined to secure its on-going work as a strong contribution to the quest for Christian unity. His long tenure, and his development of the scope and function of the office, have given the church a rich ecumenical legacy.

Much of Paul's method has been unique in enabling the insights and gifts of both the parish and the academy to find a good conjunction in service to Christian unity. Paul has faithfully served as both participant and advocate for the Faith and Order work of the World Council and the National Council, and has offered lectures in the seminary and wider church context across the country and around the world. His publication *Mid-Stream* has made a lasting contribution as a journal of opinion and discussion for the ecumenical movement.

This methodology of combining academic and pastoral insights was instrumental in Yale Divinity School's decision to grant Paul a Doctor of Divinity degree. I was privileged to accompany Paul at the time this doctorate was awarded. I thought at the time, and still believe today, that the movement we serve is infinitely strengthened by those who bring the insights of both communities to bear on the church-dividing and church-uniting issues of our day.

Paul Crow's contributions to the World Council of Churches are ably detailed by others and I have spoken of them only in passing in this brief tribute. Paul's contributions to the National Council of Churches and the development of the ecumenical enterprise within the United States is the real focus of my attention. Paul knows well, and is known by, the member communions of the NCCCUSA. Through COCU, Faith and Order, service to the General Assembly and in a host of bilateral dialogues Paul has pursued the dream of Christian unity. Amid it all he has reserved the time and energy to maintain extensive relationships with the Roman Catholic Church, and longs for a day in which we will all share in closer, deeper fellowship.

Throughout our thirty-year sojourn in the ecumenical vineyard I have regarded Paul as friend, mentor and jousting partner. We have always thought highly enough of each other to disagree on occasion. Whether on the great issues or the small, we have more than once confronted our differences with candor and the determination to persuade each other to the "correct" understanding. It is probably even fair to say that we have sometimes grown irritable and irritating to one another. Yet as siblings in the family of God we have continued to forebear with one another across the years, being led, in part, by our common calling to a ministry of unity.

Paul's friendship to me has been a reliable support over the years, my experience of a gift which he bestows on so many Christian servants around the world. From his far-flung places of ministry he has sent postcards bringing me up-to-date on the ecumenical climate, and encouraging my own ministry of the moment. When I was installed as

General Secretary of the National Council of the Churches of Christ in the USA Paul was there leading with the other ecumenical officers in the great prayer for the church in the world. Whatever the next chapter of his life may bring, Paul's "retirement" is likely to find him in the company of others working and praying for the unity of the Church. In that I shall take comfort.

[signature]

Joan Brown Campbell
General Secretary
National Council of Churches

FRED B. CRADDOCK

The career of Paul Crow as churchman and ecumenist has been of such duration and significance that modern church historians have not waited for his retirement to evaluate his work. Of course, not all have agreed with the direction of his every endeavor nor with all the causes in which he has invested his considerable influence. Only those who work is unimportant are spared criticism. All, however, speak of Paul with the respect and gratitude due one of the major voices in the church of the twentieth century. No one's respect and gratitude exceed mine. When asked to reflect on our friendship of thirty years, I had no difficulty deciding to speak more personally than ecclesiastically, attending more to the man than to the many programs and structures which bear his mark. And surprisingly swiftly came to mind three words which characterize all Paul has been and is, all he has done and does.

Affirmation

At the heart of all Paul has said or written is the fundamental affirmation of his faith: The Church of Jesus Christ on earth is one. This confession informs, inspires, and disciplines everything, and herein lies the integrity of his achievement. Some church leaders have labored under the assumption that the Church of Jesus Christ on earth *was* one and they have worked long and sincerely to restore that unity. Others have been guided by the conviction that the Church of Jesus Christ on earth *will be* one, and they have striven prayerfully toward that vision. For Paul the unity of Christ's Church is not be located in some Camelot of the past or the future. Were unity a condition of the past, then the mere passing of time would more us farther from that blessed state. Were unity a condition of the future, the slow and difficult road toward it would wear down the most fervent and prayerful among us, despairing short of that hope. But for Paul the oneness of the church is of its very nature and essence, given by Christ to his body. Every imperative of ecumenical work springs from this affirmation. Otherwise, we are trapped in the alternating moods of pride and despair which attend every partial success or failure.

Passion

No characteristic of Paul's life and work has been more remarkable than the passion which has marked his ministry to and through the church. All of us have down times, to be sure, but Paul's passion for witnessing to the unity of Christ's Church has been consistent across the decades. To appreciate this quality in him one has only to converse with those ministers who now mouth words without the fire which propelled them only a few years ago, confessing to a gradual decline of conviction, beaten down by the immensity of the task. Time itself seems to be the enemy of passion: the process of negative adaptation sets in and we become accustomed to the way things are. Add to the draining of time the other conditions which contrive to erode passion for the unity of Christ's Church. Denominational lines grow hard, then soft, then hard. New and rigid shapes of denominationalism rise and flourish under the disguise of non-denominationalism. Even among cooperating church bodies, ecumenical efforts are treated programmatically as marginal or optional. It is as though little energy is left after evangelistic efforts and stewardship drives, though a brief note about a local ecumenical gathering may make the announcement page. And time does not permit giving attention to all the new shapes and numbers of enemies of the unity of Christ's Church. Older forms of denominational entrenchment pale in power compared to the forces of sexism, racism, class hatred, belligerent nationalism, and cruel moralisms. To continue to embrace the affirmation that Christ's Church is one and to witness to it with unflagging passion is nothing short of miraculous. To see it and to hear it is to experience the active Spirit of God in a person's life. After all these years, to listen to Paul is to be reminded that something very important is at stake.

Memory

I have come increasingly to appreciate Paul's unwillingness to jettison any part of the church historical in order to purchase some gain for the church ecumenical. We do not become who we are by forgetting who we were, but apparently many congregations think so. Not only are denominational linkages being disguised or put in small print but the identity "church" is being dropped in favor of "fellowship" or "community" or "assembly." And gone also are the great hymns and the historic creeds. Such planned amnesia, regardless of its apparent immediate popularity, can only be detrimental to informed faith and disciplined hope.

Paul and I belong to a church body which learned painfully that trying to read the Bible as though there were no centuries of history in between is an illusion. Much has happened in the world, in the church, and in ourselves. In fact, this attempt at Bible study is not only an illusion, it is a denial of the continuing presence and work of Christ whenever and wherever believers have gathered to worship, to pray, and to witness to the world. Twenty centuries without the Christ we met in the Scriptures is unthinkable. Of course, no one gives blanket endorsement to all the church has said and done during those years. History has entire chapters detailing the church's cruelty not only toward unbelievers but also toward dissenting brothers and sisters. And that story has not ended in our own "enlightened" day. The church everywhere should begin each day in repentance. But God has never given up on the church or the world, and nothing could be more debilitating to the life and witness of the church than this imposed amnesia, this forgetting who we were as the way to be who we are.

Paul has consistently demonstrated that he understands the Christian life to be, among other things, an act of memory. The believer or the congregation which cannot remember prior to birth is an orphan. If we cannot remember Abraham and Sarah, Moses and Miriam, Mary and Jesus, Phoebe, Peter and Paul; if we cannot remember Augustine, Cyril, Theresa, Aquinas, Julian of Norwich, Luther, Calvin, Knox, and Wesley; if we have forgotten Nicea, Chalcedon, Constantinople, Rome, Hippo, Wittenburg, Geneva, and Canterbury, then the church is a thing dislodged in the world, without mother or father, a stranger among strangers.

But Paul remembers, not only as a church historian but as a believer. When he affirms that the Church of Jesus Christ on earth is one he is not speaking simply as a commentator on the present; he takes the long view, remembering.

[signature]

Fred B. Craddock
Bandy Distinguished Professor
of Preaching and New Testament, Emeritus
Candler School of Theology
Emory University.

VIVIAN ROBINSON

I count it an honor as well as a privilege to be asked to write this tribute for Dr. Paul A. Crow, Jr. For twenty-eight years, I have been pleasantly associated with him through the Consultation on Church Union (hereafter referred to as COCU or the Consultation); first as a member of the COCU Executive Committee and secondly as president of the Consultation for the past eight years.

When I became a member of the COCU Executive Committee, I felt a little uncomfortable because I was a lay person among so many ministers and theologians. It was Paul Crow who went out of his way to make me feel comfortable and who assured me that my years as a college professor and my years as a Christian Educator caused me to have much to offer the Consultation. Ever since then, I have been inspired and helped by his profound knowledge, his sincerity, his integrity, and his genuine interest in Church union in particular and the entire ecumenical movement in general. His accomplishments as a philosopher, a scholar, and a humanitarian did not come by accident. Early in his life he began the preparation for his achievements.

His early career prospects, however, would not have led him in the direction he has pursued. Would you believe that early in his life he wanted to be a professional baseball player with the New York Yankees and serve as a chemist with Dupont? Well, that is true. Following this plan for his life, he completed a B.S. degree in Chemistry. However, the desire to make the Christian ministry his life-long vocation overshadowed these earlier career options; and he prepared for the ministry by studying for and receiving the B.D., S.T.M., and Ph.D. degrees. His thesis for his B.D. degree was titled "The Nature of the Unity We Seek." The dissertation title for the Ph.D. degree was "The Concept of Unity in Diversity in Faith and Order Conversations from Lausanne (1927) to Oberlin (1957) Conferences." As he worked with COCU, these two themes from his thesis and dissertation were evident in all of his deliberations.

Since his beginning with COCU, Paul Crow has had a leadership role. In December, 1963, he was elected Associate Executive Secretary on the basis of a salary of only $50.00 per month plus travel and other expenses. He had been at work for COCU since September, 1963. According to the minutes of that December, 1963 meeting, the entire budget was only $4,325.08. Of course during this period, 1961-1968, he was also Professor of Church History and Historical Theology as well as Acting Dean at the Lexington Theological Seminary.

In 1965, Paul Crow helped to edit a study book interpreting the work of the Consultation. He also prepared the prospectus, at the Executive Committee's request, for *A Plan of Union.*[1] In 1968, he was unanimously elected the first General Secretary of the Consultation on Church Union. In his first report as General Secretary to the June, 1974 COCU Executive Committee Paul wrote these words:

The past three years have been a difficult time for the ecumenical movement; a time ironically when COCU was geared up to take off. What do the difficulties mean? Were we doing the wrong things? No, we were simply in a very difficult period. God was shaking up the world, and many people were losing the faith. It could not have been a worse time for COCU in a certain sense; yet we have not only survived but matured and learned to live by grace. Even small gains in a period like this are significant.

When rumors were afloat many years later that "COCU was dead," Paul Crow used this same theme of optimism to allay our fears and to assure us that God is still in control.

In 1974, Paul resigned as General Secretary of the Consultation to become president of the Council on Christian Unity of the Christian Church (Disciples of Christ). In a certificate of appreciation given to him by the COCU Executive Committee (of which I was a part) for his six years of efficient service, we find these words as printed in the June, 1974 minutes:

1. We Believe that it was in the grace and goodness of God that Paul A. Crow, Jr. was brought to us as our first General Secretary.

2. He was willing to leave a secure position in the academic field to work in the risky cutting edge of the ecumenical world.

3. He has effectively interpreted the nature and mission of COCU in this land and in other places in the world.

4. In the dark hours he has provided buoyant optimism, not irresponsibility, while seeking out positive signs of hope.

5. In his person he has embodied the qualities required for a united Church: theological insight, historical understanding, wide knowledge, infinite patience and Christian Charity.

The contributions Paul Crow has made to COCU since 1974 are too numerous to mention, but I must name a few. He has remained a member of the COCU Executive Committee until now as chair of the delegation of the Christian Church (Disciples of Christ). He has carried the message of COCU to seminaries and to many other organizations. He has served as chairperson of COCU's Commission on Church Order, and has served as lecturer and consultant on behalf of COCU nationally and internationally. Additionally, he is a prolific writer about the work of the Consultation. As editor of *Mid-stream*, a quarterly publication of the Council on Christian Unity of the Christian Church (Disciples of Christ), he has kept readers abreast of ecumenical movements today and has published many articles and special editions on the work of the Consultation.

He has helped to shape the direction in which COCU is now moving. As we moved from *A Plan of Union* to *The COCU Consensus: In Quest of a Church of Christ Uniting*[2] and on to *Churches in Covenant Communion: The Church of Christ Uniting*,[3] Paul Crow has made an invaluable contribution.

With his training and commitment to the ecumenical movement, Paul has become one of our foremost ecumenists. Not only has he been an integral part of the Consultation on Church Union, he has also participated in church union negotiations all over the world. He has had leadership responsibilities in the World Council of Churches, and of course in his own communion, the

Christian Church (Disciples of Christ). In every capacity he has served, whether in COCU or elsewhere, he has served extremely well. He has always performed his official duties with integrity and fearless determination.

He is the author of more than six books and over 200 articles. Two of his latest books are *Christian Unity: Matrix for Mission* and *The Anatomy of a Nineteenth Century Church*. As mentioned earlier, he is the editor of *Mid-Stream*, an Ecumenical Journal. Currently, he is writing *The History of the Faith and Order Movement 1910-1990*.

One would wonder what time he has for family; but in spite of all the activities in which he is engaged, he takes time for family. If you want to see him beam with pride, just ask him about his wife Mary Matthews Crow, his three children, and his six grandchildren. They are all extremely important to him and support him in the work he does.

In summary, I say that Paul is known as one whose heart is on fire with ecumenism. There is an old proverb which says, "When the heart is on fire, some sparks fly out of the mouth." When Paul speaks or writes about ecumenism, we know sparks of enthusiasm and hope for the future of the movement will come forth. May he have a happy retirement while continuing his contributions to the ecumenical movement.

[Signature]

Vivian Robinson
President
Consultation on Church Union

[1] Princeton, N.J., Consultation on Church Union, 1970.

[2] Ed. by Gerald F. Moede, Baltimore, Consultation on Church Union, 1985.

[3] Princeton, N.J., Consultation on Church Union, 1989.

HOWARD E. SHORT

Friend

Once I was invited to speak at the Christian Church in Lanett, Alabama, Paul Crow's home church. I stayed in a private home and the lady of the house said, "I want you to meet the nice young boy who lives across the street." So we went over to the Crow home and I met Paul.

After a short conversation with him, it was easy to think that this was a young man who was going places. He was alert, bright, courteous to his elders. Although we were of different generations, we were able to form a friendship that has lasted almost half a century. It is a good quality in a teenager to be able to relate to an older person without either bowing to their superiority or cringing as a lowly subordinate.

One thing that impressed me very much was Paul's college career. He majored in chemistry. When I took General Inorganic Chemistry at Eureka College, the professor told me at the end of the first semester that I did not need to come back for the second term. With Paul's native ability no doubt he could have had a career in this field if he had chosen to do so.

Student

If my memory serves me correctly, Paul served a term as President of the national student organization of the Christian Church (Disciples of Christ). At this early age he showed his ability at leadership. There are brilliant persons who are "loners," and who do not function well in a group. This fellow, however, could channel his knowledge into society and lead others into thought and action.

Soon after he entered seminary, Paul decided to major in church history, my department. In those days I taught the whole range of history from new Testament times to the present. So, Paul got a fair picture of twenty centuries of the church's life. It was quite evident that he was interested in more than denominational history. Although he was a "loyal" Disciple, he was interested in the larger church, the ecumenical field.

His thesis was titled, "The Nature of the Unity We Seek." He was not much interested in organizational or structural unity. The unity he was looking for and has advocated throughout his career, is the unity of Christians in Jesus Christ, the Lord of the Church. Although I could not foresee the leadership he would assume in the whole church, I could see that he was never going to be an isolationist who believed that his denomination was the one that had the whole truth.

Colleague

As a result of his insight into the nature of the church, I felt ready to recommend Paul Crow to my alma mater, Hartford Seminary Foundation, for graduate study. There he earned the Ph.D. degree. He also had a new type of experience that surely helped him on his way. He became the minister of a Congregational church. This gave him close contact with Christians of a different tradition and with New England culture—which is somewhat different from that of Alabama! From this point on, he was no longer just my student; he was my colleague in Christian ministry. He has continued to call me "Professor" all through the years, but we have been follow ministers, in the church and in the classroom.

When I was a graduate student, my major professor, Elmer Ellsworth Schultz Johnson, said to me one day that the greatest joy in teaching was to see your students succeed in their ministry. I thought at the time that it would be nice to have a little glory myself. Long since, I have learned that Dr. Johnson was right. True, it may reflect some glory on the instructor, but that seems secondary. Just to watch a student develop and become a leader is joy enough. This has been the case for my relationship with Dr. Crow. Through the years, as he has risen to new heights of leadership in the whole church my satisfaction has increased with each new step that he has taken.

When the Consultation on Church Union was organized by some nine denominations, Paul Crow was asked to be the head of the group—I believe his title was "Secretary of COCU." He was at home with the leaders of the various churches; he had studied about them and now he had the opportunity to meet and work with members of other traditions. If there was any friction among these people I did not hear about it.

It was a natural move for Paul to come into the leadership of the Council on Christian Unity of his own denomination, a position he fills with great ability. In spite of the heritage that Disciples have of striving for the unity of the church, not all of us have been willing to come together with others and make a common search for it. Some have felt, through the generations, that our fathers, the Campbells and Scott and Stone, had already found unity. The task then shifted from the search for unity, to an attempt to get everyone to come into the "true church."

As a result of these views our movement divided into two separate denominations by the turn of the twentieth century, and in the last half-century there has been further division. It isn't a pretty picture that we present—a three-way division in the church that claimed to have found the formula for unity.

In 1930, a World Convention was formed at a general meeting in Washington, DC This was largely the work of Jesse Bader, who was named the head of the organization. Just to show that Paul Crow is not perfect, he had some difficulty in relating to this group when he began his present work. Many denominations have world organizations but they are made up of national bodies which are quite alike in history, tradition, doctrine and practice. But our world organization included what is now the Christian Church (Disciples of Christ) and the so-called "independent" churches. (I say "so-called" because I maintain that they are no more "independent" than we are—in fact the two groups are independent of each other).

Although the World Convention continues to function and has quadrennial assemblies, Dr. Crow rightly felt that a world organization of Disciples was needed. The Disciples organizations in the respective countries join together to plan and carry out these gatherings. It is my impression that the Campbell-Stone churches in many countries have a closer relationship than we do in the United States. I have always urged our leadership, including Dr. Crow, to foster this relationship and help present a picture of one unified, historic movement to the rest of the church world. Many Disciple leaders, including Dr. Crow, have not been as enthusiastic about this as I have been.

Mentor

For many years now, I have learned more about the world church from Paul Crow than he ever learned from me. He has become my mentor in these matters. He has travelled the world and is at home with the leaders of a score of world churches. He has had more than one visit with the head of the Roman Catholic Church, the Pope, in Rome. (I prefer not to call these meetings an "audience" with the Pope. That term should be reserved for Roman Catholic pilgrims). On all these trips and at all the conferences and committee meetings, Paul has sent me a postcard, sketching the purpose of the meeting and his part in it. I suppose I have over a hundred cards stored away. Through these I have been kept up-to-date on the status of the cooperation among the churches.

Conclusion

In many churches the president, presiding bishop, or whatever the heard of the church is called, is also the chief ecumenical officer. So far as I can recall, the Christian Church (Disciples of Christ) is the only body that is structured with one major program division being allotted to unity. So, the president of the Council on Christian Unity is the logical person to represent us. I believe the statesmanship of Dr. Crow and the various presidents of the church has been at work to make our system effective.

Early in this paper I said that Dr. Crow was not much interested in structural unity. Like it or not, he is involved in the structure as president of a unit of his church. It still appears that he is not interested in structure for its own sake—just in order to view with pride a perfectly organized body with officers, committees and regular meeting dates. No; he uses structure as it is needed.

The years fly by. Now my dear student is retiring, joining those of us in our third decade of retirement. My advice to him is: "Get a life!"—a new life, that is. Your ordination did not expire with the end of your career. May your new type of ministry be as fruitful as the working years have been.

[signature]

Howard E. Short
Professor of Church History Emeritus
Lexington Theol. Seminary, Lexington, Kentucky

DESMOND TUTU

E ver since I was asked whether I would be willing to contribute to this richly-deserved tribute to Paul Crow and I had accepted this wonderful honour, I have had two biblical texts constantly in mind. They came quite spontaneously in connection with Paul.

The one occurs in the first chapter of St. John's Gospel. John the Baptist points out that Jesus is the Lamb of God, and two of his disciples then follow Jesus and ask Him where He is staying and He says, "Come and see." They spend most of the rest of the day with Him. Andrew, one of the two, presumably impressed and convinced by what he had gone and seen, then goes off to find his brother Simon and brings him to Jesus. With this action Andrew becomes the patron saint of the church's missionary endeavour. A little later Philip, who has also encountered Jesus, goes off to find the sceptical and scoffing Nathaniel who, unimpressed by Jesus' credentials of coming from Nazareth, pours scorn at the though anything good could ever come from that despised town. Philip does not argue with Nathaniel. He repeats the formula that Jesus had used with the first pair of enquiring disciples of the Baptist: "Come and see."

I found that these words were so apt for Paul Crow. In the early days of ecumenical dialogue between the different communions and denominations, one was constantly being bombarded with all sorts of sophisticated and erudite theological disquisitions setting out the reasons why the said denominations were where they were in the ecclesiastical maze. I can assure you most of these were formidable and quite intimidating, and some of us were insignificant upstarts in the international ecumenical discussions.

Paul could hold his own with the best of them in all these exchanges. And yet it was none of the *tour de force* performances that left an indelible impression on me. It was not all their theological wizardry. No, it was how deeply I was impressed, indeed touched, by Paul's gentleness with a quiet smile softening an already attractive face that seemed to speak volumes for the sort of person he was. Perhaps it should not have been surprising. After all ours is ultimately an incarnation faith. It is about a God, the transcendent invisible spirit, who tabernacles among us, who takes our flesh and through whom the divine story is made accessible to mere mortals. "Come and see"—when one accepted the invitation one would be converted by what one saw rather by what had been said, however eloquently.

The second biblical text is to be found in the Acts of the Apostles. Peter and John have been arrested after the healing of the lame man who had sat begging at the Temple gate. The Sanhedrin are amazed at the eloquence and indeed knowledge of the scriptures of Peter and John, who are clearly unlettered men—they had been fishers not noted normally for their erudition, and the Jewish Council, we are told, "took note that they (the apostles) had been with Jesus." This is slightly ambiguous, though the obvious meaning is brought out in one of the versions which translates the same passage as, "they took note that they had been companions of Jesus." This could account for their knowledge of the scriptures, for their boldness and their eloquence. But I have always had at the back of mind an understanding that I have found attractive, that the Sanhedrin realized that there was a peculiar quality about Peter and John, not just their eloquence and knowledge but a spiritual attribute, a kind of power which set them apart from those who had not been with Jesus. It was as if something of the soul, we call it the *charisma*, the attractiveness of Jesus had somehow rubbed off on His closest companions. We have been aware of it in the presence of certain people: a Mother Theresa, a Dali Lama, a Mahatma Gandhi, a Brother Roger, a Martin Luther King, Jr. You know you are in a presence, someone whose character confirms his or her utterances. Someone has said, "What you are is so loud I can't hear what you are saying." That could not be said of Paul.

What he is and what he said were all of a piece and I, for one, give thanks that I have been touched by such a transparently good disciple of Jesus, someone of whom it could be said, "We took note that he had been with Jesus." The gentleness of Jesus, His compassion, His reverence for the personhood of others, giving them space to be who God wanted them to be—all of this rubbed off on to Paul and made him such an attractive advocate for Christian unity, one who is effective without browbeating others, by letting them be their authentic selves without blotting out others.

I was a sensitive creature in my earliest forays into the world of Faith and Order and it was good that I had Paul as a mentor. He contributed to making me whom I have turned out to be, and I give thanks to God for His outstanding servant who was confident enough to say, "Come and see," depending on the fact that people would "take note that he had been with Jesus."

[signature]

Desmond Tutu
Archbishop Emeritus
Anglican Church
Cape Town, South Africa

JOHN VIKSTRÖM

Torchbearer

I once saw Paul pedal a stationary exercise cycle at an athletic club in Indianapolis. This exercise—like everything he did at the gym—was done with such determination that it would not have surprised me at all if the cycle had actually started moving across the floor. I have never seen Paul run, but when I try to imagine him running I find myself picturing him with a torch in his hand.

When the Holy Spirit created the church, uniting different nations, languages and cultures, people could see tongues of flame. Fire is thus a special symbol of the ecumenical movement and of the unity of the Church. The ecumenical movement, however, consists not only of quick blazes of Christians experiencing profound togetherness here and there, inspiring and catching as such experiences may be. The issue is rather the original and common flame which must be carried onward, toward the finish. The ecumenical movement means commitment and determined work for the visible unity of the Church of Christ.

I can still remember how the Olympic torch was carried through my home district before the opening ceremony of the Helsinki Olympic Games in 1952. The burning torch was passed from runner to runner. The fire that had been lit by rays of the sun on Mount Olympus kindled excitement in us. We felt we were witnessing a great historic event.

The ecumenical movement also means carrying and passing a torch—a torch whose fire came from heaven on the first Pentecost, a torch which, like the Olympic flame, also has a clear goal, and which therefore calls for commitment.

I have read and heard about Paul receiving his ecumenical torch from certain leading figures of this movement who had impressed him deeply. During these past years the torch has not been carried by Paul alone, of course, but we who have had the opportunity to work with him on various occasions have seen what a firm and strong hold he has had on it.

We rejoice that Paul's grip on the torch of the ecumenical movement is not loosening, though he is now entering a new phase in his life. We badly need leaders who untiringly keep the central content of faith in focus, the content without which the ecumenical movement would only be emotions, organizational structures and strategies.

Paul still has so much to give. Therefore, dear brother, keep going to the gym, so that you'll have the strength to hold the torch high!

[signature]

John Vikström
Archbishop of Turku and Finland
Evangelical Lutheran Church in Finland

G. HUGH WILSON

Dreams We Never Finish

C had Walsh in *God at Large* offers a variation on the familiar fairy tale. A princess is thrown into a death-like coma when a spindle pricks her hand. She is left to rest in state in the deserted castle, which becomes engulfed by bushes and briars. The princess has one hundred years to dream of the young Prince who will awaken her, kiss her lightly, marry her, and share a life of uninterrupted bliss.

A century later, a Prince comes across the abandoned castle. Gaining entrance is very difficult, however. The briars tear his clothing, scratch his face and hands. When he finally finds the sleeping Princess, he kisses her softly. She stirs, but a frown comes to her face. "You aren't the Prince that was promised!" His hands are dirty, his hair dishevelled, face scratched, clothes tattered.

He invites her to come with him, to be the Queen, to accept his love. "No, No! . . . I don't want to be a Queen. I don't want to wear a crown, to entertain ambassadors, to tell servants what to do. Let me sleep. Let me dream. Dreams are better than life. They never hurt you. Go away!"

That is not the typical, "lived happily ever after," kind of fairy tale. It points to the truth that dreams, though often inspiring and releasing, can be dangerous. We may dream of perfection, but life is imperfect. The prince of the dream was better than the scratched, tattered, thirty-three-year-old prince of reality.

Some hope for and search for the perfect mate, perfect friends, perfect schools, perfect jobs. Their dream can be fulfilled in the "other," only in the perfect "other." One man spent years looking for the perfect wife. Finally he found her. The bad news: she was looking for the perfect husband! When a marriage, a relationship, a school or job is less than one hundred percent satisfying, unrest seems intolerable.

Likewise, some hope for and seek the perfect government, the ideal society. Their dream can exclude any compromise, any recognition of slow or moderate development. The demand for the perfect can "eliminate the choice between better and worse."[1] If the imperfect is evil, everything is evil and distinctions of degree are lost.

Still others hope for and seek to be perfect themselves. "If I try hard enough, I can be rid of this demon, get rid of these dark thoughts, never be tempted again, and become perfectly whole and holy." It is belief in that fairy tale that some blame as a reason for the increase in teenage suicides. The good news is not that we can persist and pull ourselves up to perfection, but that God loves and accepts us. Accepting that acceptance, we are freed and live differently, though never flawlessly.

The same vanity is seen in the hope for and search for the perfect church: let's simply return to the pristine church of Paul's lifetime, or of the Ante-Nicene Fathers, or in the mind of Augustine, or Calvin, or Wesley. Whether we long for a lost model to be recovered or an emerging model to be completed, the goal is the ideal. Anything less is ungodly!

Such a fairy tale has not consumed ecumenist Paul A. Crow, Jr. One can imagine a scenario in which a young Disciple is infused with commitment to full organic union which he pursues with passion. That causes him to devote years of service to the Consultation on Church Union in order to help develop *The Plan of Union*. Utterly disappointed and feeling rejected when that failed to dissolve all differences among the member denominations, our imaginary protagonist will have nothing to do with developing a *COCU Consensus* or enlisting support for a Covenanting process. Such compromises are viewed as unfaithful distractions from the only proper goal for a perfectly united church.

That same kind of commitment could cause an ecumenical leader to work with others to find the best structure for the World Council of Churches, or the National Council of the Churches of Christ in the USA. Once that has been put in place, he defends it adamantly against any modification or development—how dare a new generation redo what we did once and for all!

A completely different scenario could describe a churchman carrying the portfolio for Christian unity who is simply a consummate politician. Putting together majorities, championing the emerging fashion, giving voice to contradictory goals, it is difficult to see any over-arching principle, any consistent vision, any faithfulness to a worthy dream.

Paul Crow has avoided those traps so well, so often. Holding to the dream, pursuing the vision, seeking the fulness of the Christian community has not caused him to live in unreality. In many discussions, debates, and decisions, he has championed the ideal but also sought the attainable. That judgment must often be a fine one: when to press for more, and when to allow people to rest on one rung of the ladder before taking the next step upward.

In one sense, of course, we do need to complete our dreams: translating ideals into action, goals into growth. But in another sense, our dreams always remain unfinished. And it is this dream—the dream that exceeds our grasp—which raises our sights, which causes us to aspire for more than we can accomplish, which calls us to seek a church that is beyond our comprehension, and to be open to what God creates, renews, and entrusts to us.

[signature]

G. Hugh Wilson
Chairperson
Council on Christian Unity

A BIBLIOGRAPHY OF PAUL A. CROW, JR.

By David McWhirter, Peter Morgan, and Phillip Dare

I. THESES AND DISSERTATIONS

The Nature of the Unity We Seek, Unpublished Bachelor of Divinity Thesis. The College of the Bible, Lexington Theological Seminary, 1957.

The Church of South India—A Free Church Interpretation Unpublished Masters of Sacred Theology Thesis, Hartford Seminary Foundation, 1958.

The Concept of Unity in Diversity in Faith and Order Conferences from the Lausanne (1927) to the Oberlin (1957) Conference. Unpublished, Doctor of Philosophy Dissertation, Hartford Seminary Foundation, Hartford, Connecticut, 1962.

II. BOOKS

The Ecumenical Movement in Bibliographical Outline. New York: Department of Faith and Order, National Council of the Churches of Christ in the U.S.A., 1965.

Where We Are in Church Union; A Report on the Accomplishments of the Consultation on Church Union. (With George L. Hunt). New York: Association Press, 1965.

No Greater Love; The Gospel and Ethics for Youth. St. Louis: Christian Board of Publication, 1966.

A Bibliography of the Consultation on Church Union. Lexington, Kentucky: Consultation on Church Union, 1967.

Church Union at Mid-Point (With William Jerry Boney). New York: Association Press, 1972.

Christian Unity: Matrix for Mission. New York: Friendship Press, 1982.

The Anatomy of a Nineteenth-Century United Church. Lexington, Kentucky: Lexington Theological Seminary, 1983.

III. EDITED WORKS

Mid-Stream; An Ecumenical Journal. Indianapolis, 1974-

Digests of the Proceedings of the Consultation on Church Union:

4th Plenary, Lexington, Kentucky, April 5-8, 1965 (With George L. Hunt).

8th Plenary, Atlanta, Georgia, March 17-20, 1969.

9th Plenary, St. Louis, MO, March 9-13, 1970.

10th Plenary, Denver, Colorado, September 27-30, 1971.

11th Plenary, Memphis, Tennessee, April 2-6, 1973.

Inside the Oikoumene; Occasional Newsletter of the Council on Christian Unity, 1981-.

Bossey; Two Vignettes from the Early Years (co-edited with Karl Hertz). Celigny, Switzerland: Ecumenical Institute Bossey, 1981.

IV. CHAPTERS, ENCYCLOPEDIA ARTICLES AND PAMPHLETS

"The Splendor of the Church." (Sermon) in *The First Congregational Church, Hadley, MA; Three Hundred Anniversary, 1659-1959* Hadley, MA: Tercentenary Publications Committee, 1959, pp. 22-27.

"The Puritan Way in the Modern World," *Ibid.*, pp. 81-87.

"In Memoriam Rev. Virginia McDowell Zierzow." Amherst, MA., Amherst Journal Record, 1959.

"Why Church Union?" (pp. 22-33) and "Emerging Issues: The Ministry (pp. 89-96)" in *Where We Are in Church Union*. Ed. by George L. Hunt and Paul A. Crow, Jr. New York: Association Press, 1965.

"Ecumenism and sthe Consultation on Church Union," Pittsburgh, Pennsylvania, Duquesne University Press, 1967.

"COCU, 1970: Report of the General Secretary." *Digest of the Proceedings of the Ninth Meeting of the Consultation on Church Union, St. Louis, MO, March 9-13, 1970.* Princeton, NJ: COCU, 1970.

"Disciples of Christ (Jünger Christi)." In Okumene Lexikon; Kirchen - Regligionen - Bewegungen," Frankfurt-am-Main, Vertag Otto Lembeck, Verlag Josef Knecht, 1987, Cols. 271-275.

Education for Church Union. Princeton, NJ: Consultation on Church Union, 1970. (Paper for WCC Faith and Order Consultation of United and Uniting Churches, Limuru, Kenya, (1970).

"The Potential of a Decade." Consultation on Church Union, a Catholic perspective. Washington: USCC Publications Office, 1970.

"Auf dem Wege zut Kirchenunion—Aufruf zur Begegnung." In *Kirchenunionen und Kirchengemeinschaft.* Ed. Reinhard Groscurtl. Frankfort-am-Main: Verlag Otto Lembeck, (1971), pp. 79-96.

"The Church—A New Beginning" (pp. 20-37) and "The Way Forward: Dynamics and Possibilities" (pp. 225-239) In *Church Union at Midpoint.* Ed. by Paul A. Crow, Jr. and William Jerry Boney. New York: Association Press, 1972.

"The Christian Church (Disciples of Christ) in the Ecumenical Movement." *The Christian Church (Disciples of Christ); An Interpretative Examination in the Cultural Context.* Ed. by George G. Beazley, Jr., St. Louis, MO: Bethany Press, 1973, pp. 253-294.

"If Not the Reunion of Christ's Church—Then What?," A Sermon Delivered at Grace Cathedral, San Francisco, California, December 3, 1971. Princeton, New Jersey: Consultation on Church Union, 1973.

Guidelines for Interim Eucharistic Fellowship (with William Jerry Boney). Princeton, New Jersey: Consultation on Church Union, 1973.

"Church Union as Vision and Experience," Geneva, World Council of Churches, 1974.

"Der Kirche der Junger Christi in der ökumenischen Bewegung" in *Die Kirche der Junger Christi (Disciples): Progressiver amerikanischer Protestantismus in Geschichte und Geganwart.* Suttgart: Evangelisches Verlagswerk, 1977. (Kirchen der Welt, Bd. XVI).

"Cathedrals in an Ecumenical Age." (sermon) Washington, DC: National City Christian Church, 1978.

"Unity and the new context for witness: 1) Mission, evangelism and unity, the crisis of mandate, 2) unity and mission, the crisis of context," the Oreon E. Scott Lectures, School of Theology at Claremont, 1979, School of Theology at Claremont, 1980.

"The Anatomy of a Nineteenth-Century United Church: The Mingling of the Christians and the Disciples." In *A Living Witness to Oikodome; Essays in honor of Ronald E. Osborn.* Ed. by Rod Parrott and Donald Reisinger. Claremont, California: Disciples Seminary Foundation, 1982, pp. 19-37.

"A Costly Unity: The Challenge of United and Uniting Churches Today." *Called to Be One: United Churches and the Ecumenical Movement.* Ed. by Michael Kinnamon and Thomas F. Best. Faith and Order Paper No. 127. Geneva: WCC, 1985, pp. 3-11. Also in *Mid-Stream*, Vol. 21, No. 2, (April, 1982), pp. 97-105.

"Three Dichotomies and a Polar Star: Christian Union in Faith and Mission Today." Indianapolis, Indiana: Council on Christian Unity, 1982.

"Impulses toward Christian Unity in Nineteenth-Century America." In *Studies of the Church in History: Essays Honoring Robert S. Paul on his Sixty-fifth Birthday.* Ed. by Horton Davies. Allison Park, PA.; Pickwick Publications, 1983, pp. 183-206.

"United and Uniting Churches," in *Called to be One in Christ.* Geneva: WCC, 1985, pp. 3-11.

"Christian Church (Disciples of Christ) Response to BEM." (With Richard L. Harrison, Jr. and Robert K. Welsh), *Churches Respond to BEM*, Ed. by Max Thurian. Vol. I, Faith and Order Paper 129. Geneva: World Council of Churches, 1986, pp 110-121.

"The Ecumenical Movement." In *Encyclopedia of the American Religious Experience.* Ed. by Charles H. Lippy and Peter W. Williams. New York: Charles Scribners Sons, 1988, pp. 977-993.

The Russian Orthodox Church and the Disciples of Christ in Dialogue in 1988. Indianapolis: Council on Christian Unity, 1988.

"Ecumenics as Reflections on Models of Christian Unity." *The Teaching of Ecumenics.* Ed. by Samuel Amirtham and Cyris H. S. Moon. Geneva: WCC, 1987, pp. 16-29. Also in Thomas F. Best, ed., *Living Today Towards Visible Unity; The Fifth Consultation of United and Uniting*

Churches, Potsdam, GDR, July, 1987. Faith and Order Paper No. 142. Geneva: WCC, 1988, pp 21-38.

"Überlegungen zu modellen Christlicher Einheit," in Gemeinsam auf dem Weg zur sichtbaren Einheit, hrsg. von Thomas F. Best, Berlin, Kirchenkanzlei der Evangelischen Kirche der Union, 1988, pp. 29-46.

"Report of the Church Order Commission." In *Digest of the Proceedings of the 17th Meeting of the Consultation on Church Union, New Orleans, LA, December 5-9, 1988.* Princeton, NJ: COCU, 1989, pp. 53-54, 60-61, 63-67, 79-85.

"The Gospel and the Glory of the Church." (Sermon) *Peachtree Sermons.* Atlanta: Peachtree Christian Church, 1989.

A Theology of a Church Building; Perspectives on a Church Headquarters. Indianapolis: Christian Church (Disciples of Christ), 1989.

"Ecumenism." *Encyclopaedia Britannica.* Chicago and London: Encyclopaedia Britannica, 1989, pp. 358-361.

"Ecumenical Education." In *Harper's Encyclopedia of Religious Education,* Ed. by Iris V. Cully and Kendig Brubaker Cully. San Francisco: Harper and Row, 1990, pp. 204-206.

"Covenanting" (pp. 244-245), "Disciples of Christ-Russian Orthodox Dialogue." (pp. 302-303), and "North America: United States of America" (pp. 735-739) in *Dictionary of the Ecumenical Movement.* Ed. by Nicholas Lossky, *et al.* Geneva: WCC and Grand Rapids: William B. Eerdman's, 1991.

"The Legacy of Four World Conferences on Faith and Order." in *Lausanne to Santiago de Compostela: 1927-1993.* By Gunther Gassmann and Paul A. Crow, Jr., Faith and Order Paper No. 160. Geneva: WCC, 1993, pp. 1-13.

"The Quest for Unity between the Disciples of Christ and the United Church of Christ: History's Lessons for Tomorrow's Church." Nashville, Tennessee: Disciples of Christ Historical Society, 1993. (2nd Forrest H. Kirkpatrick Lecture, 1994). Published also in *Discipliana,* Vol. 53, No. 3 (1993) and *Prism* [UCC], Vol. 9 No. 1 (Spring, 1994).

"My First Steps Toward Ecumenism." *Encounters for Unity*. Ed. by Gillian R. Evans, Lorelei F. Fuchs, and Diane C. Kessler. Norwich, England: Canterbury Press, 1995, pp. 47-52.

"The Ecumenical Movement in Historical Perspective, 1948-1991," in *Living Ecumenism; Christian Unity for a New Millennium*. Ed. by Denise C. Sullivan. Melbourne, Australia: The Joint Board of Christian Education, 1995, pp. 194-217.

"Ecumenical Partnership: Emerging Unity between the Disciples of Christ and the United Church of Christ." In *Built Together; The Present Vocation of United and Uniting Churches. Sixth Consultation of United and Uniting Churches, Ocho Rios, Jamaica, 1995*. Ed. by Thomas F. Best. Faith and Order Paper No. 174. Geneva: WCC, 1996, pp. 112-119.

"Ecumenism in North America, 1968-1998." *A History of the Ecumenical Movement*. Vol. 3. Geneva: World Council of Churches, 1998.

"Report of the Council on Christian Unity." in *Yearbook and Directory of the Christian Church (Disciples of Christ)*, 1974-1998.

V. VARIA

"Mission to Latin America." *World Call.* (May, 1957), pp. 26-28.

"Report of the General Secretary." *Digest of the Proceedings of the 8th Plenary of the Consultation on Church Union, Atlanta, GA., March 17-20, 1969*. Vol. VIII. Princeton, New Jersey: Consultation on Church Union, (1969), pp. 24-30.

"Commitment for a Pilgrim People." *Digest of the Proceedings of the 10th Plenary of the Consultation on Church Union*. Princeton, NJ: Consultation on Church Union, 1971, pp. 165-176. Also published in *Lexington Theological Quarterly.*

"COCU 1973 and the Image of Reconciliation." *Digest of the Proceedings of the Eleventh Plenary of the Consultation on Church Union, Memphis, Tennessee, April 2-6, 1973*. Vol. XI. Princeton, NJ: Consultation on Church Union, 1973, pp. 67-81.

VI. ARTICLES AND BOOK REVIEWS

1960

Broken Wall, a Study of the Epistle to the Ephesians. *Encounter.* Vol. 21, (Spring, 1960), p. 244.

The Ecumenical Movement and the Faithful Church. *Encounter.* Vol. 21, (Spring, 1960), p. 244.

Horizons of Christian Community. *Encounter.* Vol. 21, (Spring, 1960), p. 127.

"The Kirk in Scotland—a Disciples Version. *The Christian.* Vol. 98, No. 25, (June 19, 1960), pp. 795-796.

"A Youth Statement to Faith and Order" in *Minutes of the Faith and Order Commission, August 1960. St. Andrews, Scotland.* Geneva: Faith and Order Commission, 1960. (Faith and Order Paper No. 31).

1961

"Christian Youth in the Ecumenical Movement" in *Preparatory Materials for North American Ecumenical Youth Assembly*, 1961.

"A Cure for Local-itis: A Local Church and the Whole Church." *The International Journal of Religious Education.* Vol. 38, No. 3, (November 1961), pp. 40-41.

1962

"Science and Religion." Ed. by John Clover Monsma. *The Christian.* Vol. 100, No. 36, (September 9, 1962), p. 1148.

"Church History in an Ecumenical Era." *The College of the Bible Quarterly.* Vol. XXXIX, (January 1962), pp. 1-10. (Installation lecture)

"An Experiment in Teaching: The Portrait of a Seminar in Ecumenics." *The Hartford Quarterly.* Vol. II, (Spring 1962), p. 85ff.

"When I Think about Death." *Vision.* Vol. 55, No. 47 (October 28, 1962), pp. 5-7.

"The Christian Churches and Their Work." By Loren E. Lair. *The Christian.* Vol. 101, No. 38, (September 22, 1963), p. 1230.

1963

"Church Unity in North America: Reflections and Response." *The College of the Bible Quarterly.* Vol. 40, (July, 1963), pp. 7-16.

"Montreal and the Church in the Purpose of God." *Mid-Stream.* Vol. III, No. 1, (December, 1963), pp. 13-26.

"A Summation of and Reaction to Our Studies of the Church Union Consultation." *The Church Union Consultation and Various Churches.* Lexington, Kentucky: Central Kentucky Christian Ministers' Association, 1963.

"The Rebirth of the Laity." By Howard Grimes. *The Christian.* Vol. 102, No. 2, (January 12, 1964), p. 60.

1964

"Reconciliation and the Fullness of Unity." (Sermon to the International Convention, 1964).

"A United Church in the United States" *World Call.* (September, 1964), pp. 15-16.

1965

"Church Union Dynamics at the Fourth [Disciples-UCC] Conversation." *Mid-Stream.* Vol. 4, No. 3 (Spring, 1965), pp. 41-48.

"The Lord's Supper in Ecumenical Dialogue." *Theology Today.* Vol. XXII, (April, 1965), pp. 39-58. Also published in *Mid-Stream.* Vol. 5, No. 2, (Winter, 1966), pp. 165-184.

"Recent Reformation Studies in Review." *Encounter.* Vol. XXVI, (Winter, 1965), pp. 87-96.

"Reconciliation and the Fullness of Unity." (Sermon) *The Pulpit.* Vol. XXXVI, No. 8 (September, 1965), pp. 4-6.

"A Summary Review of the Disciples-UCC Discussion." *Mid-Stream.* Vol. IV, No. 3 (Spring, 1965), pp. 41-48.

"Luther's Works." *The Christian.* Vol. 104, No. 44, (October. 30, 1966), p. 1404.

"Unity is Freedom." By Augustin Cardinal Bea. *The Christian.* Vol. 104, No.7, (February 13, 1966), p. 220.

1966

"Church Union and the Ministry." *The Christian.* Vol. 104, No. 221, (May 22, 1966), p. 644 and *The Christian.* Vol. 104, No. 22, (May 29, 1966), p. 678.

"Tradition, Continuity and the Ministry." *Mid-Stream.* Vol. V, No. 2, (Winter, 1966). pp. 256-268.

"Ministry in a United Church." *Presbyterian Survey.* (October, 1966), p. 17. Also in *Presbyterian Life.* (May 1, 1966), p. 8. And *Church and Home.* (April 15, 1966) p. 24.

"Peter Ainslie—Apostle of Christian Unity." *World Call.* (January, 1966), pp. 13-14, 48.

"Professors and Librarians—Partners in the Oikoumene." *American Theological Librarians Association Proceedings.* Vol. XX, 1966, p. 71ff.

"The Venture of Church Union In Jamaica." *Lexington Theological Quarterly.* Vol. I. No. 3 (July, 1966), pp. 89-98.

1967

"Ecumenism and the Consultation on Church Union." *Journal of Ecumenical Studies.* Vol. 4, No. 4, (Fall, 1967) pp. 581-602. (Lecture to the American Society of Church History, Pittsburgh, PA, 1967.)

"Full Unity in Each Place" in *Proceedings of First Kentucky Faith and Order Conference.* Louisville Presbyterian Seminary, Louisville, KY, May 15-18, 1967. Ed. by Paul A. Crow, Jr. Lexington: Kentucky Council of Churches, 1967, pp. 24-33.

"Peter Ainslie and the Beginnings of Faith and Order." *Discipliana.* Vol. 27, No. 2 (July, 1967), pp. 29-31, 37.

"COCU from Dallas to Cambridge." *The Scroll*, Vol. 59, No. 2 (Summer, 1967), pp. 13-19.

"The Victorian Church" by Owen Chadwick. *The Christian.* Vol. 106, No. 14, (April 7, 1968), p. 444.

1968

"The Disciples, Reunion and the Worship of the Church." *Mid-Stream.* Vol. VII. No.4. (Summer, 1968), pp. 89-102.

"A Memorandum on the Disciples of Christ and the Patristics Tradition." Lexington, Kentucky. (June, 1968). (Memo written to the faculty of the Lexington Theological Seminary upon leaving the Seminary.)

"No Single Missionary Body is Sufficient Unto Itself." *World Call.* (November, 1968), pp. 14-15, 27.

"Luther's Works." *The Christian*. Vol. 106, No. 31, (August 4, 1969),
    pp. 988, 1276.

Luther's Works." *The Christian*. Vol. 106, No. 40, (October 15, 1969),
    p. 1276.

1969
"Ecclesiology and Ecumenism in the Midst of Social Revolution." *Papers
    presented to the Association of Disciples for Theological Discussion,*
    (December 5-7, 1969).

1970
"Church Union at the Crossroads," *The Christian Ministry*. Vol. 1, No. 3,
    (March, 1970), pp. 14-17.

"COCU at the Gateway in St. Louis," *The Christian Century*. (February 25,
    1970), pp. 231-232.

"Education and the Worship of the Church." *Mid-Stream*. Vol. 9,
    No. 2-3, (Winter-Spring, 1970), p. 82.

"Education for Church Union: A Plea for Encounter." *Mid-Stream*. Vol. 9,
    Nos. 2-3, (1970), pp. 82-100.

"The Gifts of the Disciples Heritage to the Church Universal."
    The Christian. Vol. 108, No. 8, (February 22, 1970), p. 228ff.

"Update on the Consultation on Church Union." *World Call*. Vol. 52,
    No. 6, (June, 1970), pp. 6-7.

1971
"Commitment for a Pilgrim People." *Mid-Stream*. Vol. 10, No. 2-3,
    (Winter/Spring, 1971), pp. 165-184.

"Consensus, the Eucharist, and Union." *The American Ecclesiastical Review*,
    Vol. CLXIV, No. 6, (June 1971), pp. 365-372.

"The Consultation on Church Union, the Christian Church (Disciples of
    Christ) and Their Future." *Mid-Stream*. Vol. 10, No. 4, (Summer,
    1971), pp. 81-95.

"Why this Plenary?" *Mid-Stream*. Vol. 10, No. 2-3, (Winter-Spring, 1971),
    pp. 185-186.

1972
"The Christian Church (Disciples of Christ) in the Ecumenical Movement."
    Mid-Stream. Vol. 11, No. 3-4, (Spring-Summer, 1972), pp. 253-294.

"Consultation on Church Union." *The Ecumenical Review,* Vol. 24, No. 3, (July 1972), pp. 370-371.

"Commitment for a Pilgrim People." *Lexington Theological Quarterly.* Vol. 7, (January, 1972), pp. 21-30.

"Mission, Ministry and the Future of the Church." *Encounter.* Vol. 33, (Summer, 1972), pp. 265-271.

"A Shared Eucharistic Life," *World Call.* (May, 1972), pp. 32-33.

1973

"COCU (1973) and the Image of Reconciliation." *Mid-Stream.* Vol. 12, No. 1, (January, 1973), pp. 67-81.

"Wenn es nicht zur Vereinigung der Kirche Christi: kommt—was denn?" in *Una Sancta,* Vol. 28 (1973), pp. 335-342.

"Consultation on Church Union." *The Ecumenical Review,* Vol. 26, No. 2, (April, 1974), pp. 323-324.

"If Not the Reunion of the Church--Then What?" *The Journal of Ecumenical Studies.* Vol. 10, (Spring, 1973) pp. 375-383.

1974

"Barton Warren Stone: An Ambassador of the Oikoumene." *Discipliana.* Vol. XXXIV, (Summer, 1974), p. 19ff.

"Church Union as Vision and Experience." *The Ecumenical Review.* Vol. 26, No. 2, (April, 1974), pp. 234-245.

"A Conversation with Paul Crow." Interviewed by John L. Glosser. *The Disciple.* Vol. I, (November 10, 1974), p. 9ff.

1975

"Canada Consultation Affirms Church Union." *The Christian Century.* Vol. 92, (August 6-13, 1975), pp. 711-712.

"Whither COCU. " Interview by Jim Anthis, *The Catalyst,* Vol. 7, No. 8, (August, 1975).

"Ecumenism Today and Tomorrow." *The Catalyst.* Vol. 7, No. 9, (September 1975).

"The Holy Spirit and the Unity of Christ's Church." (Sermon) *Princeton Seminary Bulletin.* Vol. LXVIII, (Autumn, 1975), pp. 60-63.

"Jesus Christ Frees and Unites." *Mid-Stream*. Vol. 14, No. 1, (January, 1975), pp. vii-ix.

"Living Our Way Toward Union: COCU's Vital Signs," *Mid-Stream*. Vol. XIV, No. 2, (April, 1975), pp. 210-223.

"From Russia with Love," *Midstream*. Vol. 14, No. 3, (July, 1975), pp. 353-356.

"Reality and Rhetoric in the Bilaterals: A Response to Harding Meyer," *Lutheran World*. Vol. 22, No. 3, (1975), pp. 235-237.

"Realität und Rhetorik der bilarteralem Gespräche," in Lutherische Rundschau, Vol. 25, (1975), pp. 249-252.

"The Toronto Consultation: Church Union in a Global Perspective," *Mid-Stream*. Vol. 14, No. 4, (October, 1975), pp. 463-475.

1976

"We Intend to Struggle Together." *The Disciple*. Vol. 3, (March 21, 1976), p.2.

"What's Ahead for the Church." *The Disciple*. Vol. 3, (August 15, 1976), p. 3.

L'Unité visibile à Nairobi." in *SOEPI Mensuel*, No. 3, (1976), pp. 7-10.

1977

"George G. Beazley, Jr.: One of a Kind Ecumenist." *Mid-Stream*. Vol. 16, No. 2, (April, 1977), pp. 151-156.

"For All the Saints," *Mid-Stream*. Vol. 16, No. 2, (April, 1977), pp. 149-150.

"The Ecumenical Institute Bossey: Symbol of Dialogue and Unity," *The Congressional Record*, Washington, D.C., (June 15, 1977).

1978

"Challenges to Our Partial Community," *The Disciple*. Vol. 5, (December 3, 1978), p. 12ff.

"A Pope and a Child." *Mid-Stream*. Vol. 17, No. 4, (October, 1978), pp. 331-333.

1979

"Elements of Unity in Recent Ecumenical Discussion--A Disciples View." *Mid-Stream*. Vol. 18, No. 4, (October, 1979), pp. 404-412.

"Unity and Hope: Faith and Order at Bangalore," *Mid-Stream*. Vol. 18, No. 1, (January, 1979), pp. 1-3.

"Unity and the New Context for Witness." (Oreon E. Scott Lectures, November 12-13, 1979). Claremont, California: Disciples Seminary Foundation, 1979.

"Reflections on the Energy Crisis of Ecumenism." *One World* (WCC) 1980, No. 48, (July-August, 1979), pp. 22-23.

1980

"Disciples of Christ Amid the Churches' Search for Global Wholeness." *Mid-Stream.* Vol. 19, No. 2, (April, 1980), pp. 132-141.

"Introduction." *Foundation for Ecumenical Commitment.* New York: National Council of Churches, 1980.

"Ministry and the Sacraments in the Christian Church (Disciples of Christ)." *Encounter.* Vol. 41, No. 1, (October, 1980) pp. 73-89. (William Henry Hoover Lecture on Christian Unity, Disciples Divinity House, University of Chicago).

"Mission and Evangelism: The Crisis of Mandate." *Impact* [Disciples Seminary Foundation, Claremont, CA]. No. 4, (1980), p. 2. Also published in *Lexington Theological Quarterly.* Vol. XV, (October, 1980), p. 114ff.

"Unity and Mission." *Impact.* No. 4, (1980), p. 16ff.

"Unity, Mission, Truth: Education for Ecumenism in the 1980's." *Mid-Stream.* Vol. 19, No. 1, (January, 1980), pp. 68-73.

"WCC 1980 Style: Celebration and Candor." *The Christian Century.* Vol. XCVII, (September 24, 1980), pp. 868-870.

1981

"Covenanting as an Ecumenical Paradigm." *Mid-Stream.* Vol. 20, No. 2, (April, 1981), pp 125-137. Also in *Austin Seminary Bulletin.* Vol. 9, (March, 1981), pp 60-72.

"Forward" in *Apostolicity and Catholicity: Report of the Disciples of Christ-Roman Catholic International Dialogue.* Indianapolis, Indiana: Council on Christian Unity, 1982.

"Disciples-Roman Catholic Odyssey." *Mid-Stream.* Vol. 20, No. 3, (July, 1981), pp. 218ff.

"Introduction," in *Bossey: Two Vignettes from its Early Years.* Celigny: Ecumenical Institute Bossey, 1981.

"John 17 and the Glory of Christian Unity," *Living Ecumenism Series*, Vol. 5, No. 2, (September, 1980), pp. 1-10. (Lecture to National Association of Ecumenical Staff, NCCC, 1979).

"Evangelism for Christian Unity: Mandates for a New Generation," *Living Ecumenical Series*, Vol. 5, No. 2, (September, 1980), pp. 11-20. (NAES)

1982

"In Memoriam: Bishop Samuel." *Mid-Stream*. Vol. 21, No. 2, (April, 1982), pp. 274-275.

"Is Your Church Large Enough?" *The Disciple*. Vol. 9, (March 7, 1982), pp. 15-16.

"Three Dichotomies and a Polar Star." *Mid-Stream*. Vol. 21, No. 1, (January, 1982), pp. 21-30.

"United and Uniting Churches; Perspectives from the Columbo Consultation." *Mid-Stream*. Vol. 21, No. 2, (April, 1982), pp. 97-105.

1983

"Critique." *The Disciple*. Vol. 10, (June 5, 1983), p. 30.

"Impulses Toward Christian Unity in Nineteenth Century America." *Mid-Stream*. Vol. 22, No. 3, (July/October, 1983), pp. 419-440.

"Growing in Ministry: Landmarks for the Disciples of Christ in Their Ecumenical Future." *Impact* [Disciples Seminary Foundation at Claremont, CA]. No. 10, (1983), pp. 22-32.

"Voices of Vancouver." *The Disciple*. Vol. 10, (December 1983), p. 19ff.

"World Conference on Life and Peace: Uppsala, 1983." *Midstream*. Vol. XXII, No. 3-4, (July/October, 1983), pp. 470-473.

1984

"Ecumenical Dimensions in the World Church." *Catholic Theological Society of America Proceedings*. Vol. 39, (1984), p. 129. (Lecture to CTSA)

"Global and Local Ecumenism in Bulgaria." *Mid-Stream*. Vol. 23, No. 2, (April, 1984), pp. 206-210; also in *The Christian Century*, Vol. 61, No. 3, (January 25, 1984), pp. 80-81.

"Response to Cardinal Ce, Patriarch of Venice" [at Disciple-Roman Catholic Dialogue], *Mid-Stream*. Vol. 23, No. 4, (October, 1984), p. 409.

"To be a Pilgrim." *Mid-Stream*. Vol. 23, No. 4, (October, 1984), p. 425.

"The Spirit and Solidarity: May Day at St. Paul's, London." *Mid-Stream*. Vol. 23, No. 1, (January, 1984), pp. 135-138.

"Christian Unity in a Wounded World." (Sermon) *The Princeton Seminary Bulletin*. Vol. 5, No. 1, (1984), pp. 50-54.

1985

"Communions Build Trust at Windsor Castle." *The Christian Century*. Vol. 102, (December 11, 1985), pp. 1142-1143.

"Frustration and Hope: The WCC in Argentina." *The Christian Century*. Vol. 102, (Aug. 28-Sep. 4, 1985), pp. 757-759.

"Introduction," *Ministry among Disciples: Past, Present and Future*. St. Louis, Missouri: Council on Christian Unity, 1985.

"The New Face of Faith and Order." *The Christian Century*. Vol. 102, (October 16, 1985), pp. 911-912.

1986

"Assisi's Day of Prayer for Peace." *The Christian Century*. Vol. 103, (December 3, 1986), pp. 1084-1085.

"The Cross of Christ Amid a Typical Lenten Season." (Sermon) *Pulpit Digest*. Vol. 66, No. 478, (March-April 1986), pp. 99-102.

"BEM: Challenge and Promise." *Theology Today*. Vol. 42, No. 4, (January, 1986), pp. 478-489.

"Unity and Renewal: Introductory Reflections." In *Faith and Renewal: Commission on Faith and Order, Stavanger, Norway, 1985*. Ed. by Thomas F. Best. Faith and Order Paper No. 131. Geneva: WCC, (1986), pp. 166-168.

"Einheit und Erneuerung: Einfuhrende Bemerkungen zum Studienprogramm," in Glaube und Erneuerung: Stavanger 1985, Sitzung der Kommission für Glauben und Kirchenverfassung, Beiheftzer Ökumenischen Rundschau, No. 55, hrsg. von Günther Gassmann, Franfurt-am-Main, Lembeck, 1986, pp. 132-134.

"Rosa's Ecumenical Song. " *Mid-Stream*. Vol. 25, No. 2, (April, 1986), pp. 1-3.

"Disciples Identity in an Ecumenical Age." *Mid-Stream*. Vol. XXV, No. 1, (January, 1986), pp. 1-13.

"Eugene Carson Blake: Apostle of Christian Unity." *The Ecumenical Review.* Vol. 28, No. 2, (April, 1986), pp. 228-236.

"The Ecumenical Reality of Theological Education." *Virginia Seminary Journal*, Vol. 38, No. 1 (July, 1986), pp. 19-21.

"Upbeat Ecumenism." *The Christian Century*. Vol. 103, (November 19, 1986), p. 1022ff.

1987

"Anglicans Ordain Women Deacons." *Mid-Stream*. Vol. 26, No. 4, (October, 1987), pp. 579-581.

"Assisi and a Day of Prayer for True Peace." *Mid-Stream*. Vol. 26, No. 2, (April, 1987), pp. 253-256.

"Ecumenics as Reflections on Models of Christian Unity." *The Ecumenical Review.* Vol. 39, (October, 1987), pp. 389-403.

"Editorial." *Mid-Stream*. Vol. 26, No. 3, (July, 1987), first page.

"Editorial." *Mid-Stream*. Vol. 26, No. 4, (October, 1987), first page.

"The Eschatology of Baseball's Spring Training." *Mid-Stream*. Vol. 26, No. 2, (April, 1987).

"One Gospel, One Church, Amid Many Cultures." *The Ecumenical Review.* Vol. 39, (April, 1987), pp. 154-162.

"Orthodoxy, Friendship and Nikos." *Mid-Stream*. Vol. 26, No. 1, (January, 1987), pp. 139-140.

"A Prayer Meeting for Peace." *The Disciple*. Vol. 14, (October , 1987), pp. 8-9.

1988

"Bearers of Ecumenism." *Mid-Stream*. Vol. 27, No. 3, (July, 1988), pp. 1-2.

Churches Respond to BEM: Official Responses to the Baptism, Eucharist and Ministry Text. *The Ecumenical Review*. Vol. 40, (July-October, 1988), p. 543ff.

Uncivil Religion: Interreligious Hostility in America. *The Ecumenical Review*. Vol. 40, (July-October, 1988), p. 543ff.

"A Conversation with Members of the Commission on Theology." (VHS video recording). Indianapolis, Indiana: Council on Christian Unity and Office of Communication, 1988.

"Editorial." *Mid-Stream*. Vol. 27, No. 1, (January, 1988), first page.

"Editorial." *Mid-Stream*. Vol. 27, No. 2, (April, 1988), first page.

"Reflections on Models of Christian Unity." *Mid-Stream*. Vol. 27, No. 2, (April, 1988), p. 116.

1989
"Arrogance, Humility and Christian Unity." (sermon) *Mid-Stream*. Vol. 28, No. 4, (October, 1989), pp. 397-400. (NCC Governing Board)

"The Crisis of Mainline American Churches and the Future of Ecumenism." *Mid-Stream*. Vol. 28, No. 2, (April, 1989), pp. 1-3.

"Creating A New History: Church Leaders and Perestroika in Moscow," *The Disciple*. Vol. 16, No. 12, (December, 1989), pp. 18-20.

"Editorial." *Mid-Stream*. Vol. 28, No. 1, (January, 1989), first page.

1990
"Calvin's Heirs Gather in An Alien World." *Reformed World*. Vol. 41, No. 3, (1990), p. 66ff.

"The Phenomenon of Pentecost." *The Disciple*. Vol. 17, (June, 1990), pp. 25-27. (Biblical Lecture to NCC Central Committee)

"Scaling Walls." *The Disciple*. Vol. 17, (November, 1990), pp. 14-15.

"Pentacost and the community which shares the Spirit; A bible study of Acts 2:1-13," Bible Study for WCC Central Committee, Geneva, WCC (mimeographed), 1990.

"The Unity of the Church and the Renewal of Human Community: A Perspective from Budapest," in *Faith and Order, 1985-1989: The Commission Meeting at Budapest*. Faith and Order Paper No. 148. Geneva: WCC, (1990), pp. 134-145.

"Die Einheit der Kirche und die Erneuerung der menschlichen Gemeinschaft aus der Sicht der Budapester Kommionstagung," in

Glauben und Kirchenverfassung 1985-1989; Sitzungen der Kommission in Budapest 1989, Beinheft zur Ökumenischen Rundschau, No. 61, hrsg. Von Günther Gassmann, Frankfurt-am-Main, Verlag Otto Lembeck, 1990, pp. 89-97.

"Three Ecumenists and the Church Triumphant." *Mid-Stream*. Vol. 29, No. 4, (October, 1990), pp. 145-148.

Michael Ramsey: A Life. *Mid-Stream*. Vol. 30, No. 4, (October, 1991), pp. 400-401.

1991
"Canberra as Hope and Struggle." *Mid-Stream*. Vol. 30, No. 3, (July, 1991), pp. 181-191.

"The Unity of the Church and the Renewal of Human Community." *Mid-Stream*. Vol. XXX, No. 2, (April, 1991), pp. 130-138.

1992
"The Ancient Vision in New Wineskins." *Mid-Stream*. Vol. 31, No. 1, (January, 1992), pp. 1-3.

"Ecumenism, Spirituality, and the Dark Night of the Soul." *Impact* [Disciples Seminary Foundation, Claremont, CA]. No. 29, (1992), p. 30ff.

"A Summons to the Church's Imagination." *Mid-Stream*. Vol. 31, No. 2, (April, 1992), pp. 75-78.

1993
"Ecumenism, Spirituality, and the Dark Night of the Soul." *Mid-Stream*. Vol. 32, (January 1993), pp. 5-20. Also published in *One in Christ*. Vol. 29, No. 2, (1993), pp. 100-112. (Paul Wattson Lecutre on Ecumenism, San Francisco, 1992)

"Fatigue and Renewal in the Ecumenical Movement." *Mid-Stream*. Vol. 32, No. 1, (January, 1993), pp. 1-3.

"Have Disciples Lost Their Christian Unity Zeal?" *The Disciple*. Vol. XIII, (January, 1993), p. 12ff.

"The Legacy of Four World Conferences on Faith and Order." *The Ecumenical Review*. Vol. 45, (January, 1993), pp. 13-26.

"The Lure and Languishing of Disciples–United Church of Christ Unity." *Mid-Stream*. Vol. 32, No. 3, (July, 1993), pp. 1-8.

"Ecclesiology: The Intersection Between the Search for Ecclesial Unity and the Struggle for Justice, Peace, and the Integrity of Creation," in *Costly Unity.* Ed. by Thomas F. Best and Wesley Granberg-Michaelson. Geneva: WCC, 1993, pp. 53-58.

"Martin Luther King, Jr., Was My Man Too." *The Disciple.* Vol. CXXXI, (July, 1993), p. 20ff.

1994

"Daily Bread for Pilgrims: A Santiago Diary." *Mid-Stream.* Vol. 33, No. 1, (January, 1994), pp. 1-10.

Orthodoxy, Friendship, and Nikos" in *Nikos A. Nissiotis: Religion, Philosophy and Sport in Dialogue.* Athens: Privately Published, 1994, pp. 362-364.

"What Happened at Santiago?" *One in Christ.* Vol. 30, No. 3, (1994), pp. 291-294.

1995

"Ecumenical Lessons from COCU's History, 1960-1995. *Mid-Stream.* Vol. 34, No. 3, (July-October, 1995), pp. 13-41.

1995

"Ecumenical Partnership: Emerging Unity between Disciples of Christ and the United Church of Christ." *Mid-Stream.* Vol. 35, No. 1 (January, 1996), pp. 63-70.

"God Doesn't Operate on Our Time; A Time for Unity," *The Disciple.* Vol. CXXXIV, (July/August, 1996), pp. 9-11.

1997

"Christian Church-Disciples of Christ Ecumenical Partnership," in Thomas F. Best and Union Correspondents, "Survey of Church Union Negotiations, 1994-1996." *The Ecumenical Review,* Vol. 44, No. 2, (April, 1997), pp. 223-262. Reprinted as Faith and Order Paper. No. 176.

"The Struggle for Newness: Faith and Order's Tanzanian Sojourn," *Mid-Stream.* Vol. 36, No. 1, (January, 1997), pp. 1-7.